LETTERS
TO THE
EDITOR

TWO HUNDRED YEARS IN THE LIFE OF AN AMERICAN TOWN

EDITED BY
GERARD STROPNICKY, TOM BYRN, JAMES GOODE, AND JERRY MATHENY

A Touchstone Book
Published by Simon & Schuster

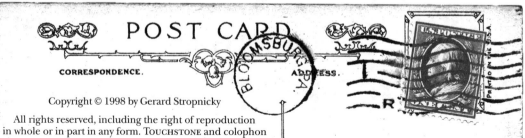

POST CARD

CORRESPONDENCE.   ADDRESS.

Design and typography by Sam Potts
Manufactured in the United States of America

1   3   5   7   9   10   8   6   4   2

Library of Congress Cataloging-in-Publication Data
Letters to the editor : two hundred years in the life of an
American town / Gerard Stropnicky . . . [et al.].
p.   cm.
"A Touchstone book."
1. Bloomsburg (Pa.)—Social life and customs.
2. Bloomsburg (Pa.)—History. 3. Letters to the editor—
Pennsylvania—Bloomsburg. I. Stropnicky, Gerard.
F159.B64L47   1998
974.8'38—dc21   98-10198
                                        CIP
ISBN 0-684-84853-8

TOUCHSTONE
Rockefeller Center
1230 Avenue of the Americas
New York, NY 10020

ACKNOWLEDGMENTS

In the creation of *Letters to the Editor,* the four of us experienced anew what it is to be part of a community. We have so many to thank.

First, we express appreciation to our employer, Bloomsburg Theatre Ensemble, this region's not-for-profit professional theatre company, which provides the artistic home that makes it possible for this group of actors, directors, and stage managers to create. We also thank the thousands of donors and subscribers who have made BTE possible over the past twenty years.

There were ten collaborators on the theatrical version of *Letters to the Editor;* four of us continued on to make this book. We offer a special thanks to the six other play collaborators: David Moreland, Sharon Pabst, Seth Reichgott, Leigh Strimbeck, Jane Wellington, and Rand Whipple. Their wisdom, playfulness, and creativity made the play and infuse this book. The same must be said of our design collaborators on the play version: lighting designer A. C. Hickox, set designer Wendy Ponte, costumer April Bevans, and Learning Tomorrow for computer graphics. A healthy collaboration on an original stage work softens the borders of job descriptions. Their insight and good-humored advice influenced the play in ways that still shine in this book.

Thanks to the National Endowment for the Arts/Expansion Arts Program for funding the first theatrical workshops of *Letters to the Editor,* and to the Pennsylvania Council on the Arts for their steadfast support of BTE over decades. It is a sad footnote that, because of the congressionally mandated restructuring of the NEA, the Expansion

Arts Program was eliminated. The grant that made *Letters* possible was among the last of its kind.

A special appreciation must go to George A. Turner, a retired professor of history from Bloomsburg University who helped us throughout as an advisor and who generously shared his ever-fresh astonishment at the human side of history. We are honored to count ourselves among the fortunate few who can call themselves his students. And thanks to Craig A. Newton, a professor emeritus of history at Bloomsburg University who is now the pastor of Emmanuel Methodist Church in Windsor, Pennsylvania, for biographical information on Private Christian Reice that was published in "Local War Letters from the Philippines: 1899–1900," *The Columbian,* vol. 3, no. 4, April 1974.

The course of research brought us to many libraries and historical societies. We'd like to thank the following institutions and their patient staffs:

Harvey L. Andruss Library, Bloomsburg University, Bloomsburg, Pennsylvania
Thomas Beaver Library, Danville, Pennsylvania
Ellen Clarke Bertrand Library, Bucknell University, Lewisburg, Pennsylvania
Berwick Historical Society, Berwick, Pennsylvania
James V. Brown Library, Williamsport, Pennsylvania
Columbia County Historical and Genealogical Societies, Orangeville, Pennsylvania
Historical Society of Pennsylvania, Philadelphia, Pennsylvania
Historical Society of Schuylkill County, Pottsville, Pennsylvania
Library of Congress, Washington, D.C.
New York Public Library, New York, New York
New York State Library, Albany, New York
Northumberland County Historical Society, Sunbury, Pennsylvania
Pennsylvania Historical and Museum Commission, Harrisburg, Pennsylvania
Pennsylvania State Archives, Harrisburg, Pennsylvania
Pennsylvania State Library, Harrisburg, Pennsylvania
Joseph Priestley House, Sunbury, Pennsylvania
Wyoming Historical & Geological Society, Wilkes-Barre, Pennsylvania

Among the joyful discoveries on *Letters to the Editor* was the magnificent historical record held in postcards, trade cards, and other paper ephemera. A special thanks to Roy H. Shoop of Watsontown, Pennsylvania; to Mary and Reuel Hartman of Bloomsburg; to Harry Ward of Bloomsburg; and to the Susquehanna Valley Post Card Club, Inc. These folks selflessly shared their expertise not only about postcards, but also about the communities they lovingly record.

Thanks to our talented contemporary photographers, and to our good friends Marlin R. Wagner and Gordon R. Wenzel, who did more than fulfill assignments.

Many others interrupted their lives in one way or another to help bring *Letters to the Editor* to the page, including J. Scott Atherton; Diane Baas; Kathleen H. Baas; everyone at BTE, especially administrative director Steve Bevans, board president Luther J. Black, Peter Brown, ensemble directors Elizabeth Dowd and Sharon Pabst, Gerry Edwards, Keith Fernsler, Jamie Kurtz, Marge Killian, Laurie McCants, Erin Oestreich, Mary Powlus, Nick Troisi, Mary Lou Wagner, and the BTE Board of Trustees; Cee Tee Photographic, Lewisburg, Pennsylvania; Glen Edwards Studio, Bloomsburg, Pennsylvania, and its owner, Dale K. Morris; Paul Gallagher; Columbia County Prothonotary Tammy Kline; Ray Orley; Jeffrey G. Pope of Rising Sun Antiques, Danville, Pennsylvania; Veronica Snyder-McHenry of Mazzy's Shotz; Leigh Strimbeck, Joe Jurchak, and their family; and Peter Van Leeuwen of NewsBank, Inc. Thank you for your help and encouragement.

A huge debt of gratitude is owed to the contemporary newspapers the *Press Enterprise* in Bloomsburg, Pennsylvania, and *The Danville News* in Danville, Pennsylvania, which granted BTE and the editors of this book permission to use letters that first appeared in their publications. For only momentarily looking at us like we were crazy, and then doing everything in their power to make this project possible, a special thanks to publisher Paul R. "Pete" Eyerly III, treasurer James T. Micklow, and editor James P. Sachetti of the *Press Enterprise* and to editor and general manager Pamela Christine of *The Danville News*. Thanks too to Tom James of James, Mihalik, Buehner & Leipold, Attorneys at Law, Bloomsburg, Pennsylvania, and to Carolyn Langdon of Wagner & Langdon, Attorneys at Law, Danville, Pennsylvania. These lawyers worked hard to find the way to say yes.

This book owes its existence to Laura Langlie of the Kidde, Hoyt & Picard Literary Agency. Laura had heard a story on National Public Radio about BTE's play version of *Letters* and called the next day to say she thought it would make a fine book. It took some convincing, but she prevailed on us to take the next steps and devoted her close attention to this project every step of the way. Special thanks to Sam Potts, our designer at Simon & Schuster, who so lovingly crafted the look of this book, and to Denise Roy, our editor at Simon & Schuster, whose belief in this project sometimes surpassed our own.

And, of course, our deepest gratitude to our letter writers. Those still living whom we have met have been unanimous in their enthusiasm for this project. We thank them for their hope. Implied in every word these authors wrote to their local newspapers is the hope that things can get better. That hope defines America.

DEDICATION

This collection of voices
from Main Streets and rural roads
is dedicated to the people of our community,
from past to present to future,
who take the time
to make an issue their issue.

CONTENTS

Foreword by Gerard Stropnicky   15

Prologue   19

1. *This Gentle Hint*   21
2. *New Nation/New Ideas:*
   1790–1810   23
3. *Kids and Dogs*   33
4. *Setting the Record Straight*   37
5. *Flights and Fancy: The 1840s*   41
6. *"30 Seconds"*   47
7. *Women and Men: Courtship*   49
8. *Thanks to the Fair*   56
9. *Crime Log*   58
10. *Women and Men: Marriage*   61
11. *"30 Seconds": Trailer Court*   65
12. *The Breaking*
    of the Bounds: 1861–1865   67
13. *Thy Sons and Thy Daughters*   76
14. *"30 Seconds": Karaoke*   78
15. *Last Act/Last Hope*   80
16. *John Q. Timbrell*   83
17. *Boss K*   85
18. *Happy Holidays*   97
19. *Gumption*   100
20. *The Constant Tramp*
    of Progress: 1890–1900   104
21. *Citizen Abroad*   114
22. *God's Housecleaning*   123
23. *The President Is . . .*   138
24. *A Silent Message*   148

25. *Standards of Behavior:*
    The 1920s   149
26. *A Town Tour: The 1930s*   162
27. *The Out-of-Towner*
    vs. the Farmer   169
28. *The Old Job*   171
29. *Women and Men:*
    Sex in Society   180
30. *The Game*   185
31. *Happy Days: The 1950s*   193
32. *Lost and Found*   208
33. *The Fatal Death*   211
34. *"30 Seconds": Utterly Fed Up*   212
35. *1970*   215
36. *One Million Years Behind*   219
37. *Catawissa Galileo*   222
38. *Earth Day*   223
39. *Mother Nature*   227
40. *Faith*   233
41. *Human Nature*   241
42. *No Harm Is Meant*   242
43. *Your Next-Door Neighbor*   246
44. *"30 More Seconds"*   248
45. *The ABCs*   251
46. *Parting Thoughts*   255

Epilogue   259

Afterword: Letters to the Editor
as Theatre of Place by Todd London   261

Bibliography   265

LETTERS TO THE EDITOR

FOREWORD

BY GERARD STROPNICKY

Few of us choose our hometowns. We just wind up at a particular spot on the map by accident of family, birth, work, or education and learn to call it home. Neither do we choose the friends and neighbors who live and work all around us, yet somehow each disparate group of people thrown together in time and place learns to live together—for better or worse—as a community. Whether we remain close to home or set out for the wider world, most Americans hold a special spot in our hearts for our first hometown.

Bloomsburg, Pennsylvania, nestled in the Susquehanna River Valley of the western foothills of the Appalachian Mountains, is a lovely little town of twelve thousand, about three hours west of New York City on Interstate 80. The river flows past as it winds its way toward the Chesapeake Bay. The town is bordered on the south and east by the anthracite coal region, though there is no coal here. To the north there are the great woods, which once provided a thriving lumber industry but are now best known for their natural beauty, streams shimmering with trout, and, they say, fine deer hunting in season. To the west there are farms, mostly dairy and corn. Bloomsburg, with its county fair and its university, has always been a kind of crossroads.

It is a rural community sociologists might describe as vertical: There are rich families and poor families, industrialists and factory workers, farmers and professors, and all their kids go to the same schools. There are trailer courts and magnificent Queen Anne mansions; there is a Little League and a busy welfare office. For most of its history, Bloomsburg has never been quite prosperous enough to attract much in the way of ethnic migrations, and it remains 98.5 percent Caucasian.

Bloomsburg spent the better part of this century as a "one-company town"—the Magee Carpet Company, the Mill of Two Thousand Dinner Pails—but in recent decades it has become more diversified, which is the polite way of saying that the carpet mills pretty much shut down in 1972. After some difficult times, unemployment is now only slightly higher than the state average. In or out of work, there is a love of life here, and a firm belief that, even as times change, the town will preserve the neighborliness that has often flourished here.

What is special about Bloomsburg? Everything and nothing. It's where we are, so it's where we look. No president ever came from here, though Harry S. Truman passed through twice on whistle-stop campaigns; once the train paused long enough for him to give a five-minute speech. Richard Nixon visited Berwick when he was vice-president. In the 1930s, Columbia County native Frank S. Laubach inspired literacy efforts worldwide. In the 1980s, Lacy J. Dalton went from Bloomsburg to Nashville and made some successful country albums. Perhaps the most famous Bloomsburger in recent years was Kip Simons, a member of the 1996 U.S. Olympic men's gymnastics team. After the Atlanta games, the town gave Kip a parade down Main Street. Bloomsburg likes parades.

In a sense, *Letters to the Editor* is its own walk down Main Street. The book is not a history in the strictest sense, and neither is the play that was its inspiration. We are not historians, but what could be a more perfect project for a community-centered professional theatre than to revisit two centuries of life in its hometown and honestly present the townspeople's voices? In search of the juicy stories and colorful characters of our town's past, the members of the Bloomsburg Theatre Ensemble temporarily abandoned the stage for the library, where we spent hours poring over the letters to the editor in old newspapers. As actors, directors, and dramatists, we were less interested in the specifics of personages and plot that a traditional historian might treasure than we were in the drama, the surprise, the small but telling stories.

As we leafed through thousands of letters, we sensed we were on to something. Sure, there were plenty of the angry diatribes and political screeds long regarded as editorial stock in trade, but there was also something more. Again and again, we found citizens speaking freely and from their hearts, recording a personal yet public diary of our community. There were expressions of thanks, expressions of pain. Here was a marvelous sense of humor, there a deep need to set the record straight. And under it all was a resilient faith that no matter the crisis at hand, things were bound to get better in time. In these letters we learned how our fellow citizens talk, how they listen, how they live as a community.

As a common person's chronicle of America, *Letters to the Editor* was a local success on stage. Unexpectedly, it was no less interesting to people outside this valley, as these two hundred years of commentary on events in

American history spoke volumes about the character of our nation. Our production attracted the attention of the national media, which prompted invitations to *Letters to the Editor* at state and national gatherings of editors and publishers.

Even at book length, we could not touch on every issue. Some burning controversies of today, such as abortion and gun control, don't appear here because the local letters on these topics, though often thoughtful, seem to express the opinions of interest groups, not individuals. Many of the letters we do include read like extended conversations over a backyard fence, on just about any aspect of daily life, from sports and romantic gossip to politics (local and national), education, and faith. What we hope emerges is a portrait of a town, a portrait of community, a portrait of a nation. We hope we have provided a window into our past and a new mirror for our present, sometimes contradicting, sometimes confirming what we expect to see in its reflection.

Our hope is not so much that you might regard Bloomsburg as some special, magical place (though it may indeed be just that), but rather that you might take a fresh look at your own town, your own local newspaper—that you might listen anew to your neighbors and think about those who walked the same streets in generations past and who have given us, for good or ill, this astonishing, troubled, funny, diverse, and heartbreaking nation.

⧩ PROLOGUE ⧩

MAIN STREET, BLOOMSBURG, PENNSYLVANIA.

Dear Editor:

I feel it is about time someone said something good about Bloomsburg.

First I want to say a good thing for our schools. They never went on strike as far as I know and they have turned out some fine students.

Our police aren't unionized and they work well. Our county officers are as good as average. Our streets are bad in spots, but no worse than our State roads. A lot of streets are being repaired.

We have good churches but too few attend them. So let's be thankful that we are here instead of some of the trouble spots around us.

    Gomer Auten, Bloomsburg
    The Morning Press
    February 23, 1978

◢ THIS GENTLE ◣
HINT

THE HAND OF ART

Mr. Ingram,

There are few villages more beautifully located than Bloomsburg, and very few, I imagine, of the same size and population, in which more business is transacted. But what matters the delightful situation, unless the hand of art be employed in giving a cheerful and neat aspect to its streets and dwellings?

There are but few, very few dwellings, whose fronts have been touched with the brush of a painter; and but few also who have the advantage of pavements. This is certainly nothing but sheer neglect. The cost would be trifling to each owner of property, when compared with the advantages; and I sincerely hope that this gentle hint may have the desired effect.

A CITIZEN
Columbia Democrat
July 22, 1837

THE NORMAL SCHOOL

What business has Bloom to be continually growing and increasing, and wanting to lay out more lots, and build more houses, and open more streets and alleys? Some people thinks

CARVER HALL,
BLOOMSBURG STATE NORMAL SCHOOL
(LATER BLOOMSBURG STATE TEACHERS
COLLEGE, LATER BLOOMSBURG STATE
COLLEGE, NOW BLOOMSBURG UNIVERSITY).

the more the town increases in population, and size, and beauty, and schools, and churches the better it is for the whole county. I don't see it.

It makes us all work a great deal harder to keep the town supplied with provisions than it used to. I know the time when I could hardly sell a bushel of potatoes for forty cents, now I could sell a wagon load of them at two dollars a bushel. I used to sell my butter at eighteen cents, now you pay fifty cents a pound for it. You see we can hardly keep you going now, and if you keep on growing, it will be worse yet.

They say you're going to get a Normal School at Bloomsburg; and that will bring about five hundred more people there to help eat up meat and bread, and potatoes and butter, etc. If we have to keep you all in provisions, I don't know what will happen.

A Countryman
The Columbian
May 8, 1868

THE CARPET WHISTLE

Dear Sir:

I recently spent a few days in Bloomsburg, after a long absence. The thing I missed the most was the Magee Carpet whistle. I hope to be in Bloomsburg for the Fair. I was just wondering if the whistle will be in operation for the Fair?

Yours truly,
Franklin Sherman, Cleveland, Ohio
The Morning Press
September 17, 1971

THE TRAFFIC LIGHT

I think the traffic light at Route 487 and Central Road should be timed better. On Dec. 1, 1982, I timed it for 15 minutes, from 1:50 to 2:05 p.m. and again on Jan. 4, 1983, from 12:05 to 12:20 p.m. I was at the same place and used the same watch, which may not keep perfect time, but not too far off.

On Dec. 1, the times varied from three seconds to 17 seconds. Again on Jan. 4, the variation was anywhere from three to 16 seconds. As you can see, the time was nowhere even. I am a local resident who must use this intersection.

J. E., Bloomsburg
Press Enterprise
January 11, 1983

THE MAGEE CARPET COMPANY.

CHAPTER 2

✎ NEW NATION/ ✎
NEW IDEAS:
1790–1810

A LARGE QUANTITY OF VALUABLE LANDS TO BE SOLD.

The public are hereby informed, that the whole manor of Pomfret, consisting of sixteen good farms, containing near 300 acres each, will be sold at public vendue, at the house of Martin Withington, in Sunbury. The sale to commence on the SEVENTEENTH day of JUNE next, and to continue from day to day, till the whole is disposed of.

The improvements on these farms are valuable—Good comfortable log houses, and convenient barns and stables, on all of them; on most of them, a large quantity of excellent meadow, in the best order, and a considerable proportion of arable land cleared; and on some of them are good orchards.

The situation of these farms further recommend them to the public attention, being adjacent to the town of Sunbury, in the county of Northumberland. This town always affords a ready market for all produce that may be raised on the above described plantations.

There will also be sold at the same time and place, a number of very valuable OUTLOTS, containing about five acres each; most of them of the first rate meadow.

Indisputable titles will be given for the whole, by JOHN PENN and JOHN PENN, jun., Esquires, late proprietors of the state of Pennsylvania.

John Penn & John Penn, jun.
The Oracle of Dauphin and Harrisburgh Advertiser
May 27, 1793

ADVICE TO INNKEEPERS

As a great deal of custom is necessary to make good markets and good inns, and as there is but little traveling, except on public roads, the question is, how shall taverners on private roads, where there is but little traveling, make provision for entertaining gentlemen well, without suffering great losses. I speak not of provisioning for country people, for these are willing to take cider and pot-lucks, or the common fare

THE CHANGING ROLE OF NEWSPAPERS

———•———

Rural newspapers of the era are weeklies, whose grander purpose is to chronicle the activities of Congress and the new government. The nature of that government is far from settled, and each paper has a clear political bias. Some newspapers, including *The Sunbury and Northumberland Gazette,* are critical of the Federalists—its editor is tried and convicted of libel against President Adams under the Alien and Sedition Acts.

But most readers have far more practical needs—from purchasing supplies to providing for personal safety—so newspapers are also called upon to serve as community bulletin boards, where notices might include periodic militia call-ups in defense of Indian attacks.

While some letters to the editor follow the modern format of open expression—to air the views of a particular individual or to set the record straight, others serve the same purpose as classified ads today—general announcements, notices for stray livestock, missing indentured servants, runaway slaves, or an offer for sale of any of these. Still others are intended to entertain, through poetry, anecdote, or essay.

Newspaper designs are austere, consisting mostly of tightly printed text. What few illustrations there are—farm views, horses, a runaway slave—recur again and again. Even in rural Pennsylvania, the image of the slave appears frequently.

of the taverner's own family; but I speak of people who have been accustomed to a city life, and better cookery and liquors. It appears to me, that provision for the latter may be made, without needless waste.

You cannot, for example, buy a pipe of Madeira wine of the first quality, but you can keep a gallon or two for many months, and when gentlemen find a good glass of wine in the country, they are willing to give a good price for it. But, I will recommend it to you to be more careful in the choice of your wine; for when you purchase, the wine-sellers turn you off with any adulterated mixture they please. After a great number of experiments, I can safely declare, that nine times out of ten, the wine I have called for in the country taverns, has been a mixture of cider, molasses, and a little real wine; or brandy and wine, and not unfrequently with a strong tincture of sugar of lead. Such mixtures pass, in the country, for Malaga, or other sweet wine. To avoid impositions in purchasing wine, get some gentleman to choose it for you, and keep a little of the *best* quality for such passengers as are willing to pay for it.

With respect to spirits, the same advice is necessary; but of the quality of spirits you are better judges, and therefore less liable to imposition. Keep also a little of the best kind of teas, as hyson, gun powder, or souchong, and good loaf sugar. A small quantity of each will serve you for perhaps five or six months. Most passengers will not want these articles; they will not be able or willing to pay for them, but a few will wish for them, because they have always been accustomed to them; and you must make a difference of price between a breakfast or supper of Bohea tea and fried pork, and one of hyson tea and loaf sugar.

With respect to meat, there is no difficulty, if you will have a little foresight. You cannot indeed have fresh meat every day, and gentlemen do not like boiled pork and cabbage, cooked and dished together. But if you will every winter provide a number of *good hams* and *beef tongues,* you may, in the warmest weather, spread a table that no gentleman will find fault with.

In cooking, take a word of advice. Use the gridiron instead of the frying pan. Do not roast or broil meat until it is as dry and tough as sole-leather. Meat slightly done, is both more palatable and more

NOVEMBER 26, 1792.

healthy. Do not boil meat and vegetables together, unless you put the vegetables in a bag. Do not bring upon the table different kinds of meat in the same dish. Let each be brought out in a separate dish. Do not kill a fowl and put it warm over the fire. A fowl is tough and good for nothing, unless it has been killed 24, or at least 12 hours. When you bring on liquors, endeavor to give every one a separate glass. If you have not enough in the house, you will be excused; but gentlemen do not like that all the company should drink out of the same vessel.

Endeavor to accommodate different companies with different rooms. Nothing is more disagreeable than to crowd a number of strangers into the same room; or to oblige travellers to sit down with grog-drinkers in the bar-room. Furnish yourselves if possible with beds enough to give every lodger one to himself. It is monstrous indecent, as well as unsafe practice for persons, perhaps total strangers, to sleep in the same bed. It is an affront to a man to request it.—And a word to you about keeping your beds clean. Give every decent man a decent bed. Every one ought to have clean fresh sheets: it is an imposition to ask a man to lie on sheets, that have before been slept in by you know not who. You say it is great trouble: very well, then make your lodgers pay for the trouble. Those who expect clean beds are willing to pay for them. In the hot months, take special care that the beds are not infested with bugs. This is an article of advice very necessary for many of you. It is a filthy, infamous negligence, which suffers these animals to trouble your lodgers. Nothing is more offensive to travellers, and nothing does more towards injuring the reputation of a tavern.

P. Q.

The Oracle of Dauphin and Harrisburgh Advertiser
August 8, 1807

THE AFRICAN LYON

FOR SALE OR RENT,
A TAVERN

In the town of Bloomsburg, (at the sign of the African Lyon) in the county of Northumberland, near the mouth of Big Fishing Creek, on the great road from Northumberland, to Berwick, Wilkesbarre &c.

A WELL FINISHED FRAME HOUSE,
KITCHEN & CELLAR,

Together with a large Shed, a Stable and two Lots of ground, & a well of excellent water, near the door, the whole in good order. In point of situation it is allowed to be one of the best stands for a Tavern, or Large Store, in the county, as there are several well travelled roads, which intersects the main road near the Tavern. The roads which are thus situated run through a fertile country, whose produce must be conveyed to market, by the Turnpike road from Berwick to Easton, or by Catawissa to Reading; in either of which cases this stand is well situated to accommodate travellers.

Whoever wishes to live in the public line, and keep a good Tavern, may apply to the Subscriber on the premises who will make a good title clear of all incumbrances.

JOHN CHAMBERLIN

Bloomsburg

The Republican Argus
October 30, 1805

☞ There is a convenient Out-lot of 5 or 6 acres which perhaps might be purchased if application be made soon.

THE RIGHTS OF MAN

If the much boasted EQUALITY really means no more than "an equal right to personal and mental liberty—to property, and protection of the law," (the sense in which I take it to be used in the bill of rights) he must be an aristocrat indeed who will not subscribe to it. But does this rational and sober explanation of it account for the enthusiasm with which it is celebrated, or by any means justify the levelling spirit which prevails?

Anonymous
The Oracle of Dauphin and Harrisburgh Advertiser
March 18, 1793

THE RIGHTS OF FISH

Fish are a species of animals which ought to be exempt from our tyranny. They inhabit an element of their own: they encroach not on our rights; nor do they destroy our property. We have no claim on them for their food, nor can we have any prejudice at their situation. To see a harmless and inoffensive creature tortured and dragged from the bosom of its home, its companions and attachments, to feed the luxurious appetite of man, is a scene so inconsistent to a rational mind, that it ought to be discountenanced with the whole force of precept and example.

Besides, angling, though every day practiced on the banks of the Susquehannah, is an unmanly and ungenerous sport. To beguile to death under the semblance of giving sustenance, is mean and treacherous, and beneath the dignity of a man of noble and tender feelings. There are animals whose natural ferocity and destructive disposition require correction and death: but to see the harmless trout driven from one end of its habitation to the other, in the most agonizing distress, till spent and breathless, he yields to his destiny, and the savage arts of man.

M. S.
The Sunbury and Northumberland Gazette
October 9, 1793

TEN DOLLARS REWARD

RAN AWAY,

On Sunday the 24th of April, from Hope furnace, Derry township in Mifflin county, a Negroe man named Carlos, above 23 years of age; about 5 feet, 2 or 3 inches high. He had on when he went away, a fine linen shirt, a nankeen coat, a white dimity jacket, yellow corded pantaloons, a pair of clouded cotton stockings and a pair of fine round-tip shoes. He is very talkative, and full of spirits. As he is a good workman in a forge, he will probably offer himself for employment, in some part of this state. Ten dollars will be given if he is secured in any jail, so that the subscriber may get him again; and if brought home, reasonable charges will be paid, by

> ROBERT GOOD
> Living at Hope furnace
> *The Republican Argus*
> May 25, 1808

6 CENTS REWARD

Ran away from the subscriber, Hatter, in the Town of Danville, on the eighth day of this instant, an apprentice lad named James Persten, about seventeen years of age, five feet six inches high; had on and took away with him a brownish Sailors jacket of striped swansdown, and black linsey trowsers. Whoever takes up said runaway and secures him in any jail, so that his master may have him again (or brings him home) shall have the above mentioned reward, but no costs.

JOHN REYNOLDS
The Republican Argus
April 27, 1804

EXTENDING EDUCATION

Mr. Editor,

All men of any liberality of mind, or who wish for a strong foundation for Morality, Religion or Republican government, must desire of having Education extended to the rising generation, females as well as males: and the only question remaining is, how is this to be effected.

If ever we expect general, necessary, Education to take place, we must leave people to erect schools whenever they may find it convenient, and hold out all the encouragement we can to induce poor people, especially, to send their children—If the poor can be encouraged to send their children; there is little danger, but those in better circumstances will take care that their children shall receive necessary learning, either at school within their vicinity, or by boarding them out, give them the advantage of a better style of education.

Become acquainted with the population of the country and learn how many children there are, between five and twelve years of age, on every three mile square; for at a greater distance they cannot well attend, and boarding out will ruin the scheme.

Then he will have laid some proper foundation for his calculation. Every thing short of this, will be illusory and deceptive, as to any general and necessary system of Education, adapted to the general interest of Morality, Religion, and Republican government.

M.
The Republican Argus
September 14, 1804

AROUND TOWN

- The Town of Bloomsburg is established in 1802, though settlers scatter about the vicinity before that.
- The neighboring communities of Berwick, Catawissa, Danville, and Millville all incorporate earlier. The entire region is part of Northumberland County, which covers nearly a third of Pennsylvania. The nearest settlements of any size and ability to support newspapers are Harrisburg, Northumberland, Sunbury, and Wilkes-Barre.
- In 1805, Lorenzo Da Ponte, Mozart's librettist on three of his greatest operas (*The Marriage of Figaro, Don Giovanni,* and *Così fan Tutte*), emigrates to America, and from 1811 to 1818 settles in Sunbury, Pennsylvania. There he starts a general merchandise business, trading between Sunbury and Philadelphia and eventually becoming one of the wealthiest men in Northumberland County. Family and business difficulties overwhelm him in 1818, and he moves to New York, where he joins the faculty of Columbia College.
- Land speculation is rife, as the earliest yearnings to "head west" begin to stir. Much of the territory still belongs to the descendants of William Penn, the Quaker who formed the colony in 1682, and much of it is for sale.

POOR LOUIS

FOR THE ORACLE:

LOUIS, then, has at length ascended the scaffold!—is at length—BE-HEADED!—Cruel fate!—Humanity supposes the crown might have sufficed, supposes that, stript of the trappings of royalty—deprived of regal power—Louis might, nay, ought to, have been permitted to live—a citizen of France. However perfect the republican system of France may be; however conducive to the establishment of universal liberty; it will be viewed with horror by posterity when found sealed with the blood of Louis XVI. Inhumanity and insult do not, cannot, constitute republicanism: but behold Louis! hapless fellow-creature! Insulting him in the moment of death, while yet his soul hovered over the verge of eternity, with the sound of drums and trumpets, was an instance of contempt never exhibited before; derogatory to the characters of French republicans; and which has fixed an indelible blot on the historic page of France! May such conduct never be imitated!

All this contempt and ignominy was imposed by the French on Louis—who was once a monarch beloved—the pride of Frenchmen—for aspiring to the dignity which he once possessed. Is it not the most eligible position, that under the influence of a similar education, and expectations, he would have ranked among the foremost patriots in France? But where is the man who, nursed in the lap of royalty, imbibed with his first milk, the principles of hereditary right; and whose whole plan of education had been calculated to inspire him with a firm conviction of his indubitable right to sway the sceptre, would have acted otherwise? Then let us drop a tributary tear to the memory of a man, whose peculiar situation in life exposed him to sufferings, of which no other man was capable, and whose only crime (if he was guilty of a crime) was merely the effect of education. The real service he rendered us (when a king), in our struggles for freedom, every circumstance considered, was alone sufficient to counterbalance all the political errors of his life, and demands our warmest gratitude.

A FREEMAN.

The Oracle of Dauphin and Harrisburgh Advertiser
April 8, 1793

FROM HERE TO THERE

DANIEL WITMER begs leave to present his most grateful Thanks to his Friends in Northumberland county for the many Favors he has received during his residence in *Sunbury*—As he intends removing to the House lately occupied by *Mr. George Moore* in *Lancaster,* where he will keep a House of Entertainment, he takes this opportunity of soliciting a continuance of their kindness, and he flatters himself, from the exertions he will constantly use to have everything as commodious and accommodating as possible—He will not be found unworthy of it.

> *The Sunbury and Northumberland Gazette*
> July 21, 1792

PHILIP BERGSTRESSER informs the inhabitants of Northumberland county, and strangers in particular; that he has lately purchased that noted house, formerly belonging to *Daniel Witmer* in Broad way, at the sign of the *Waggon and Flat,* and opposite Mr. Howerant's Ferry, where he proposes to ferry over the main branch of the Susquehanna, upon the following conditions, viz.

A single man, three-pence, a man and horse, six-pence, waggon and four horses, three shillings and nine-pence, and everything else in proportion.

> *The Sunbury and Northumberland Gazette*
> November 17, 1792

COPY OF A CURIOUS HAND BILL, LATELY PICKED UP IN A RESPECTABLE TOWN.

ADVERTISEMENT

WANTED, for a sober family, a man of light weight, who fears the Lord, and can drive a pair of horses. He must occasionally wait at table, join in household prayer, look after the horses, and read a

CARRYING THE MAIL

PROPOSALS

For carrying the mails of the united states on the following Post Roads, will be received at the General Post Office, in Washington City, until the 12th day of July next, inclusive.—

IN PENNSYLVANIA

From Philadelphia to Germantown, Norristown, Trapp, Pottsgrove, Reading, Hamburg and Sunbury to Northumberland once a week. Leave Philadelphia every Wednesday at 4 *p.m.*, arrive at Reading on Thursday by 6 *p.m.* Leave Reading on Friday at 6 *a.m.*, and arrive at Northumberland on Saturday by 3 *p.m.* Returning—Leave Northumberland every Sunday at 5 *a.m.*, arrive at Reading on Monday by 5 *p.m.* Leave Reading every Tuesday at 5 *a.m.* and arrive at Philadelphia on Wednesday at 8 *a.m.*

From Northumberland by Lewisburg, Aaronsburg, Milesburg and Bellefont to Centre Furnace once a week. Leave Centre Furnace every Friday at 10 *a.m.*, and arrive at Northumberland on Saturday by 6 *p.m.* Leave Northumberland every Monday at 6 *a.m.* and arrive at Centre Furnace by 3 *p.m.*

From Harrisburg by Halifax, Sunbury, Northumberland, Danville, Catawissee, Berwick, Salem and Plymouth, to Wilkesbarre, and from thence by Hanover, Newport, Lee's Ferry, Salem, Berwick and the same route to Harrisburg, once a week. Leave Harrisburg every Thursday at 4 *a.m.*, and arrive at Wilkesbarre on Saturday, by 8 *p.m.*, leave Wilkesbarre on Monday at 4 *a.m.*, and arrive at Harrisburg on Wednesday by 8 *p.m.*

> *The Aurora General Advertiser*
> Philadelphia, Pennsylvania
> June 10, 1802

THE GRAVE OF LUDWIG EYER, FOUNDER OF
BLOOMSBURG, ROSEMONT CEMETERY,
BLOOMSBURG, PENNSYLVANIA.
THE EPITAPH READS:
"IN MEMORY OF LUDWIG EYER, BORN JANʳ. 8. 1767.
DIED SEPʳ. 20. 1814. IN THE 48, YEAR OF HIS AGE. HE
LEFT A WIDOW, 6 SONS, & 4 DAUGHTERS TO DE-
PLORE HIS LOSS. HE WAS PROPRIETOR OF BLOOMS-
BURG, LAID OUT IN 1802, AND PRESENTED THIS
SQUARE, TO THE LUTHERAN & PRESBYTERIAN CON-
GREGATIONS, FOR A CHURCH & BURYING GROUND,
IN 1807.
 COME PILGRIMS VIEW THIS SILENT TOMB,
 PAUSE AS YOU PASS IT BY,
 REFLECT UPON YOUR CERTAIN DOOM,
 LIKE ME YOU ALL MUST DIE!
 YOUR DAYS ON EARTH THEY ARE BUT FEW.
 GIVE NOT YOUR SOULS FOR DRESS,
 BUT THINK ON HIM, WHO BLED FOR YOU,
 AND DIED UPON THE CROSS;
 AS I DEAR FRINDS, HAVE SPED MY WAY,
 GOD'S WARD IS THUS TO YOU.
 PREPARE YOUR SOULS, WHILE YET YOU MAY
 TO PASS THE GRAND REVIEW."

chapter in the bible. He must, God willing, rise at 7 in the morning, obey his master and mistress in all lawful commands. If he can dress his hair, sing psalms, play at cribbage, the more agreeable.

N. B. He must not be too familiar with the maid servants of the house, lest the flesh should rebel against the spirit, and he should be induced to walk in the thorny paths of the wicked.—Wages 16 guineas a year.

*The Oracle of Dauphin and Harrisburgh
Advertiser*
June 3, 1793

THE AMERICAN LOCUST

Sir,

In your paper of June the 2d, information is requested on the subject of the American Locust. This insect has made its appearance three times within my memory: The first was in the year 1766; the second in the year 1783, and now in 1800.

Their appearance in different parts of America are in different years. Information respecting the times and places of their appearance would be gratefully received, as they are a useful animal, palatable for human food; and their visitations a blessing and not a curse to the country. I am, sir, yours, &c.

E. L., Lewisburgh
*The Oracle of Dauphin and Harrisburgh
Advertiser*
June 16, 1800

KIDS AND DOGS

A COLD PUP

Dear Office Window:

I am a nice light tan puppy. Last fall I was small, loved and protected. Then I started to grow and thus I became a little too much trouble. Now I am tied to a clothesline pole from early morning until late at night. Ever so often I get wrapped around the pole. All my barking does not bring help, so for hours I can hardly move.

These last few days have been pretty cold. If I had a rug to sleep on or a pen to crawl into, I wouldn't complain. It gets very cold with nothing to sleep on.

Is there some way I can make my owner understand that even if I am a dog, it isn't so pleasant to live a dog's life?

> Signed,
> A cold pup from the 400 Block
> West Third Street, Nescopeck
> *Berwick Enterprise*
> January 27, 1955

RICK & HERB
GO TO THE MOVIES

Dear Sir:

We just returned from up town. We were planning on going to the movie, because it sounded like it was a racing picture.

When we arrived at the ticket box, we were informed that it was a SKIN movie. So, we walked to the other theatre. This was also the same type as the other, R. (Restricted)

We had our homework done and our chores, too. We didn't know what to do, so we decided to write to you.

We wish you could influence the public with your fine column, "Letters to the Editor," to help get movies for our age group. After we finish this letter we are going to play Monopoly, but we wonder what other kids our age are doing tonight.

> "Rick" Steinruck (age 14)
> Herbert Kline (age 11)
> *The Morning Press*
> November 18, 1970

A FUNNY MISTAKE

Dear Morning Press:

This morning Feb. 2, 1971, I found a mistake in the Funnys. You called Blondie . . .

. . . Bettle Bally . . .

. . . and you called Bettle Bally Blondie. I didn't see any others.

> Lisa Wolfe
> *The Morning Press*
> February 4, 1971

NEVER FORGET

The people have heard from the people and from the parents and now we think that it is time they heard from the kids.

All of us did something that was wrong and could have done some damage but we were lucky. When it was all over, we wished we would not have done it.

But it was all over with and there was nothing we could do to take it back. Many people say that the arrest was not enough but to us it was. No punishment to us could ever compare to being arrested. We learned a great lesson from this and it will be something that we will "never forget."

Signed,
The Six Misfortunes
Bloomsburg Area
The Morning Press
November 5, 1975

BELLOWING COW

A cow penned up in close quarters or some other neglect is continually bellowing to the utter discomfort of the neighborhood. Why the owner does not try in some way to stop it I cannot say. I think it is a case for the officers for Cruelty to Dumb Animals or Board of Health—which?

Citizen
The Bloomsburg Daily
March 26, 1900

BELLOWING COW OWNER

People that live in alleys must put up with such things. I will say for the benefit of the officers for Cruelty to Dumb Animals that the cow has a yard 10x20 feet and a stable almost as large as that citizen's house, and the Board of Health can examine the place at any time.

CITIZEN
The Bloomsburg Daily
March 28, 1900

THE DOG TAX

There are without doubt from 1500 to 2000 dogs in Bloomsburg; and the same were here last year. Yet the assessors last year assessed less than 300 dogs. The assessor asks "Have you a dog?" the taxpayer answers "No," and the assessor goes on to the next taxpayer and the next gives the same answer. Now, they

MAIN STREET, BLOOMSBURG, CIRCA 1900.

both had a dog or dogs but they satisfied their own consciences and the assessor thus: "The dog or dogs are not mine but my son's, my daughter's or my wife's," and thus the lying ones escape dog tax while the honest ones pay. It is the duty of assessors to assess property owners the dog or bitch or dogs and bitches harbored or kept on his or her premises. If he or she be in this way assessed wrongfully he or she can be righted on appeal day. This is the only way to get the just tax on dogs. Let the assessors govern themselves accordingly in 1894 else they may bring trouble to themselves.

> Francis P. Drinker
> President, Town Council
> *The Bloomsburg Daily*
> March 28, 1894

WISH I COULD FORGET

I am writing this in hopes that I can reach the young mother with her child. I met you at J&D Tasty Freeze this month. I wish I would of asked you for your name.

I witnessed you shaking your child. It was just this month.

I saw you shake your baby hard. You shook him not once, not twice, but three times and then I spoke up to you.

I told you it was illegal to shake your child and your answer to me was he likes it.

I just can't forget this. My mind won't let me forget. I wish I could have taken him home. I felt so sorry for him. Here I am, childless, and you shake your child. I hope she was from our area and sees this letter. If you have to shake him, please give him to me. I'll raise him and if I ever see you again, it is my prayer that I certainly will report you.

I remember your face. If you do this in public, you do him at home as you told me he likes.

Wish I could forget it.

> Mrs. Irene Hower, Catawissa
> *Press Enterprise*
> August 6, 1993

CHAPTER
4

☞ SETTING THE ☜
RECORD STRAIGHT

NEWS ITEM

OLIVER M. KOPP

Oliver Kopp, of near Slabtown, was lodged in the county jail last evening after being unable to pay the fine and costs on a charge of operating a motor vehicle without an operator's license.

The Morning Press
March 5, 1933

COLUMBIA COUNTY JAIL.

Oliver Kopp was committed to the county jail not because he was unable to pay the fine and costs in violation of the State Motor Code as previously reported in these columns, but because he deliberately chose to be committed for his own personal experience and to study jail conditions.

> OLIVER M. KOPP
> *The Morning Press*
> March 10, 1933

MARY E. WALTERS, EIGHTH STREET

To Editor of the Daily and Sentinel:

Dear Sir—I was very much surprised when stopped on East Street last evening and asked when I had returned from Sunbury with Calvin R. Kressler. I want the people of Bloomsburg to understand that I am the Mary E. Walters, of Eighth Street, and that the other young lady, who is with him, and myself, are two entirely different persons. I will thank the people of this town not to get my name mixed up with hers.

> Mary E. Walters
> Eighth Street
> Bloomsburg, Pa.
> *The Bloomsburg Daily*
> September 25, 1902

ONE WHO MINDS HER OWN BUSINESS

Dear Editor:

I wish you would inform some of the people of this borough of Berwick that what my husband and I gave to the Community Chest is strictly our own business and no one else's. Furthermore I don't want our contribution in the paper. Some of our nosey neighbors who happened to know we gave a dollar made remarks about what they call our "high living" and our new car, which they say cost $4,000. For their information, they are several hundred dollars off on their estimate. If they don't keep their big mouths shut we won't give anything next year. If we think $1 is enough then who is to tell us that it isn't and if we want to buy a car and enjoy life I guess that's our business too.

> One Who Minds Her Own Business
> *Berwick Enterprise*
> November 8, 1954

We are grieved to think that the dollar of the above party is in jeopardy next year. It is true, however, that the neighbors shouldn't be "nosey."

Editor

A BERWICKIAN

Dear Editor:

I am sending a note about this daylight savings plan. To my mind this is a lot of bunk. Let the clocks as they are so that if you want to go on the bus or train it's OK without extra figuring. If the shops want to work on fast time let them start an hour earlier. Let the clocks as they are. Changing the clocks is just plain nonsense. Let's stay with the sun. This is no gripe. It is a plain fact.

A Berwickian
Berwick Enterprise
March 26, 1955

W. T. MORGAN

Bloomsburg Daily:

In regard to my being locked up in Chicago I have this to say: I was never in Chicago in my life, neither have I given an hypnotic entertainment either public or private since I left Bloomsburg. The fact is I did not pose as a professional hypnotist. I have studied the science thoroughly and am perfectly satisfied of its existence and feel positive I could put a man to sleep for seven days just as easy as one, but having a good position at present I never felt like giving it up and traveling as a professional hypnotist. The week spent in your town was one of four weeks vacation and I put three weeks in giving hypnotic entertainments simply as an experiment. The experiment cost me over one hundred dollars and I have done nothing whatever with it since.

Yours respectfully,
W. T. Morgan, Hazleton
The Bloomsburg Daily
October 19, 1896

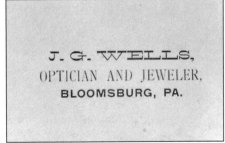

J. G. WELLS,
OPTICIAN AND JEWELER,
BLOOMSBURG, PA.

TRADE CARD, FRONT AND BACK, CIRCA 1885.

THE SILVERWOODS

Caution: Eloped from my bed and board, my wife, Mary Silverwood, without my consent or any provocation whatever. All persons are hereby cautioned against trusting her on my account as I am determined not to pay any debts of her contracting after this date; and the law shall decide on her behaviour towards myself, my family and my concerns.

    James Silverwood.
    The Sunbury Times
    December 3rd, 1813

Mr. Printer, I observed a caution to the public in your paper not to trust me on my husband's account, and that I left him without any provocation; but I wish the public to know the facts. I think it provocation sufficient when a man takes his wife by the throat and drags her over the floor, striving to cut her throat with a razor; and I am able to prove all this and more too. He has made several attempts to drown me in the river, and if he does not settle with me, I will prove all this before the court.

    Mary Silverwood.
    The Sunbury Times
    December 24, 1813

FLIGHTS AND FANCY: THE 1840s

MINDING MY BUSINESS

Messrs. Tate & Gangewer:

Sirs—It seems there is a certain class of persons in this place, who understand my business better than I do myself. I hereby give notice that I shall leave this place on or about the 30th inst. for Texas, calculating never to return, I therefore would feel extremely obliged to those persons if they would take the entire charge of my business hereafter, for which they shall receive my warmest thanks.

STEPHEN MANSFIELD
The Berwick Sentinel
January 21, 1841

THE TOWN EXQUISITES

Messrs. Editors—

It happens occasionally that a mania (if I may so term it) for some particular fashion, takes possession of the first or second grades of *polite life*. It is not only such polished characters as Beau Brummel, or Count D'Orsay, I may further remark, who give this sudden turn in the current of Fashion, but frequently second or third rate actors. From what source, however, a new fashion originates, no sooner does it begin to be popular, than all "the faithful" consider themselves bound to adopt it. If, for instance, an extra ribbon decks the brow of some fairer miss, all the better and more beautiful part of mankind must most certainly have the fascinating top-knot attached to their own.

Gentlemen's hats are metamorphosed every-now-and-then into all shapes, dimensions and colors. The bell-crown and straight-crown and low-crown, and the black and white at different epochs succeed each other, and are each for a time the *ne plus ultra* of taste and propriety. But it is principally concerning a fashion recently becoming popular that I propose to speak—which is that of *carrying Canes*.

From all the lights in my possession on this important subject, I am led to conclude that Canes were intended for the support of the aged, whose *bodies* had become weak, and of that portion of the young, whose *heads* were naturally so. Any other conclusion would be in opposition to facts plain and notorious. For these are principally the two classes who use them—the *old* for *use,* the *young* for *fashion.* There is, certainly, a *dignity* and *gracefulness* in the custom with young men! How advantageously they appear! And the custom with them is so *useful* and *necessary!* With what admiration, bordering on ecstasy, would persons from the country look at some of the town exquisites promenading the streets of our goodly borough, with that useful, beautiful and important aid to their walking organs, denominated a cane? They might not see any use to it, but the appearance would surely be captivating!

I would, however, suggest to the "literati," as they style themselves, a new custom, or way of locomotion, which I think would be found as convenient as it would undoubtedly be graceful; that is, to *use crutches.* The old men have long enough monopolized that fashion, so much so, in fact, as to make it a little *vulgar.* But let the *respectable gentlemen loafers* adopt the crutches, and it will immediately be found to be the most fashionable, convenient and beautiful practice introduced lately into *Number One* society.

DIKEMAN
The Berwick Sentinel
May 6, 1841

A FASHIONABLE REPLY

Messrs. Editors—

I see by your paper of the 6th inst. a communication signed "Dikeman," against the present fashionable custom of carrying canes. Now if the truth were known, I have no doubt it would be found that this loafer who signs himself "Dikeman" had lost his borrowed cane, (as I presume he never owned one) or that someone had stolen it, which makes him so ill-natured at those who were not so unfortunate or so careless as himself. Thus much for "Dikeman's" mo-

tive. Now what great harm is there in carrying a cane, that it should so excite the spleen of this petty scribbler? "Dikeman" pretends to object on account of its uselessness. As well might he object to the thousand and one other nameless customs now in vogue—to the ladies' fashion of wearing *bustles,* for instance; and I would like to catch at *that.* I would make him *bustle* out of the way pretty quick, or my name is not Harriet. A pretty thing, indeed, that a fashion is to be objected to on account of its want of *use.* Why by and by, we shall have some contemptible whiffet scribbling against the use of wigs, curls, lacing, and all the paraphernalia of a lady's toilette. Away with the thought.

A word to "Dikeman." If you will but remove your lion's skin, and expose your length of ears, I will read you a lecture, to which the above is no comparison. I hope to hear a better account of you in future. And you one of the *"literati,"* too. Ain't you ashamed of yourself? I have written the above for your especial benefit, and I hope you will conduct yourself in future, as Tony Lumpkin would say, in a "concatenation accordingly."

HARRIET
The Berwick Sentinel
May 20, 1841

A GAPING CORPS

Mr. Editor:

I saw an advertisement, a few days since, in a German paper entitled *Der Westbot,* printed at Columbus, Ohio. As perhaps few of your readers have an opportunity of reading this paper, I have translated the article with a view to its publication in the *Lewisburg Chronicle,* if it meet your approval. It is as follows:

"A good Chance for some
who may wish employment!

175 young gentlemen, of every age, figure, and size, from the tall, slender exquisite with mustachios profuse enough to stuff a cushion, down to the beardless urchin. The object is a good one, namely, to form a GAPING CORPS, whose business it shall be to station themselves every Sabbath, before service, at the church doors, to gape at the ladies, and to make tasty remarks about their persons and dresses. All those feeling desirous to join the aforesaid corps are requested to meet the first three Sundays, from half past ten to half past eleven, at the different church doors in this town, when they shall be received in due form, their names, sizes, &c., after being registered in a book kept for this especial purpose, shall be published in the different papers in town. To prevent, however, too great a rush, we would wish it understood that no one professing the least share of good mother wit need expect encouragement—they had therefore better not make application."

Now, Mr. Editor, you perhaps may wish to know my object in transferring this advertisement to your columns. It is simply this: It appears that they have not quite enough of this class of bipeds in Columbus, Ohio. We have them, of the right stamp and to spare with us. Hoping that this article may meet their eyes, we heartily wish that a few of them may wend their way to the destitute regions in the valley of the Mississippi.

C.

Lewisburg Chronicle
May 5, 1848

Time Capsule

AROUND THE WORLD

- In 1840, the penny post and the first adhesive postage stamps are introduced in Britain.
- In 1842, Austrian Christian Doppler describes the effect of velocity on sound and light waves.
- In 1843, Charles Dickens writes *A Christmas Carol.*
- In 1845 and 1846, the potato crop fails in Ireland. Famine spreads throughout that country.
- In 1846, German astronomer Johann G. Galle discovers the planet Neptune.
- In 1848, Friedrich Engels and Karl Marx publish the *Communist Manifesto.*
- In 1849, Frenchman Armand Fizeau measures the speed of light.

AROUND THE NATION

- William Henry Harrison is inaugurated as the ninth president in 1841 but dies a month later. Vice-President John Tyler becomes the tenth president, followed by James K. Polk in 1845 and Zachary Taylor in 1849.
- In 1844, Samuel F. B. Morse transmits a message from Washington to Baltimore via electric telegraphy. John Deere invents a plow with a steel moldboard.
- In 1846, the United States goes to war with Mexico. Gold is discovered in California in 1847.
- In 1848, Stephen Foster writes "O Susanna."
- Amelia Bloomer introduces trousers for women in 1849. The costume will be known as "bloomers."

FROM THE JAWS OF A PANTHER

I was only six or eight years of age at the time—but never can I forget the thrilling details of the escape of a young man from the jaws of a panther which occurred near my boyhood's home.

One afternoon, the youth went over the "chestnut ridge" (at the time covered with the original forest a distance of about two miles) to visit an especial favorite of the other sex. Night came upon him just as he was about emerging from the wood, and almost in sight of the house he wished to reach, when a long, shrill cry, as of a person in distress, roused him from his delicious reverie.

His first impulse was to return and succor the person calling so plaintively, but he had gone back only a few paces when he was convinced by the rustling of the underbrush and the appearance of two glowing eyes, that his help was not needed. Instantly turning, he ran for the house—he heard the animal after him, and rapidly gaining—he seemed to feel its very breath—every nerve was extended to the utmost, to reach the low fence before the house—with the assistance of one hand he cleared the fence, but as he did this one of the panther's paws struck upon the rail and in so doing "conquered a piece" from the flap of the man's frockcoat! The proximity of the house seemed to deter the animal—but not the youth, who pushed for the house, and had just closed the door when the heavy feet of the panther (which had made another spring) struck upon the door! then uttering a cry of anger he bounded away.

The terror of the *subject*, and HIS *object*, and their joy withal, I can not describe. It may be as well to add that this adventure caused a speedy consummation of the union of the lovers (for what woman would long expose her lad to such a danger?).

It also made young men thereabouts more circumspect in their times of visiting, and no great exertion was necessary to get "the boys" home *early*—a "consummation devoutly to be wished" in these latter days when there are no panthers to chase home truant husbands and boys.

O.

Lewisburg Chronicle
February 25, 1848

THE AERONAUT

We publish below, Mr. Wise's account of his 28th aerial voyage.

Mr. Editor:—

I took my departure from the Court House yard at five minutes past two o'clock, the wind blowing from the W.N.W. drifting the vessel S. by E. until I reached the Roaring Creek furnace, and fast gliding toward the mountains. The atmosphere was very hazy, which limited my prospect to an area of about 35 miles in diameter: the confluence of the two branches of the Susquehanna, with the two bridges and the towns of Northumberland and Sunbury made a beautiful view. Catawissa, Bloom and Berwick, up the North Branch, fell more distinctly to my view, which rendered the scene up the North Branch most interesting. At 2 o'clock 35 minutes I lost sight of Danville, and a few minutes after, passed into the rays of the sun; the balloon began to expand from the heat, which caused it to ascend very fast. The river was soon lost to my view by the intervention of the clouds, and the country beneath presented one vast wilderness as far as the eye could reach. The atmosphere became extremely cold as I crossed this extensive coal region, the clouds being sufficiently broken to give me a constant view of the earth. I never before found the clouds so extensively diversified in height; the lower strata was cumulo-stratus resembling high and rugged precipices, the upper level more of the cirrostratus, indicating the approach of a storm. My vessel, however, soon attained a height of two and one half miles, sufficiently high to avoid any thunderstorms.

At 2 o'clock 45 minutes I crossed the Pottsville road between the Bear Gap and the Northumberland road, travelling at the rate of 55 miles an hour. At 3 o'clock I crossed Pottsville, and again brought to view the cultivated fields of the husbandman. My altitude was so great that I could not at first recognize the town until I crossed Schuylkill Haven and got in sight of Orwigsburg. The cold atmosphere became so unpleasant that I made preparations to descend; but after lowering some distance, I found that I had only passed the valley to reach the chain of Blue Mountains, and was again obliged to seek refuge in the clouds.

At 3 o'clock 40 minutes the clouds began to thicken beneath me, so that I could at intervals only see the face of the country, and in crossing a little village I threw overboard a bread-basket that was lying in my car. Its descent presented a beautiful appearance to my view; it acquired a rapid rotary motion giving it the appearance of a fancy wheel. At 4 o'clock I crossed the Harrisburg and Reading Turnpike about three miles to the east of Reading. The white streets crossing at right angles, and the beautiful steeples newly painted, with their glittering balls and vanes, made the prospect highly interesting.

I found the atmosphere much colder in crossing the mountains than it was at the same height in crossing over level and cultivated land. During the voyage I observed a peculiar motion in the Balloon: when sailing along with a steady current, whilst the balloon is in equilibrium, it revolves slowly. On this occasion it drew my particular attention, on account of the regular pulsations that it moved with.—At first I attributed the regular vibrations to the pulsation of my body, but on holding my breath I found it to continue more perceptively. In fact the less motion I produced in the car, the more regular were the vibrations of the vessel. Whenever the Balloon, by the discharge of ballast or gas, would ascend, or descend, the pulsation was suffi-

WISE'S 20th

BALLOON ASCENSION.

On Saturday, September 5th, from the Prison Yard, in the borough of Chambersburg, at half past 2 o'clock, P. M.

Mr WISE, the æronaut, respectfully informs the ladies and Gentl men of Chambersburg and vicinity, that he will make his 26th grand ærial voyage, (being his second from Chambersb'g,) from the above named place and time, with his superior ærial ship, Great Eastern, containing 470 yards of silk, and holding 56,000 gall ons of gas or upwards of 8000 cubic feet.

ORDER OF ASCENSION.

JOHN WISE ADVERTISEMENT FOR AN ASCENSION IN CHAMBERSBURG, PENNSYLVANIA. *CHAMBERSBURG REPOSITORY,* SEPTEMBER 3, 1840.

THE CHRONICLE.

W. B. SHRINER, EDITOR AND PROPRIETOR

LEWISBURG, PA.

Saturday Morning, Aug. 14, 1847.

ciently arrested not to be observable. This phenomenon caused me to remain in the atmosphere nearly an hour longer than I intended to, and on another occasion I will continue the further investigation of this subject. The pulsations worked at intervals of two and one half seconds, and made a revolution in fifty seconds. This was the result of five successive tests. There is no motion in nature that I can as yet attribute it to, and to me it has opened another remarkable and very wonderful source of investigation. The cause of dizziness or vertigo, as I have before stated, is now beyond a doubt in my mind, destroyed by isolation, and invites the attention of anatomists and oculists to the further investigation of that delicate and most essential organ—the eye.

At 25 minutes past 4, I made a descent near the home of WM. MCILVANE, near Morgantown, and was cordially received by this gentleman and his hospitable lady. I proceeded from this place to Downingtown, where I took the Cars and returned to Danville via Lancaster and Harrisburg.

My numerous and respectable audience, also the gentlemen who assisted me during the arrangements and inflation, will accept the warmest thanks and good wishes of

> Their most obedient servant,
> JOHN WISE, Aeronaut
> *The Berwick Sentinel*
> June 17, 1842

The balloon was visible at Danville about 30 minutes. By the course it took, Mr. Wise travelled 110 miles in 2 hours and 20 minutes, and landed in Berks, close by the lines of Chester and Lancaster counties, being about 90 miles, in a direct line, from Danville.

> Editor

☆ "30 SECONDS" ☆

THE CALL
A NEW WAY TO MAKE
YOUR OPINIONS HEARD

Exactly 200 years ago, when the Bill of Rights was added to the Constitution, newspapers consisted of almost nothing but opinion. Towns were so small there was little need for "news" in the sense we understand it today; most everybody knew everything worth knowing long before it was set into type.

So newspapers were journals of opinion—strong opinions—that brought revolution to a boil, forged the fiery debates that forged a new nation, then banished the evil of slavery.

Sad to say, very little remains of this great legacy of debate in the daily press, even in the largest papers.

Obsessed since the early 1900s with fairness, accuracy and objectivity, journalism has driven opinion out of the news columns and corralled it on one or two pages: a couple of editorials, some letters to the editor, a few columns.

And a lot of what passes for opinion is like watered-down whiskey: It may look like, smell, even taste like the real thing. But it ain't got much kick.

This has not been good, for the republic or for journalism.

"Historian Christopher Lasch argues that democracy is not served well by a stream of neutral information," writes Bruce DeSilva of the Hartford, Conn., *Courant*. "Instead, it requires vigorous public debate. [Lasch] longs for the days of partisan newspapers, and notes that the high point of popular participation in politics coincided with the 19th century heyday of partisan journalism." But because the economics of publishing has turned all but a handful of cities into one-newspaper towns, partisan journalism cannot be revived.

The next best thing is for newspapers to encourage the broadest possible range of opinions on their commentary pages, which is what this column is all about.

Although we published almost 800 letters to the editor last year, we'd like to do more to stimulate debate among area residents on all kinds of topics and issues.

So we're opening up a special phone line for readers to call in and say what's on their minds. Then we'll publish as many of the comments as we can, and perhaps throw in a few of our own.

We're calling it "30 Seconds," which is how much time you'll have to speak up on any subject.

Unlike letters to the editor, we are not going

to insist that callers give their names. We are just going to ask that you tell us the town where you live.

Because your comments will be published without your name, we will edit them to remove personal attacks, allegations of wrongdoing, political endorsements and the like.

The actions of public officials are fair game for criticism, but not the officials themselves, unless you're willing to put your oral signature on your remarks by telling us your name and giving us a phone number for verification.

Or, to put it another way, if you want to turn the kitchen stove into a blast furnace, you've got to be willing to identify yourself so you, too, can absorb some of the heat.

Our hope is that "30 Seconds" will take on the tone of a town meeting, where people feel free to discuss anything and everything, but to do it with respect for their fellow citizens.

It's an experiment. We hope it works. Either way, we can think of no better way to celebrate the 200th anniversary of the Bill of Rights, which begins by giving every citizen—not just we in "the media"—the right to be a reporter and a commentator.

Jim Sachetti, Editor
Press Enterprise
January 7, 1992

THE RESPONSE

I'm tired of this baloney on homosexuality, cats and what have you. I happen to believe Jesus Christ died on the Cross to forgive our sins. I also believe God is love. He is not the hateful, revengeful God that some local people say. The same ones that beat their wives, hit their kids, throw boiling water on cats and quote the Bible, then go to church every Sunday. I didn't ask to be a man, I didn't ask to be a woman, I didn't ask to be a homosexual. I am what I am. I believe God is love and can save me as well as

the wife beater and cat scalder. Oh ye of little faith, where is your compassion?

Bloomsburg R.R. 4
Press Enterprise
April 17, 1992

I like Cal Thomas and Mike Royko. Cal's column is the main course: clams, crabs, shrimp, sharp cheese, filet mignon, french fries, salad, lasagna, meatballs, spaghetti, roast beef, mashed potatoes, and gravy. Mike Royko's column is the delicious dessert: apple, pumpkin, coconut custard and coconut pies, banana splits, hot fudge sundaes, custard-filled doughnuts, chocolate marshmallow, butter pecan, and french vanilla ice cream, and Polish cookies.

Salem Township
Press Enterprise
January 30, 1992

I am a free spirit. I like to sleep naked. No sheets or nothing. But when I get up every morning at noon, I've got scratches all over from this pesky tag I daresn't cut off. Hows come you ain't allowed to yank it off? What's the big deal? Do they really check? Can I go to jail?

Sleepless in Slabtown
Press Enterprise
February 23, 1996

On the bombing in Iraq: I approve of it very much, but I would like to see it continue every hour, just like it was before, until this man is finished. I mean F-i-n-i-s-h-e-d. We do not need this nut. We have enough of them. Get rid of the nut.

Danville Woman
Press Enterprise
January 16, 1993

WOMEN AND MEN: COURTSHIP

CALLING CARD, CIRCA 1880.

When we dwell on the lips of the lass we adore
   Not a pleasure in nature is missing;
May his soul be in heaven; he deserv'd it, I'm sure
   Who was first the inventor of kissing.
Master Adam, I very well think was the man,
   Whose discovery will ne'er be surpass'd,
Well, since the sweet game with creation began,
   To the end of the world may it last!
      Peter Pindar
      The Oracle of Dauphin
      and Harrisburgh Advertiser
      June 22, 1795

TRADE CARD FOR VAN HAAGEN SOAP, CIRCA 1875.

THEORY: 1854

Girls, you want to get married don't you? Ah, what a natural thing it is for young ladies to have a hunkering for the sterner sex! It is a weakness that woman has, and for this reason she is called the weaker sex. Well, if you want to get married, don't for conscience sake act like fools about it. Don't go into a fit of the nips every time you see a hat and a pair of whiskers. Don't get the idea into your heads that you must put yourself in the way of every young man in the neighborhood, in order to attract notice, for if you don't run after the men they will after you. Mark that.

A husband hunter is the most detestable of all young ladies. She is full of starch and puckers, so puts on many false airs, and she is so nice that she appears ridiculous in the eyes of every decent person. She may generally be found at meeting, coming in, of course, about the last one, always at social parties, and invariable takes a front seat at concerts. She tries to be the belle of the place, and thinks she is—Poor girl! You are fitting yourself for an old maid. Just as sure as the Sabbath comes on Sunday men will flirt with you, and flatter you, simply because they love to do it, but they have no more idea of making you a wife than they have of committing suicide. If I was a young man I would have no more to do with such fancy than I would with a rattlesnake.

Now girls, let Nelly give you a piece of her advice, and she knows from experience that if you practice it you will gain the reputation of being worthy girls, and stand a fair chance of getting respectable husbands. It is all well enough that you learn to finger the piano, work embroidery, study grammar, etc., but don't neglect letting grandma, or your dear mother, teach you how to make bread and get a meal of victuals good enough for a King. No part of a housekeeper's duties should be neglected, if you do not marry a wealthy husband you will need to know how to do such work, and if you do, it will be no disadvantage for you to know how to oversee a servant girl, and instruct her to do these things as you would have them done. In the next place, don't pretend to be what you are not. Affectation is the most despicable of accomplishments, and will only cause sensible people to laugh at you. No one but a fool will be caught by affectation—it has a transparent skin, easily to be seen through. Dress plain, but neatly. Remember that nothing gives a girl so modest, becoming, and lovely appearance as a neat and plain dress. All the flummery and tinsel work of the dressmaker and milliner are unnecessary.

If you are really handsome, they do not add to your beauty one particle, if you are homely, they only make you look worse. Gentlemen don't court your laces and jewelry but your own dear selves.

Finger rings and folderols may do to look at, but they add nothing to the value of a wife—all young men know that. If you know how to talk, do it naturally, and do not be so distressed polite as to spoil all you say. If your hair is straight, don't put on the curling tongs to make people believe you have negro blood in your veins. If your neck is very black, wear a lace collar, but don't be so foolish as to daub on paint, thinking that people are so blind as not to see it. If your cheeks aren't rosy, don't apply pink saucers, for the deception will be detected and become the gossip of the neighborhoods.

Finally, girls, listen to the counsel of your mothers and ask their advice in every thing. Think less of fashion than you do of kitchen duties—less of romances than you do of the realities of life—and instead of trying to catch beaux, strive to make yourself worth being caught by them.

NELLY
Democratic Investigator
March 16, 1854

PRACTICE . . .
AT THE BALL, 1792

Messrs. Printers,

I HAVE observed at regular balls in this place, that the masculine part of the assembly is, not always, but generally, made up of three different classes, viz. those, that surround a large table, smoking segars, talking politics, &c. The next class dance with the ladies; and the third, stand fronting the ballroom,

POSTCARD, 1916.

COLUMBIA PARK, 1913.

with their reverse to the fire, useful at the end, but very disagreeable at the beginning of a dance in cold weather.

At the request of Philochoras, I had the honour to be at one of those balls on Thursday evening last, and without ceremony, took a place in the third class; where I enjoyed a very great share of happiness, from a fair opportunity of observing a number of accomplished ladies, setting forth all their beauties, seemingly with a desire to please. The majestic sweetness, the agreeable figure, the modest air, the virgin shape, the gentle mien, the becoming demeanor, the pleasing gesture, and the gaining aspect, are graces which were all displayed before me: not any two ladies were alike; yet every one seemed to possess a peculiar beauty, and being in motion, exhibited every charm in its highest exertion. I returned them many thanks, by way of soliloquy, for affording me such a number of agreeable ideas; and could easily figure out to myself the modest virgin, the indulgent mistress, the tender wife, the generous friend, and the kind mother, in every one of their set dances.

Gentlemen, please to recommend in your *Oracle,* to the bachelors, who frequent those assemblies, to take alternate nocturnals, or horary stands in the third class; and in my opinion, if they comply, it will have a very great tendency to hasten the legitimate population of the united states.

I am, messieurs, your very humble servant,

PHILOKALAS.

The Oracle of Dauphin and Harrisburgh Advertiser
November 26, 1792

. . . AT THE FAIR, 1871

Mr. Editor:

Of all the sights at the Fair, the Fair itself is the greatest sight to see. There were cakes and candies, apples and cider, ice cold lemonade and raspberry syrup. There were chickens and pigs, horses and cattle, sheep and mules. There were wild men from Africa, sword swallowers, thimble riggers or something of the sort, and all kinds of devices, good, bad and indifferent, to make money.

I know of no place where you can study human nature to more advantage than at a country fair. The sharper, the business man, the mechanic, and the farmer congregate there. The young fellow who has a sweetheart goes and takes her, and the one who has none goes to find one. Girls who have lovers promenade quietly in a state of bliss, and those who have none are to the fore, as the Scotch say, to secure one. The younger girls keep their eyes upon the older ones to learn, but the boys are staring round for the purpose of chaffing older ones, who are for the first time, looking sheepishly at calico.

You see there young fellows who think themselves gentlemen, puffing a cigar, and gallanting a lady. It was not so in the olden days—gentlemen did not smoke even in the presence of ladies—and indeed *gentlemen* do not now. But what else can you expect, when the man who should be the first gentleman in the republic, is a horse-racing, cigar smoking, whiskey drinking moss trooper! It is a bad example for our young men to have, and still worse to follow.

You see there beautiful girls, dressed in the highest art of the milliner and mantua maker, whose under-skirts, as they pass through the crowd, turn up and prove they have not seen the wash-tub for months. You can also observe, as they smile sweetly at the compliments of their gallants, that their teeth have seldom, if ever, been brought in contact with a tooth brush. Nothing is more utterly disgusting than a foul mouth, and nothing is more positively unjustifiable and inexcusable. For a young lady, faugh! when a brush and a tumbler of salt water, to cleanse the mouth after every meal and before retiring, would preserve the teeth, purify the mouth, and sweeten the breath!

> VIATOR
> *Columbia Democrat*
> October 20, 1871

U. S. GRANT ON A TRADE CARD FOR
J. W. LEMAISTRE DRY GOODS,
PHILADELPHIA, PENNSYLVANIA, CIRCA 1870.

. . . ON THE STREET, 1878

Messrs Editors:

I observe that the Town Council propose to light the streets of Bloomsburg. It is a good thing—it ought to be done. The moon and the stars ought to have some little assistance, they don't need much, but what little they do need they ought to have. No doubt it is a waste of the raw material to help them out with the brilliant gas now used for that purpose, and therefore the move in the direction of economy, to put in coal oil lamps with nice chimneys in place of gas. Now certainly we don't need anything so expensive as coal oil. Would not a tallow dip, which could be got for a penny, be a great deal cheaper, and much more beautiful and picturesque, especially in a dark night than the glare of a gas light? Besides all that, if you see a young lady home you can't give her a good night kiss at the gate, without having every body on the street looking on, which is very disagreeable, and spoils the effect.

Wherefore I say down with the gas and up with the tallow dip. Tallow dips will give all the light we want, and I hope this great reform of this great reform Town Council will be carried out, and they will have the thanks of

> A Roving Blade
> *The Columbian*
> June 14, 1878

. . . IN THE SNOW, 1881

Mr. Editor:

Mahoning Township is still alive and sleigh riding is all the rage. The party that passed through your town on their return from Mt. Pleasant had a pleasant time and safely returned in the morning at 6 o'clock. Miss McKay, who was about to return to Philadelphia, was suddenly and unexpectedly detained by an ex-sheriff into whose hands she quietly fell. The sleighing was excellent and the sheriff passed rapidly with his charge several times between Danville and Bloomsburg as if in doubt as to which jail would afford the best security. The lady however by superior tact and skill, managed to make good her escape and last week she quickly fled to her city home.

> Local Gossip
> *The Bloomsburg Journal*
> January 26, 1881

. . . AT HER RESIDENCE, 1849

You remember I wrote you a letter telling you I had lost my heart. As I was entirely unwilling to do without it, I made the excursion I told you I contemplated and as luck would have it on the third drive I accidentally came across the residence of my charmer. I need not tell you a long story about the matter, for the whole thing was done in a hurry. She had seen me at the celebration and we were mutually pleased with each other. It was "love at first sight," and no mistake.—Perhaps, Mr. Editor, you don't believe in that sort of thing. If you don't, I pity you. Well, I talked with Jane, an hour or so, and then took my leave promising to call again soon. I did call. You know that these are moonlit nights; (well they are) great for making love, and with this heavenly aid, you may be sure I did not idle my time.

I boldly accused her of having stolen my heart and taking it away with her. She denied the "soft impeachment," but I was firm. She was not cognizant of having such a possession and thought from out of that acquaintance it could not possibly have happened. We discussed the matter for some time and finally succeeded in convincing her of the fact and proving the point. She was somewhat loath to restore it, and I agreed to take hers in exchange. We are mutually pleased, and I am,

HENRY
Columbia Democrat
July 14, 1849

. . . AND IN CHURCH, 1871

We know several parties who have a habit, in church, as well as elsewhere, of keeping up a continual cooing to the thorough disgust of everybody about them. If they, like Armand and Heloise, think themselves consecrated to the "artful god," whose arrows have stuck deep in their soft hearts, they should stay at home and enjoy their faith, and not parade it in public places to annoy and disturb the more high-minded.

JUST SO
The Montour American
March 9, 1871

⚞ THANKS TO ⚟
THE FAIR

Gentlemen:

Some years ago I used to hear that you had such a wonderful Fair.

So about 6 or 7 years ago I went with a Roamer Tour to your Fair, enjoyed it so much that I have been to your Fair every year since. I was

up to your Fair last Wednesday but I did not "fair" so well. . . . When I came to the grounds, I went immediately for dinner which I always had at some Lutheran church at the upper end of the grounds where they always served a banquet instead of a meal. When I was about a stone's throw away from the Church stand I felt that something was not right. I tried to hold myself at one of the stands but missed and fainted. The first thing I noticed when I regained consciousness was that I was surrounded by Boy Scouts, who offered their help, and also one of

your Ground Police who offered his help. I heard one say to the other, "get the ambulance," and the person said "I have it at the gate already."

They had blankets and put me on a litter and carried me in the ambulance, took me to the hospital. They treated me in a way that could

THE BLOOMSBURG HOSPITAL.

not have been kinder, had I been their own father.

A king could not have received nicer treatment than I did. I hope you will overlook the form of this letter. I am not fit yet to send this letter as you may readily see by my writing. I could not help sending this to you but I wanted you to know my feeling of thankfulness to all who were concerned. The Fair Board who conducts such a nice Fair, the Boy Scouts who were right there to help, your ground police, the hospital and all who helped when I was down. The Fair police and, everyone who was so kind and ready to help in such a time of need. And I want to say "Thank you to all," and may God Bless you for the kindness shown to me.

William M. Greenawald, Kutztown, PA
P.S. I am 76 years old and you may know that I appreciate the kindness I received.

The Morning Press
October 9, 1971

⚒ CRIME LOG ⚒

ARSON

To the Bloomsburg arsonist: I don't know what reasons you have to be doing all of this with the fires, but it can't be that bad. Please turn yourself in to someone.

The police can be understanding. A close friend could help you, but talk to someone. You have only burned places that had no people around, so I know you care.

So, stop before you hurt someone or kill someone. It's not that bad, really it's not.

A High School Student, Espy
Press Enterprise
February 23, 1983

DISTURBING THE PEACE

To the Editor of THE TABLET

I find an article in a recent issue of your paper, denouncing in no uncertain terms, a party of gentlemen for stealing a chicken and disturbing the sleeping inhabitants of our village. Your informant says that while the "gang"— gang, understand—was howling and wailing, one of their number was stealing chickens.

To the first clause of the sentence we plead guilty to a certain degree, inasmuch as we were singing, but did not think we were creating the awful heart-rendering, ear-splitting discord your correspondent has described. If we are permitted to entertain any conceit of ourselves, we always thought there was a little music in our makeup, but if our singing is productive of such awful results, we will never sing again.

As for stealing chickens, we are hardly prepared at present to refute the charge. We do, however, plead guilty to the charge of cooking a chicken and having a feast, but supposed we came by it in a legitimate manner, and if not the member who furnished it will have to plead guilty to the charge of theft unless he can vindicate himself. We also admit that we cooked it in a putty bucket, but the bucket was clean. We hope that no act of ours will ever cause a disturbing wave to ruffle the calm peacefulness of our little town, and in the future, should our palates tickle for chicken we will—well—we will eat chicken.

ONE OF THE GANG
The Millville Weekly Tablet
January 8, 1896

know whether or not we'll spend any of our firewood profits in his store after the way he's acted.

Wood you?

John Harter and Bob Thomas
Berwick Enterprise
March 5, 1955

P.S. For new orders dial 9085 and ask for Mr. Collins, our general manager.

Dear Office Window:

Seems to us that the fella with the twinkle in his eye who influenced you to call us culprits in last week's *Office Window* column, for putting firewood in his car, while he was shopping, is certainly an ungrateful cuss.

You see, we know that this young man would like to build a little lovenest for Wanda, as we heard him whispering in her ear while we were having a cup of coffee in his store (Jessup and Summerhill). Well, we thought we were really being Good Samaritans by putting some high grade lumber and a first class cement block in his car to help him get started. And he has the gall to call it firewood.

How he could misconstrue our act of kindness as anything but such is beyond our comprehension. However, thanks to you for writing our names and numbers in the *Office Window*. We are now doing a thriving business, but we don't

CIVIL DISOBEDIENCE

Please allow me to comment on the law adopted by the Bloomsburg Town Council concerning the new mandatory recycling.

I have never participated in the volunteer recycling program. After getting up at 5:30 a.m. to get my husband to work and my children to school by 7:30 a.m., I then put in eight hours on my feet at my job.

When I come home at night and open a jar of spaghetti sauce for supper, side dish of a jar of instant coffee, I'm in no mood to stand at the sink washing these jars and peeling off labels. I believe that piece of glass became my property when I purchased it from the store and I'll do with it as I please. I use my empty jars to throw away such things as grease, coffee grounds and leftovers.

When the town council supplies me with a dishwasher, several garbage cans, twine, extra

garbage bags or cartons, pays me for my time, and lowers my monthly garbage bill, then I'll be glad to give them my recyclables.

Figure this out: Two days in jail for drunk driving; 30 days in jail for a garbage violation! I think this new law needs to be recycled.

I don't drink, but I'll probably see you in jail!

E. S., Bloomsburg
Press Enterprise
April 15, 1983

HIT AND RUN

Friday night, April 28, between 8 and 10 p.m. in the municipal parking lot in Bloomsburg. "She" dented the left, back side of our Lincoln Town Car! "She" left "her" name, address and phone number on our windshield . . . but . . . the phone number was someone else's, there is no such address, and no Jensens live in Berwick!

"She" scribbled this phony identification on the back of a menu plan and grocery list! If you were planning to have tacos, chicken parmesan, pork and sauerkraut, quiche and meat loaf, maybe your "daughter" should be telling you something!

Incidentally, you write legibly . . . your "daughter" can't!

Mr. and Mrs. Martin Sembach, Millville
Press Enterprise
February 3, 1989

TO MY PERSONAL UNDERGARMENT THIEF

You must be close enough to watch me hang out my family wash on the lines in my yard. Of all the assortment of clothing, you choose to steal my underwear and bras. This leads me to believe you are a male, too embarrassed to admit you like dressing in women's undergarments and can't bring yourself to the local department store to purchase your own. The theft on Saturday, Nov. 4 between 5 and 8 PM was the third time and for me that is three too many!

My neighbors beware, we have a demented person running loose in our neighborhood. Please contact me with any information that could help me catch this person that only wants women's undergarments. He is in our neighborhood.

Linda Jarrard, Bloomsburg
Press Enterprise
November 16, 1989

⊿ WOMEN AND MEN: ⊾
MARRIAGE

LOVE

"Dan Cupid" is said to be the greatest archer of all ages. When he smites the love smitten, the love-smitten hearts are helpless victims before the bond of matrimony. But, if true affinity has not met, in the love-smitten hearts, how serious are the consequences of such a divided union!

People of tender years are naturally drawn into the matrimonial meshes, before the riper years of experience have asserted themselves, and hence, many people have married before they were fully developed, in judgment and physical manhood or womanhood. And often, their folly became manifest, when too late to retract.

Many a clergyman has been so highly censured, and often fined for uniting juvenile lovers in the bonds of matrimony. Hence, nearly all the clergy of our state petitioned the Legislature to pass a law for their own protection against censure and fine, by irate parents, who so strongly protested against clandestine marriages, that parties desiring to be united in matrimony should first procure a license from the Courts before they could be united in matrimony.

Hence many young people go out of their own state, to be united in marriage, in another state, where no such license is required. Is this right? Is it just?

A marriage is a very solemn step and seals the destiny of every individual that enters upon it, for better or worse, so long as both shall live, is a thought that should be well pondered before taking such a step.

> J. C. Wenner
> *The Columbian*
> May 30, 1907

POSTCARD, 1914.

HONOR

This is to announce to the public that Brigadier General Charles M. Blaker Esq. was married to Miss Anne E. Morris, on the 14th of March, 1859, and cohabitated with her as his wife, about nine months, when he discarded her and went about boasting that he was never married to her, and refused to maintain her. She took him at his word and arrested him for seduction. When he found he had no other way to escape the penitentiary, he took the position that he was married, proved it, and the Justice very properly sustained his position and discharged him on that ground.

> Alpha & Omega
> *The Star of the North*
> March 21, 1860

OBEY

Said Sylvia to a Reverend Dean,
  "What reason can be given,
Since marriages are holy things
  That there are none in heaven?"
"There are no women," he reply'd.
  She soon returned the jest:—
"Women there are; but I'm afraid—
  They cannot find a priest."

> Anonymous
> *The Oracle of Dauphin
> and Harrisburgh Advertiser*
> March 8, 1797

IN SICKNESS

Wm. S. Kase—Dear Sir:

With pleasure I reply to the inquiry in regard to reports said to be in circulation in your neighborhood, reflecting upon the domestic relations of Mr. & Mrs. Wm. Keeler. They are

POSTCARD, 1915.

my very near neighbors, and I meet them every day. They live in their own house and are industriously employed in their pursuits, sharing the confidence and respect of this community. They are members of one of our leading churches at whose services they may be seen every Sabbath. Any reports that their domestic relations are unhappy are surely unfounded.

> Respectfully,
> L. L. Brasher
> Supt. of Station A. Cin. P. O.
> *The Columbia County Republican*
> June 30, 1887

AND IN HEALTH

Heaven forbid that my beloved young friends should ever meet (if they enter the marriage state) with a husband like sir William S——; or, if they unfortunately should do so, may they be enabled to imitate the transcendent goodness of his admirable wife. I found her yesterday weeping over a letter which lay before her, and which she said I was entitled to read.

I hastily ran over the contents and could not help dropping a tear of compassion for the unhappy writer, who, I found, was an unfortunate young woman, who had been seduced by sir William S—— some years since; by whom he had two children; and now was so inhuman as to abandon both her and the little innocents to want. I could not help feeling much when I came to this line: "Little Billy is now standing by me, crying for bread; alas! I have not a morsel, either for him or for myself."

The postscript, too, greatly affected me, in which were only the following words: "You promised to pay for Tommy's schooling."

I asked lady S—— what she intended to do?

"I shall order an handsome annuity to be settled on this unhappy object for her life; and I will send immediately for the poor boys, and provide every necessary comfort for their relief."

A tear here forced its way. She that moment sent a bank bill to the unhappy mother, and ordered the children to be brought back by the bearer of her bounty.

They were two fine boys. Lady S——, with her own hands, began dressing them with some suits she had procured for that purpose; and they were expressing their joy and innocent surprise at what they called their finery. "Look, brother Billy, at my coat;" and, "See," said Tommy, "what fine stockings this kind lady has given me."

"Poor babes!" said lady S——, her eyes suffused with tender emotion, "Alas, ye guilty parents of your neglected offspring, what a refined delight do you lose by your shameful neglect of such engaging little prattles!"

That moment the door opened, and sir William entered; he started. "See here my dear! Whose brats are these?"

"Alas!" replied this excellent woman, "Why do you neglect and why have you left to perish these lovely boys, with their unhappy mother? Why, my dear, would you not inform me of their unfortunate little pledges? I have a heart, I hope enlarged enough to receive them as my own, for are they not my husband's?"

"Thou heavenly woman," returned he, lost in astonishment at her unequalled generosity, "Is it thus thou upbraided me for my infidelity to the most admirable woman that ever existed? O, my love, forgive; but that's impossible! I am—I will be only yours. But where is the unhappy woman, which—"

"I have taken care of every thing," replied the

THE KNOCKER.

A KNOCKER IS A GROUCH'S COUSIN,
AND JEALOUSY'S A BROTHER,
YOU'RE A MEMBER OF THAT FAMILY
I HAPPENED TO DISCOVER.

POSTCARD, CIRCA 1915.

angelic lady S——, "I shall remit her a very sufficient sum, yearly, for her support; as to these children, these lovely little ones, their education shall be my —"

"Good God," interrupted sir William, "This is too much! O my Harriet! What a generous triumph have you gained!" He fondly clasped her to his breast (on which he leaned) whilst a silent tear stole down her cheek.

But I was too much affected myself with this tender scene, not to take the first opportunity of retiring; lost in admiration of a woman, who does honour to her sex.

> Adieu for the present,
> Ever yours,
> Emilia
> *The Oracle of Dauphin and Harrisburgh*
> *Advertiser*
> September 28, 1795

'TIL DEATH DO US PART

Dear Colonel,

Four years ago, I stood as groom by the side of as fair and happy a bride as I ever saw. Health

MILLVILLE WEDDING, CIRCA 1920.

played upon her cheek, beauty sparkled in her eye, love breathed in her voice, grace was in all her actions. In the course of time she became a mother, and a long life of happiness and usefulness seemed open before her. But disease came on! Slowly, insidiously, the destroyer overcame its victim. Sometimes she was hotter and soon she was worse—hopes and fears disturbed her friends.

I thought I perceived that she could never recover, and I said so. Friends were unwilling to believe what they felt must be true. Yet when I held her emaciated hand in mine, when I surveyed her wasted frame, when I gazed upon her sunken cheek and hollow eye, I knew that she was near the end of earth.

She is dead! How I regret now that I had not courage enough to part from her as I even then wished to do. I felt that I should never see her again in this world, and yet I parted from her with outward calmness. I regret it now bitterly. She is now an angel of light.

How many of us part from our friends *for the last time,* without knowing it?—Part in perfect health, and yet, the separation proves to be eternal. Death unlocks the door of his dungeon, and carries off the victim in the heyday of his activity and usefulness, and before his companions are aware, a rescue is too late. But it matters not, the crowd push for his place, some one obtains it, and the race goes recklessly on as before.

How many acquaintances and friends in this world, have met *"for the last time?"* Every person can recall an instance of unexpected separation, of sudden death. Three weeks ago I met an acquaintance on the Packet Boat, well as usual; yesterday he fell down dead! We had met *for the last time.*

Anonymous
Democratic Investigator
November 17, 1853

CHAPTER 11

"30 SECONDS":
TRAILER COURT

I'm a Christian lady that lives in the trailer court in Danville. My husband moved out of my trailer into his girlfriend's house next door. I pray every night that he would move out, but the landlord would not move him out. I cannot say who I am, but I pray there is a God after all. I know there is. My attorney and I are fighting this case that he moves out and there are things that go on in front of his wife sees every night with his girlfriend. I do not believe in adultery, but my husband has done it right in front of me.

    Anonymous Caller
    Press Enterprise
    July 11, 1994

I'm calling about the comic strip "Nancy." She used to be different and now in the Sunday comics she's different and she looks more weird. I was just wondering whatever happened to her. If you're able to bring the other one back, will you? Because the other one's kind of better.

    Berwick Resident
    Press Enterprise
    February 12, 1996

I live next door to a lady who says that she is a Christian in a trailer park in Danville. She says that her husband left her and that she does not believe in adultery, but that her husband is doing it right in front of her. The lady I live alongside of threw her husband's clothes out and told him to get out and is now considering this adultery, which I do not. I do believe in God.

    Danville
    Press Enterprise
    July 14, 1994

We have a pressing situation at hand. The disarmament of nuclear warheads and the towers of Snow White's Castle at Disney World. For decades, the theme park has been accepting the highest bid from world dominating countries, in exchange for the privilege of multiple warheads that on command can fire. These missiles are low flying. Henceforth, they will not be detected until they reach their target and obliterate millions of lives. My secret informant, Keith, has briefed me on the volatile subject. And I am sure that the time to act is now.

    Bloomsburg Man
    Press Enterprise
    June 3, 1995

I'm calling in response to the person who stated that all the people who call 30 Seconds are stupid and illiterate and they make this person sick. Well, you called didn't you?

Danville Woman
Press Enterprise
July 7, 1994

To the Danville woman that lives in the trailer court of Danville, the Christian, she did not throw her husband's clothes out. She told him to please leave because he threw her up against the wall and hurt her back and now when it rains her back hurt. She was abused by her husband many years. She found out what brought this fight on that he was having an affair with the neighbor woman for some time, a supposed to be her best friend. Now she has asked the person that has said that adultery is adultery and he is still committing adultery. She has asked to be left alone at night. Don't prowl around her trailer at night. If you want to know who is in the trailer, please come in and she'll let you know who is in there as she has told us.

Anonymous Caller
Press Enterprise
July 18, 1994

I'd like to respond to the man who called in yesterday about the cars being parked in Sherwood Village. I know who he is talking about and he says that we park five cars in our yard. I'd like to correct that. It's not five. We have nine cars.

Anonymous Caller
Press Enterprise
January 16, 1993

To the Christian lady who lives in the trailer park in Danville and says that her husband is committing adultery right in front of her with her next door neighbor, I would tell that woman give him a divorce and quick.

Danville
Press Enterprise
July 16, 1994

THE BREAKING OF THE BOUNDS: 1861–1865

AN EXCHANGE OF IDEAS

FALMOUTH, VA.
Colonel Freeze,
Dear Sir:—

I generally employ my leisure moments in riding about the country for the purposes of learning the sentiments of the people, their manners of living, and encountering adventures. I have met with many strange incidents, which I promise myself much pleasure in recounting to you in case I live to return home.

I have become acquainted with quite a number of old Virginia families. Last Sunday I visited one of this class in Prince William's Co., with which I had contracted a slight intimacy. I received much instruction and was highly entertained. The head of the family was about 80 years of age, but his memory and powers of conversation were undiminished.—He had a lively recollection of Washington, Lee, Madison, Monroe and many other distinguished Virginians. He was a near neighbor to the former and attended the same church in Alexandria. A short time previous to his death, a military gen-

tleman formed a company in Alexandria consisting of small boys. This company assisted at the funeral of Washington.—Only two of the number yet live;—my friend being one of them. He showed me a pair of silver-mounted pistols, once the property of Washington. They had been gilted over to suit the rank of Major General, and on the handles were engraved "Gen'l G. Washington."

My entertainer held a position in Government during the former part of Madison's Administration, and upon the breaking out of the war of 1812 took a commission in the army. Several swords taken from British officers were shown me, and many interesting anecdotes related.

One part of the house formed a picture gallery, which was very interesting. There were many old pictures by renowned artists of rare value; but what chiefly amused me were the old family portraits. Here was an antique lady with huge skirts, and an immense stomacher, while by her side was the "old Virginia gentleman" arrayed in buff waist coat with flaps to the thigh, dainty silk stocking, snow-white frills and ruf-

THE CHANGING ROLE OF NEWSPAPERS

———

The Civil War is fought not only on the great battlefields of Bull Run, Antietam, and Gettysburg, but also in the homes, taverns, and churches of towns like Bloomsburg. And the conflicts spill onto the highly politicized pages of the era's newspapers. Readers on both sides of the heated national debate that ignited the flames of war write passionately to the three local newspapers of the day: *The Columbia County Republican, The Star of the North,* and *Columbia Democrat.*

The Columbia County Republican supports the Union cause and all its trappings, including the Lincoln presidency, the abolitionist ideology, and the necessity for active participation in the war to uphold these beliefs. The other two papers had definite "Democratic" or "Copperhead" leanings. They support the war insofar as it is fought to restore "the Country as it was, and the Constitution as it is." The editors and their readers oppose the secessionist rebellion, but they see Lincoln and the Republicans as unworthy dictators. They oppose the draft, and they want slavery "left alone" in the states where it is practiced. The "Copperheads" decide that the Emancipation Proclamation "subverts" the purpose of the war for Union as they had understood it and take the signing of that document as a personal betrayal. As the carnage continues, these letter writers take up an ever more acid pen.

fles, and an enormous wig. The books were old and *orthodox.*

His extreme politeness almost shamed my blunt manner; and I was on nettles till the formal and lengthy dinner was over. The ladies then entertained us with music and singing.

His politics were "State's Rights," which here means *Secession.* He has five sons in the rebel army. He informed me that so long as there was a United Government he clung to it, and that his County had sent a Union delegate to the Virginia Convention; but after the fall of Fort Sumter he changed sides. He argued "that a man's *first* allegiance was to his State, and his *second* to the United States; the latter being the creation of the former, and entrusted with only certain delegated and enumerated powers. He fought for the Union as long as he could, but he went with his State."

This is the rock upon which this people split. Of course I endeavored to argue against these fallacies. He thought the war would be long and bloody, and finally would degenerate into a guerilla struggle; that the South were taking their armies from the coast to be out of range of our gun boats, and then to wait for sickness, &c., to do its work.

I am pained to learn that Gen. Hunter has declared the slaves free in Georgia, South Carolina, and Florida; and that he is forming negro Brigades out of them. I am sure that President Lincoln will disclaim this act, as he did Fremont's proclamation. Nothing more unwise could be done at this time, when our troops are everywhere victorious, and when ultimate success is so nigh. Perhaps the abolitionists, seeing that the Union is about to be restored with the rights of States unimpaired, and fearing that among those rights the privilege of "regulating their domestic institutions" will be retained, have brought all their influence to bear to have emancipation declared, even at the expense of a protracted war. My only hope is that the President will abide by the policy laid down at the commencement of his administration. I enlisted in this war to restore the Union *as it was,* and to see the Constitution literally carried out. So did thousands of my countrymen. When *that* ceases to be the object, I no longer wish to remain in an army procured by such fraud and perjury. Therefore, if the President maintains Gen. Hunter, my resignation, with hundreds of others will be sent to the Department.

The effect of bringing negroes into service will not only give them the rights of citizenship contrary to a decision of the Supreme Court, but will have a tendency to degrade our white soldiers. *We cannot acknowledge ourselves so weak as to need their assistance.* Not only will the precedent be dangerous, but it gives the blacks a fearful power, and the end will be rebellion of *their* side. I have watched them carefully, and from observation in this and other counties, am convinced that they are not fit for citizens, nor of the right stamp for soldiers. But you can reason on this matter better than I can, therefore I will not tax your patience further.

ARTILLERIST
Columbia Democrat
June 7, 1862

Time Capsule

AROUND THE NATION

- In both his elections, Lincoln wins Pennsylvania, but not Columbia County. In 1860, Lincoln loses handily in the district to John C. Breckinridge, the southern Democrat states'-rights candidate; in 1864, he loses by an even greater margin to General George B. McClellan, whom Lincoln had dismissed as Commander of the Army of the Potomac, and who ran against him on a peace platform.
- April 12, 1861—South Carolina Militia fire on Fort Sumter in Charleston harbor, beginning the Civil War.
- September 23, 1862—Lincoln's Emancipation Proclamation is published, declaring the freedom of all slaves in the Confederacy. Enlistments in the North decline.
- July 1–3, 1863—In the Battle of Gettysburg, about ninety miles southwest of Bloomsburg, Lee's armies are turned back in their northward drive. This is as close as the smoke of war gets to Bloomsburg.
- April 9, 1865—Lee surrenders to Grant at Appomattox Court House. Five days later, Abraham Lincoln is assassinated at Ford's Theatre in Washington, D.C.

STAR OF THE NORTH, MAY 25, 1864.

STAR OF THE NORTH, DECEMBER 25, 1861.

CRAVEN APOLOGISTS

Dr. P. John———

Enclosed please find amount for subscription to *The Republican*. I send you the amount more willingly because I like the paper—*it is interesting*, which cannot be said of many county papers; and then your political sentiments (if one may call a hearty support of the present Administration, and its war policy, *political*) I endorse.

How strange that any man who wishes to be called loyal, should express anything else than an unqualified endorsement of President Lincoln's conduct. How tenaciously these old Breckinridge Democrats cling to their sinking platform! As if it were a revelation from heaven, and infallible in its principles, the *Magna Carta* of your liberties and the salvation of the world! I have met them in Maryland and in different parts of Pennsylvania, and everywhere they favor the peace policy; oppose the Government, and withhold all sympathy from those who are fighting, and suffering, and dying for the defense and perpetuity of this, the *best* of governments—the government which has *made them*, and which Buchanan, Breckinridge, & Co., well nigh destroyed.

They deserve the same obloquy and punishment as the leaders of this unholy and unjustifiable rebellion, in the South.

Surely the institution of slavery which they foolishly imagine they are divinely appointed custodians of, has no particular attractions, or special rewards for them—its Northern advocates—that they should so zealously defend it. And from what we know personally of most slaveholders, the ambitious tyrants who have originated this civil war, we know they would not condescend to recognize most of their craven apologists in the North, *except on election day.*

Yours &c

——— ———

The Columbia County Republican
June 19, 1862

THAT PROCLAMATION

CAMP NEAR BELLE PLAINS, VA.
COL. JOHN G. FREEZE
My Dear Sir:—

From the beginning I have been hopeful, and did all in my power to keep others so; but a deep gloom has settled upon the army. From every side, day after day, comes tidings of disaster and defeat. The men for over six months, have been unpaid. To add to their discontent, a proclamation has been issued, freeing millions of blacks, placing them in the army and many on the same footing as white men; notwithstanding the protests of the latter, and the disgust the soldier has for the Negro. Two weeks have gone by since that proclamation was issued, and as a war measure it has not had the least effect upon our enemy other than to increase discontent.

My duties requiring it, I have been in almost every Corps and Division of the army of the Potomac, and have found both officers and men opposed to the present policy of the Administration. I have yet to find *one man* in favor of the Proclamation. Hundreds of officers are resigning, and numbers of others would do so could they get an honorable discharge. Every officer of a certain Pa. Regiment sent in his resignation, and the Government refused to accept them.

My sole object is to place before the people

of my county, the state of things as I see them. My *judgement* may be wrong, but my *intentions* are correct. No one wishes more ardently to see the prospect brighten, our army victorious, rebellion crushed— and peace throughout the land, than Yours—

ARTILLERIST
Columbia Democrat
January 24, 1863

THE EPITAPH READS:
"LIEUT. J. STEWART ROBINSON,
OF 7TH REG. P.R.V.C.
WAS SHOT BY A REBEL
SYMPATHIZER IN BENTON TP
COLUMBIA CO. PA. WHILE
ASSISTING A U.S. OFFICER IN ATTEMPTING
TO ARREST DESERTERS
JULY 31, 1864.
AND DIED OF THE WOUND
NOV. 3, 1864
AGED 29 YRS 7 MO'S
& 24 DAYS."
(BETHEL HILL CEMETERY IN FAIRMOUNT TOWNSHIP,
LUZERNE COUNTY, PENNSYLVANIA).

MESSENGERS OF SATAN

Permit me, through the columns of your excellent journal, to speak a few words in regard to the manner in which our would-be ministers of the Gospel, but messengers of Satan, conduct themselves in this part of our once happy, but now distracted country.

On Sunday eve last, I proceeded to the Methodist

Time Capsule

AROUND TOWN

• The fact that the farmers and workers of Columbia County are not themselves slave owners does not mean they embrace the ideology of abolitionism. They fear future competition for jobs, believe that Emancipation will prolong an already devastating war, and absolutely oppose any concept of racial equality. While both "Abolitionist" and "Copperhead" fight and die bravely for the Union, the Union cause is far from united.

• Antiwar dissent and draft resistance, common throughout the North, combine in Columbia County with rumors of preparations for an armed uprising. An army lieutenant is shot and mortally wounded while seeking deserters in northern Columbia County. The federal government deploys several hundred troops to the Bloomsburg Fairgrounds in August 1864 to occupy the county and seek out dissenters "up Fishing Creek." Forty-four men from the Benton area are arrested in their homes before dawn on August 31 and shipped to Fort Mifflin in Philadelphia harbor, where they are imprisoned for a period of up to seventeen weeks. One dies in captivity. Only twelve ever face trial (in military court, according to the Lincoln administration's declaration of martial law), charged with aiding and abetting resistance to the federal draft and uttering disloyal statements; seven are found guilty and sentenced to fines and imprisonment. By the spring of 1865, all have either been released without charge or are granted presidential pardons. The episode is known as "The Fishing Creek Confederacy."

Church, hoping to hear the word of God expounded according to the laws laid down in the Holy Bible. But instead of that, to the utter shame and disgrace of the Christian community, we were presented by the would-be minister, but in truth political negro head, with a stump-speech, too offensive to be uttered in the house of God, and what was still more outrageous, on the Sabbath, which should be devoted to the praise of God, and not to political affairs. After discussing the manner in which our armies had been conducted, their progress, etc., and giving as might be expected of these negro-loving ministers, a "hint" to Copperheads, he ended by reading and asking the choir to sing a National Song, but what he called a hymn.

Such Mr. Editor, was the manner in which the word of God was presented to us. The congregation was horrified to think that this church should be devoted to a political stand, instead of a place where the lovers of God might assemble and praise Him according to divine truth. What in the name of common sense will our Christian Community come to if we let in power Abolition minions instead of just men for our rulers? White men's rights have been imposed upon, and these political fiends and desperate tyrants go so far as to trample on the church and turn it into a political stand. It is time that something should be done to save our country from ruin and nothing short of the election of George B. McClellan, can save our country from eternal destruction. The people have had their eyes opened of late and they are going to rush to the ballot-box this fall with a determination that Abraham Lincoln shall be their ruler no longer. Let the people in every State do so, and Satan who has been loose for nearly four years, will be chained again.

> William
> *Columbia Democrat*
> September 24, 1864

FISHING CREEK CONFEDERACY

Hon. C. R. Buckalew, United States Senator
Sir:—

I wrote you a few days ago directed to Washington. Learning Congress has adjourned I suppose it has not reached you: Therefore I'll write to you again. My trial has again come to a close. I have heard nothing yet as to the result, only rumors. I have had a very tedious time: I was arrested in the morning of the 31st of August; was aroused from my slumbers just at the break of day by rapping at the front door of my house. Dressed myself; went down stairs and opened the door; perceived my house was surrounded by armed soldiers. They came in and searched my dwelling from cellar to garret, in search, for arms as they said but finding none, as I never owned any. Then, one of them tapped me on the shoulder and said, "You can consider yourself a Prisoner."

I asked to have time to eat my breakfast, and my wife insisted upon their giving me time for that purpose, but it was not granted. I was taken with others up to Benton, four miles above where I live, and put in Benton Church with a large party from the neighborhood. In the course of an hour Col. Stewart made his appearance and took the pulpit. After considerable whispering, winking and significant grimaces, forty-five of us were selected out and put under strong guard, and ordered to march. I'll not attempt to depicture to you with what difficulty that force march of sixteen miles to Bloomsburg was accomplished by some of the old men who had nothing to eat from the evening before. I was forced past my home; not allowed to go in to get a change of clothes. My wife followed me with some cakes and a few articles of clothing. Was forced past parents, sisters and brothers who stood by the way-side; not allowed to take them by the hand and bid them farewell. Their expressions were full of feeling which came from the heart, and their eyes were filled to overflowing. It caused tears to course freely down the bronzed cheeks of the guards beside me. It was very trying, though I did not allow my feelings to overcome me. The outrage made me indignant or I should have been completely overcome. We were hurried to Bloomsburg, got there about 8 P.M.; stopped but for a short time and were put on the cars, not knowing our destination. Were brought on to Harrisburg; stopped but a few moments; were not allowed to get anything to eat; started off again we knew not whither; arrived at Philadelphia about 8 A.M. and were marched to 5th and Buttonwood and put in barracks. At 11 o'clock we had some rations furnished us being the first in 40 hours. Those of us who were not too much exhausted partook with a keen relish.

Started from the barracks about 1 P.M.; marched to the Arch Street wharf; were put on board the *Reybold* and forwarded to Fort Mifflin. There we were marched up in front of the Colonel's quarters and detained there something near an hour in the scorching sun. Sir, it was a pitiable sight to see the exhausted appearance of the men, particularly the old and infirm, as there were several such among us. There was a cellar cleared in the meantime in the Bomb-proof for our reception. It was in very filthy condition, full of vermin. I have not space to give you a description of the place where we were confined. It never was intended for and is entirely unfit to hold men for any length of time. Its location and construction will break down the strongest constitution in a short time as the emaciated condition of the Columbia County prisoners fully verifies. The suffering endured whilst confined in that

STAR OF THE NORTH,
MARCH 2, 1864.

filthy place beggars description. Fortunately for me, I was not confined there as long as some of the others. I was brought to Harrisburg about three months ago for trial, and (as you are aware) my condition here has been more tolerable. The worst feature of my confinement here has been the miserably filthy and corrupt society I have been compelled to endure. Their vulgarity and profanity I cannot portray. The confusion at this writing renders it almost impossible to write. The anxiety of mind has been great, being on trial so long, and I was aware of the effort they were making to convict me. I never shunned an investigation, but desired it. All I ask was a fair trial, but was so closely confined that I had but little chance to prepare for defense.

In conclusion; I never violated any law, civil or military, to the best of my knowledge. If I ever did it was an error of the head and not of the heart. I have been taught from my earliest boyhood, by kind and religious parents, to observe the laws of my country, and I have regarded them as second only to the laws of God. My imprisonment I consider an outrage, and I have never begged for my release. I have spurned the idea. Liberty is dear, but I cannot and will not sacrifice principles of manhood to obtain it. I hope the day is not far distant when a full exposé will be made public.

Excuse this lengthy scrawl.

> Your Friend,
> Daniel McHenry
> *The Star of the North*
> January 4, 1865

Charles Rollins Buckalew, a Bloomsburg Democrat, is a United States senator from Pennsylvania. He attempts to intervene on behalf of the Columbia County prisoners. Daniel McHenry, accused of conspiring to defy the draft, and "commission of acts of disloyalty against the Government of the United States," which included "uttering disloyal sentiments and opinions," faces a military commission and is found "not guilty" on all counts.

A PINT OF CORN CHOP A DAY

Dear Colonel:

There is a Soldier home here who was taken prisoner about six months ago. He was down to Charleston in prison. He got only a pint of corn chop a day. He is now a mere skeleton. He says that the reason our brave boys are starved is contrariness on both sides. He said that our side would not exchange prisoners because the Rebels will not exchange the nigger, and say they are their property. So our dear Husbands and Brothers are left there to be starved to death, because the rebels will not give up their property.

He came right out and said, that the party in power think more of the

Niggers than they do of our brave White boys in the army: and more, he said that if any had to be where he was, they would not become black abolitionists. They would be DEMOCRATS. But I must tell you what one of our lying loyal leaguers told him—He said, that there were copperheads in the North that went in for the South starving our men! Now he knows that he told a willful black-hearted Lie, for he cannot find one Democrat, that goes in for starving them; and he knows it too; but he had to lie a little.

But great God, how long are we to live under such a black administration as this?

A SOLDIER'S WIFE

Columbia Democrat

January 14, 1865

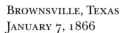

Early in the war, both Charles B. Brockway, age twenty, and Samuel Knorr, age twenty-three, volunteer to serve in the first Civil War unit assembled in Bloomsburg, the Columbia "Iron Guards," Company A of the Thirty-fifth Regiment of Pennsylvania Volunteers, Sixth Pennsylvania Reserves. Brockway is a Democrat "Copperhead" who often writes under the name "Artillerist"; Knorr is a staunch Republican and abolitionist. Though each transfers in time to other units, Brockway and Knorr are both at Second Bull Run; Brockway is captured, but is later exchanged and "paroled," and goes on to see action at Fredericksburg, Chancellorsville, Gettysburg, and elsewhere. He remains opposed to emancipation through the end of the war. In 1863, Samuel Knorr lives his ideals, when he accepts an appointment as captain of Company A of the Nineteenth United States Colored Troops, one of the first "Negro" units, and with them sees action in eastern Virginia from the Wilderness to the fall of Richmond. Brockway, the "Artillerist," takes part in these same battles. The following is Samuel Knorr's farewell message to the men of the Nineteenth Regiment, a year after war's end.

BROWNSVILLE, TEXAS
JANUARY 7, 1866
Officers and Men of the 19th Regt. U.S.C.T.

Having at length received my discharge it is befitting that I should say a parting word.

I was with you in camp of instruction. I marched with you in the field, and with you I endured all the fatigues, privations and dangers incident to long and rapid marches, again many battles and a bloody siege without parallel in history.

Together we have witnessed the breaking of the bounds of four millions of slaves and the restoration of the authority of the United States throughout all her domains and over a free people.

I part with you as with heroic companions of many achievements.

Accept my gratitude for your uniform kindness and respect.

I will always rejoice to meet you and honored to do you a favor.

May you all be allowed ere long to return to your homes, become useful, peaceful citizens, with honor pure as the evergreen, fragrance as the Rose—and lasting as eternity.

Samuel Knorr

Civil War Military Service Record

National Archives, Washington, D.C.

After the war, both men return to Bloomsburg as honored veterans, to become active in politics and the community. Charles Brockway remains a Democrat, and in 1875 becomes the editor of *The Columbian,* formed by the merger of the *Columbia Democrat* and *The Star of the North.* Samuel Knorr remains a Republican, and becomes the proprietor of Bloomsburg's Keystone Foundry.

☑ THY SONS AND ☑
THY DAUGHTERS

I have in my possession the transcript of a taped conference (telephone) call, between two ladies and a gentleman, who are seriously involved in and with this country's public school systems.

If the gentleman's name were to be mentioned, readers would know of him (and his wife's) monumental work uncovering the religion of secular humanism and other subversive materials and subjects in school textbooks. This phone conversation between the three parties took place in 1985.

In the transcript, they speak of the manner in which teachers are trained, in some instances, to hypnotize their captive audiences. It is done, they said, by speaking for several seconds, then being silent for several seconds, alternating, until they get the rhythm down.

At one point in the conversation, the gentleman tells about receiving a complaint 2 years ago (from the 1985 date) from a distraught mother in Oregon, in which she tells him of her child's experience with hypnosis in the classroom. (From my daughter's personal experience many years ago I can vouch as to the veracity of that statement of complaint.)

Also discussed are the various other methods of mind-control being used in the classroom,

such as visualization, guided imagery, telepathy, clairvoyance, E.S.P., and some of the Eastern occultic religious practices like yoga.

Many Eastern religious tenets are taught in schools as routinely as any of the legitimate curriculum. Children are taught the "art" of yogic breathing, purportedly to manage stress, and are prompted to do it on a regular basis, until they can enter the quieting reflex in six seconds flat!

Often they are told not to tell parents they are learning the basics of these Eastern religions because parents are too old-fashioned to understand anything about it.

Further explained as to the whys of these exercises is that at the peak of the trance-like state entered into through yogic breathing, the child is instructed to "call for a spirit guide."

In one case, where this exercise had been completed successfully, the guide told the child not to pray, nor to speak to mother about the experience! At this point, readers should keep in mind that those two Christian ladies have "come up" through the systems and have their doctorates in education, so they know whereof they speak.

The information they have revealed regarding Eastern occultic, religious practices being taught in the classrooms across America have come to them directly from teacher training manuals.

The practices, they further declare, are begun in the earliest grades, such as kindergarten and pre-K. This coincides with methods and means of "Education in the New Age," advocated by the United Nations' "spiritual" arm, Lucis Trust (former Lucifer Trust), which also appears in the former Secretary General's (Robert Mueller of the U.N.) "World Core Curriculum."

In the conference call, the ladies also discuss classroom use of what is called psychosynthesis, which is restructuring of the personality through inner mental activity! (Parents need not wonder why, or how it is that their children change after attending only a few years of school, when such as these mind-altering techniques are being used against them.)

It's been my experience that the only way parents can protect their children from the harm those teachings bring upon them and families is to carefully monitor all textbooks and inquire daily from your child as to what all classroom discussions were about.

When any of the above mentioned is found, dislodge it from your child's mind as soon as possible and replace it with thoughts, words and actions from your own belief systems and your family values.

For whatever it's worth, you still do have recourse in protecting your child from forced foreign religious training and discussions taking place in school under the Hatch Amendment to the Education Act, which forbids such intrusions into those aspects of your personal family life. If you are careful with yourself and yours the warning of Deuteronomy 28:32 need not come to pass in your case.

> Ruth Gonzalez, Barnesville
> *Press Enterprise*
> December 22, 1993

JOE AND RUTH GONZALEZ.

> Thy sons and thy daughters *shall* be given over to another people, and thine eyes shall look and fail *with longing* for them all the day long: and *there shall be* no might in thine hand.
>
> Deuteronomy 28:32

⚔ "30 SECONDS": ⚔
KARAOKE

This is to a certain contestant of the Karaoke contest at the Chatterbox who came in fifth and went down to the IGA in Bloomsburg and shot his mouth off about the contest being rigged. I think that he had better take a look at the videotape that was made and see why he came in fifth. He had no real costume, except a cowboy hat that he doesn't even own, whereas the other contestants were decked out and also played the song up more than he did.

Anonymous Caller
Press Enterprise
July 24, 1995

I am a teenage marijuana user. I am calling about those idiots who think marijuana may make people want to fly and jump out of windows. You are crazy. Using marijuana makes me want to have sex and listen to Rock & Roll. Let's party.

Anonymous Caller
Press Enterprise
July 28, 1992

I'm calling to thank the people that stole my grill from the back porch. If they would come by, they could pick up the instructions. Because if they don't have the instructions, and they put it together, and if they start it up, it'll blow up.

Berwick woman
Press Enterprise
August 16, 1995

This is about the Karaoke contest. First of all, I never shot my mouth off. I said I felt that I was robbed and I still do. But there will be more contests. And I have a videotape of that contest and a lot of people agree with me. I also felt my costume was fine. Who cares where I got the hat? The point was, I had a cowboy hat on. And I felt that I played my song better than I was given credit for. At least I was in the contest finals.

Should have done better
Press Enterprise
July 29, 1995

If chicken is the tuna of the land, then President Clinton is the Paul Bunyan of the East.

> Bloomsburg man
> *Press Enterprise*
> July 19, 1994

This is in concern to getting your services hooked up when you're moving into a new home. I was just wondering if anybody can give suggestions to what you are supposed to do when the different types of companies would like you to be at your home or to verify identification. I don't know what to do. I work during the time that they're open also. Can you give any suggestions?

> Bloomsburg Woman
> *Press Enterprise*
> February 22, 1996

This is for the Karaoke contest complainer. He says he played his song better than he was given credit for. First of all, he didn't play the song. The machine did. And he doesn't play songs, he mimics them. I'm a musician. I play songs. He just sang along.

> Anonymous Caller
> *Press Enterprise*
> August 4, 1995

CHAPTER 15

⊿ LAST ACT/ ⊾ LAST HOPE

On October 21, 1868, the *Columbia Democrat* reports the "sad and shocking news relating the fact that Alexander W. Rea, esq., Superintendent of the Locust Mountain Coal Company in this county, had been horribly murdered." The news rocks the Anthracite Region just south and east of Bloomsburg. Suspicion falls upon four alleged members of the "Mollie Maguires"—a rumored organization within the Irish-American "Ancient Order of Hibernians" that responds to exploitation by mine owners with terrorism, intimidation, and murder. At their trial in Bloomsburg, three of the men are acquitted; the case against the fourth, Patrick Hester, is dismissed for lack of evidence.

Seven years later, new testimony from a "Mollie" turned state's evidence leads to the arrest of Hester plus two others. Once again, the trial is held in Bloomsburg, and is one of several sensational "Mollie" trials throughout the region. From Bloomsburg, Mr. Fielder, a native of Shenandoah, Pennsylvania, tells the story in a series of letters to *The Shenandoah Herald*.

ALEXANDER W. REA.

POTTSVILLE EVENING HERALD,
MARCH 26, 1878.

PRETRIAL MOTIONS

The excitement regarding the coming trial is still on the increase, and the increasing crowd is even growing larger. Nothing but trial is talked of and there are more stories in circulation about the murderers and the murdered than would fill a very respectably sized volume. In this part of Columbia County, the people seem to know as little about "Mollies" as they do in California I would say. In Schuylkill county, the name stands for all that is bad, but here a "Mollie" is more of a curiosity than anything else. The preparations for the trial are on a scale of unheard of completeness. Counsel are so numerous as to be almost unrecognizable from outsiders, and almost every second lawyer you meet is introduced as "counsel for Hester" or some of the rest of the gang.

Mr. Fielder
The Shenandoah Herald
February 8, 1877

The trial lasts three weeks. All the men are found guilty and sentenced to hang. While awaiting appeals, they spend a year in the Bloomsburg jail.

PATRICK HESTER.

POTTSVILLE EVENING HERALD,
MARCH 26, 1878.

"THE JAIL"

Whenever you ask a Bloomer to show you "the jail" he goes and points you to the very door, otherwise you would be unable to find the haven of people who should have died in their youth. Situated nowhere in particular but behind the court house by which it is hidden is "the jail." You see an ancient looking weak-kneed and altogether miserable looking brick dwelling house of medium size. Climbing some narrow stairs you arrive at the front door—a very ordinary door, and one which a first-class kick would very easily demolish. Entering and passing along a very narrow passage, the traveler is stopped by an iron latticed door. This door having been unlocked, I stepped inside and stood in the jail proper. There are four cells in the building. In the first cell to the right are the three prisoners, although in the opinion of the warden the prisoners ought to be separated. I said "Why don't you separate them then?" "For a very good reason," was the answer "but you'll probably see for yourself before you leave us." I did. In the cell above, a prisoner could crawl quietly up the chimney and make his way to the roof. The third cell can be mined in a very short space of time and with little trouble, and as the miner would drop into the fourth cell, it can easily be seen that "the jail" is the poorest apology for a jail that was ever built.

Mr. Fielder
The Shenandoah Herald
March 1, 1877

Their appeals denied, on March 24, 1878, the men are hanged. A large crowd observes the assembly of the gallows borrowed from another "Mollie" execution in Mauch Chunk (now Jim Thorpe), Pennsylvania, and the arrival of a "stained ice box" sent by an undertaker to transport one of the bodies back to Pottsville.

NO STAY OF EXECUTION

That there are serious evils connected with the execution of the death penalty must be confessed by any one who has observed the morbid interest of a large part of our community, which began several days before the execution, and culminated in the eager and excited crowd of fifteen or twenty hundred people outside the prison walls during the hours of 9 and 11 on Monday morning. The throng was not within limits of either age or sex. Women and children, men and half-grown boys, were on the tip toe of expectation, eager to catch the sound of something going on within the walls, and all the while discussing every imaginable detail of the revolting spectacle, from which they were properly excluded. The day of the execution will live in the memory of many boys of our town, not as a day of expiation and misery, but as a day which afforded unexampled opportunities of sight-seeing and excitement. The impression of the day on their minds will be one of absorbing interest, rather than of painful sorrow.

A disposition to lionize the men, positively made itself felt and was upheld by scores of people. This was but a natural outcome of the universal talk about the impending execution, which was ever present in the public mind. The last act in a tragedy always leaves a more vivid impression upon the average mind than the first. It would be hard to say who received the greater share of tender consideration in the common talk of the town—the innocent victims or the brutal murderers. I believe that one of the greatest evils attending the execution of the death penalty, is the misplaced sympathy of a large class of people. It is this that makes so many advocates of the abolition of capital punishment, and in a large measure neutralizes the beneficial results that follow its execution, *viz:* the diminution of murder and crime.

If capital punishment could be administered without its attending evils its beneficial effects would be largely increased. It seems to me this would be possible, if we had in each separate state, a single locality where all executions should take place. The novelty and excitement in such locality would soon wear away on account of the frequency of the punishment, while the effects upon the neighborhood from which the criminal goes forth, would be what they ought to be—a wholesome restraint upon the lawless—the absence of any popular demonstration and the silent acquiescence of hundreds of good people who, in the excitement of the hour, would always express undue sympathy with the murderers.

L. Z.
The Columbian
March 29, 1878

A century after the murder of Alexander Rea, the "Mollies" again attract a crowd in Bloomsburg. On June 5, 1968, *The Morning Press* reports that "several hundred people lined Route 11" to observe a film crew shooting Richard Harris and Sean Connery in scenes for Paramount Pictures' *The Molly Maguires.* That night, during a victory celebration after the California primary, Senator Robert F. Kennedy is assassinated.

LAST HOPE

Each of us is asking what can I do?

President John F. Kennedy, Dr. Martin Luther King, Senator Robert Kennedy—

We feel helpless and frustrated. Many of our leaders talk of gun control. Legalized gun control is not the answer. The answer in part is:

1. News media, teachers, churches and individuals must stop honoring the old unrealistic western tradition of winning a battle with your fists, a knife, a club or a gun. Every time one of us honors the fighter, we put the act of peace below the act of violence. Each day when a person speaks in pride of killing any animal or speaks in pride of war or aggression, he opens the door to kill for the border-line psychotic person. He gives that person the OK to destroy.

2. Mass media, teachers, and churches must take on a new role. These powerful influences on people must begin to talk about more than love. They must begin to talk about the honor of settling a problem with intelligence.

Our minds and our hearts are our last hope. If now, tonight, tomorrow and every day after, we do not honor the peaceful ways of handling our problems, then tomorrow, the next murder may be close to you and be your fault.

William Evans, Bloomsburg
The Morning Press
June 8, 1968

JOHN Q. TIMBRELL

WHAT?

Dear Sir:

Certain officials of the local College published an announcement recently; RE: the visit of Black congresswoman Shirley Chisolm to the campus. The article reports her district to have 70 percent blacks and Puerto Ricans with the rest being Jewish, Polish, Ukranian, and Italian. What? No Americans? Would it be better for her to stay home and get these people naturalized so that they can vote? Or is this racism?

> John Q. Timbrell, Bloomsburg
> *The Morning Press*
> February 22, 1972

IT'S A LOTTERY

Dear Sir:

The Pennsylvania Lottery was approved by the Public, IF the money was handled by banks, and IF the earnings was used to help the elderly with property tax and room rent for those who did not own real estate.

The general public regards the teachers as underworked and overpaid. If any of this money is grabbed for teachers pay raises, I, for one will buy no more lottery tickets.

> John Q. Timbrell, Bloomsburg
> *The Morning Press*
> September 15, 1978

BRIDGES

Dear Sir:

Secretary of Highways T. Larson wants to update Routes 15 and 220. For what? The deer and bear don't need a 4-lane, divided fast road. Or is it intended to provide a convenience for the Governor, Philly and Harrisburg politicians to go hunting and fishing in Sullivan, Bradford and Tioga counties? We need new bridges.

> John Q. Timbrell, Bloomsburg
> *The Morning Press*
> June 26, 1979

CHINESE

In 1949, when the Communists took over China and established a totalitarian Dictatorship Government (they call it a "People's Government"), the Chinese masters immediately made the growing of poppies and the production of morphine and heroin a complete Government monopoly. All of the elderly who used opium and heroin were liquidated as unworthy of continuing to live.

The heroin getting into this Country from China is worth $5.5 billion on the street. The heroin getting to our troops in Vietnam comes from China. The Red Chinese delegates at the U.N. in New York are paying their bills with new U.S. $100 bills. Any questions?

> John Q. Timbrell, Bloomsburg
> *The Morning Press*
> March 31, 1972

RUSSIANS

Dear Sir:

25,000 persons killed yearly on the roads. Not one has been killed by a Nuclear Accident. Yet, 20,000 people traveled in cars to a protest rally in California. 15,000 attended a anti-nuclear rally in New England.

Who gets these people organized? Who makes up the chants? Who are the cheer leaders of the chants? Who pays the expenses, buys the meals, buys the gasoline? Should we be suspicious of money from the Russian Embassy?

> John Q. Timbrell, Bloomsburg
> *The Morning Press*
> July 24, 1979

WE DON'T WANT . . .

We don't want hippies, yippies, zippies and dippies in Washington, or anywhere in Government. We don't want permissiveness. We don't want surrender to Communism. We don't want amnesty to the cowardly draft dodgers. We don't want coddling of prisoners. We don't want the electric chair in storage. We don't want pinkos and reds running to Hanoi. We don't want low bail and early paroles.

> John Q. Timbrell, Bloomsburg
> *The Morning Press*
> November 15, 1972

⊿ BOSS K ⊾

WHISKEY FOR VOTES

MR. EDITOR,—

The practice of treating beer and whiskey for votes should be spurned by every voter with contempt, as it is a direct insult to his manhood and independence, for the one that offers it too often estimates it as the price of the vote of the one he treats. Voter! it is an insult to your manhood! it is the price of your citizenship! Spurn the candidate who offers you drink only during an election campaign as one who offers you the greatest insult to the dignity of the American citizen.

> A VOTER
> *The Danville Intelligencer*
> March 14, 1884

A CARD FROM MR. KRICKBAUM

BLOOMSBURG, PA., JULY 22, 1884
EDITOR *Catawissa News Item:*

In your issue of July 10th, you submit several questions to me, over the signature of a name-

THE CHANGING ROLE OF NEWSPAPERS

The 1880s mark the beginnings of a struggle between those in the newspaper business who genuinely hope for an impartial press and work for political reform and those who would wield the growing power of the press as a blunt political instrument for party or personal gain. Or both.

less correspondent, who demands an answer under oath.

I deny the right of an anonymous scribbler to put any questions to me, and assert my right to refuse an answer to them. But, if your correspondent will, over his own proper name, assert that what he implies therein is the truth, and give also the names of those to whom he alludes, he shall have a full, complete and satisfactory answer. If he refuses his name, and the names of the persons he implicates, then I pronounce him a *sneak* and a *coward*.

Yours, &c.,
WILLIAM KRICKBAUM
The Columbian
July 25, 1884

WILLIAM KRICKBAUM ANSWERS

The affidavit published below was made in answer to the questions printed in the *Catawissa News Item* of July 10th. The questions, which come from Benton in the north of the County, are as follows:

1st. When you were up through here electioneering, a short time ago, did you not give some parties five, some ten and another twenty dollars to electioneer for you?

2d. Did you not send those two demijohns of whiskey up to this place, about two weeks ago, to your friends to electioneer for you?

3d. Have you not made arrangements to attempt to carry the primary elections with money, whiskey and beer, wherever they can be used to an advantage?

4th. Did you not purchase and roll a barrel of cider into your friends cellar last fall, in this town, for this purpose, and have you not a barrel of whiskey at the new jail at present?

AFFIDAVIT OF WM. KRICKBAUM
COLUMBIA COUNTY   sworn and subscribed:

Before me, John M. Clark, a Justice of the Peace in and for said county, personally came Wm. Krickbaum, who being duly sworn according to law, deposeth and saith:

That to all of the above questions except 4th deponent says, No.

As to 4th question deponent has this to say:

"Sometime in October of last year, arrangements were made with the committeemen of Fishingcreek, Benton, Jackson and Sugarloaf townships to meet the county chairman and me at Benton, for the purpose of making arrangements to get out the Democratic vote in the aforesaid townships; having met at the time appointed and when about ready to proceed to business Mr. Everhart of Jackson stopped in front of the Hess Hotel, and when requested by me to come into the house, replied, that he had a barrel of sweet cider to dispose of first. I, wishing him to assist in the caucus, thought the only way to make sure of it was to get rid of the cider, asked Mr. Weirman if he wanted it, and upon his answering in the affirmative, I ordered it to be taken to Mr.

Weirman's and then paid for it. What Mr. Weirman did with it I have no knowledge. As to the barrel of whiskey I say, that I have no barrel of whiskey at the new jail nor anywhere else.

"In answer to slanderous reports circulated by Wm. H. Snyder that I sent out demijohns of whiskey by the Benton stage to Daniel Karns, James Weirman or to any other person, are untrue; and for the purposes of deceiving the voters and to injure me.

"WM. KRICKBAUM."

Sworn and subscribed before me, July 29th 1884,

JOHN M. CLARK, J.P.
Bloomsburg
The Columbian
August 1, 1884

EDITORIAL

Early in the spring the COLUMBIAN invited correspondence touching the political situation in this county, but received only two or three communications, and to these the writers were unwilling to sign their names. The COLUMBIAN has boldly denounced all political methods that have a corrupting tendency, and insisted that the campaign should be conducted entirely within the law and the rules of the party.

We have insisted that if any person know of improper practices on the part of any candidate, that the fact should be published, openly, honestly and fearlessly, and have offered to print anything on the subject that was accompanied by the name of a responsible person. We have frequently criticized the practice of circulating charges against candidates, and have insisted, and always will insist, that such charges shall be fairly made and openly sustained, or be looked upon with suspicion. We have endeav-

COLUMBIA COUNTY COURTHOUSE, CIRCA 1884.

ored to be strictly impartial, and have had no regard for persons in the applications of these principles, seeking only that which, as a general rule, we believed to be for the best interests of the party.

All that can be done now is to urge all voters to attend the delegate election on August 9th, and cast their ballots for those who they believe are best qualified for the positions to be filled. If you believe any candidate incompetent, do not vote for him; if you believe any one dishonest, vote for some one else; if you believe that improper means have been used to secure votes, vote accordingly. At all events, GO TO THE POLLS AND VOTE.

The Columbian
August 1, 1884

WHAT WHISKEY?

BENTON, JULY 25TH, 1884
TO WM. KRICKBAUM, Esq.

MY DEAR SIR: In answer to your question I will say, that you never sent whiskey in a demijohn or otherwise, by me for James Weirman,

AROUND THE NATION

- "Boss" William Tweed dies in prison in 1878, following his conviction on multiple counts of political corruption, but his "Tammany Hall" power base in New York continues to exert great force, transforming favors, kickbacks, and patronage positions into political power.
- With sensational slogans like "Rum, Romanism, and Rebellion" and new terms like "mugwump" (one who deserts his political party for another), the 1884 presidential election between Democrat Grover Cleveland and Republican James G. Blaine is one of the ugliest on record.

AROUND TOWN

- Through the spring and summer of 1884, a bitter campaign is waged between William H. Snyder and two-term incumbent William Krickbaum for the Democratic party nomination for the Columbia County row office position of prothonotary. The primary election is held Tuesday, August 12, 1884.
- *Prothonotary*—from the Greek meaning "keeper of records." The prothonotary is responsible for maintaining such civil files as lawsuits, judgments, abuse petitions, marriages, and divorces.

Daniel Karns or any other person. Nor have I carried whiskey to those persons, from anyone else.

E. P. ALBERTSON,
Benton Stage Driver
The Columbian
August 1, 1884

A CARD

A report having been circulated in this township that William Krickbaum has left a keg of whiskey with me for campaign purposes, I desire to state that there is not a word of truth in it. Neither he nor any one for him has ever given me money or whiskey for that or any other purpose, and I would not have taken it, had it been offered.

Yours truly,
W. A. KILE
Warden, Columbia County Jail
The Columbian
August 1, 1884

THAT WHISKEY

SUGARLOAF TOWNSHIP
RED MILL, JULY 25TH, 1884

On Monday July 21st, 1884, Wm. H. Snyder while at this place electioneering told myself and sons, that Mr. Krickbaum had two demijohns of whiskey sent with the Benton stage to Benton, one for Jas. Weirman and one for Daniel Karns, and he also

CAUGHT IN THE STORM, IN OLDEN TIME.

stated that they would put circulars all through the county a few days before the delegate meeting which were intended to the injury of Mr. Krickbaum.

GEO. W. DRIESBACH
The Columbian
August 1, 1884

EVEN MORE QUESTIONS

BENTON, PA., JULY 26TH, 1884
EDITORS COLUMBIAN:

A few weeks ago I requested Mr. Krickbaum to answer a few questions over his affidavit in some paper in the county, which he refuses to do because the communication contains an anonymous author.

I would ask Mr. Krickbaum again if he did not purchase a barrel of cider from Augustus Everhart of Jackson township, and place it in James Weirman's cellar to be used for electioneering purposes?

2nd. I also ask him if he did not invite Messrs. D. Karns, James Weirman and Jesse Hartman to go with him to the Mountain a few weeks ago, keep them clear, give them money and after he returned to Bloomsburg, send Messrs. D. Karns and Jesse Hartman each a demijohn of whiskey up in the stage?

3rd. I also ask him if he did not get a barrel of whiskey, directly or indirectly, at Fowler's distillery, and have it hauled to the new jail, and if his friends do not congregate there at night and on Sunday to drink it?

4th. I also ask him if he has not requested persons to bring their demijohns to him to get them filled, during the present campaign, and if he has not had one in the vault of his office?

5th. I also ask him if he has not had boxes of beer delivered at the Lime Ridge back of Afton, and in private cellars at different places, and if he has not taken whiskey with him electioneering?

6th. I also ask him if he has not given men money, whiskey and beer in violation of the rules governing our County Convention and the election laws?

I have not the slightest prejudice against Mr. Krickbaum, but I am violently opposed to any candidate corrupting the people to secure his election, which is a shame and disgrace to any civilized community. If Mr. Krickbaum is innocent let him make a clear, clean and positive statement in his affidavit.

Let it be *definitely* understood that we want an *honest, unequivocal* statement, containing *positive* facts, not one in which he screens himself and places the responsibility upon his hirelings.

Yours Respectfully,
J. F. Smith
The Columbian
August 1, 1884

The Columbian, August 8, 1884

The Prothonotary Fight

GETTING RED HOT.

William Krickbaum Charged with Violation of the Election Law

His Answer to the Charge

Affidavit of James E. Weirman

State of Pennsylvania,
County of Columbia, ss:

Before me the subscriber, a Justice of the Peace in and for said County, personally came James K. Weirman of Benton, said County, who made the following affidavit, to wit:

"That during the month of September, A. D. 1883, William Krick-baum of Bloomsburg, approached me with reference to his candidacy for Prothonotary and earnestly solicited my support for the nomination of Prothonotary; thereupon I consulted some of my friends in Bloomsburg and asked them whether it would be advisable for me to encourage said Krickbaum in his advances for my support and gain his confidence so as to get into the secrets of his disreputable and outrageous methods of electioneering, and I was advised to pursue such a course.

"This course having been advised and determined upon, I gave said Krickbaum to understand that he should receive my support. As soon as I promised said Krickbaum my support he asked me whether it would not be advisable to use some money to exert an influence for said Krick-baum in that part of the county where I live, and, wanting to see how far said Krickbaum might go in his disreputable methods, I answered, 'yes.'

"During said month of September I was serving as a Grand Juror at Bloomsburg, and received from said Krickbaum the sum of fifteen dollars to be used for electioneering purposes; and from that time to the present, at various times, have received from five to ten dollars, for the purpose of influencing votes for said Krickbaum, at the same time keeping my friends posted as to his plans in the upper end of the county, and using all the power I could, under the circumstances, to prevent said Krickbaum from gaining a foothold in Benton and vicinity. The last money got from him was on Monday, July 21st, 1884, when I received the sum of five dollars. The day before Krickbaum wrote to me as follows:

BLOOMSBURG, JULY 19th, 1884

MR. JAMES WEIRMAN, *Dear Sir:* I wish you would come down on Monday and stay over night. Come if you can. Important matter to be looked after.

W. KRICKBAUM

"On Sunday, July 20th, I went to Bloomsburg, and on that day I received from said Krickbaum five dollars, and on the following day five dollars. I have received in all from said Krickbaum about one hundred and seventy-five dollars since last September; each time I received the money from him I was instructed by said Krickbaum to do with it all I could for said Krickbaum's nomination for Prothonotary.

"The course I have pursued has not been a pleasant one to me, but having once entered the field to unearth said Krickbaum's corrupt and degrading practices I have been determined from the beginning to keep it up till the last, and as the campaign is now about closed, my unpleasant task is ended, and before God and man I here submit and substantiate by affidavit the result of my efforts, hoping that all those who have seen my actions and impugned my motives for making what appeared to be an alliance with said Krickbaum, will now count me in the great majority of Democrats in their determined march for the victory they will achieve in the overthrow and downfall of Krickbaum and his methods.

"JAMES K. WEIRMAN."

Sworn and subscribed before me this 4th day of August, 1884, after hearing the contents of the above affidavit.

JAMES B. HARMAN, J. P.

MR. KRICKBAUM ANSWERS

MESSRS. EDITORS:

Mr. James K. Weirman of Benton, takes an oath that he has been acting the spy, sneak and informer in his intercourse with me, William Krickbaum, at the instance and under the advice of some of his (Weirman's) friends in Bloomsburg. He does not name the "friends in Bloomsburg" under whose advice he acted, but the name of one at least will be exposed in the course of this reply to the affidavit.

Mr. Weirman having by his own "disreputable and outrageous methods" got himself into the shadow of the Quarter Sessions of Columbia County, the District Attorney, Robert Buckingham, and Wm. H. Snyder, candidate for Prothonotary, seem to have entered into a conspiracy to squeeze him; and seem to have been so far successful, as to add to Mr. Weirman's previous "disreputable and outrageous methods," those of the traitor, pretending friendship to betray his friend.

The "disreputable and outrageous methods" of District Attorney Buckingham, in this business will most fully appear by the following letter; and it shows also the "friend in Bloomsburg" who advises Mr. Weirman to make himself additionally notorious:

BLOOMSBURG, PA., Feb. 27, 1884.

JAMES K. WEIRMAN, Esq.,

Dear Friend:—Our *friend* was here to-day, and has so arranged matters that you will not be troubled for three months with the Wilson matter. He was perfectly willing to enter into the arrangement as soon as he came, and he has stopped the possibility of your being prosecuted for three months. I am pleased that they have given you three months' time to prevent the prosecution which they might institute against you, and for which there is a heavy penalty. I know you too well to think that you will not pay the amount in that time, and I congratulate you upon your safety for the next three months, and I know that you will raise the amount in that time. If you do not, you know Wilson's disposition, and it may be that another attempt to help you out of the difficulty may not succeed. Now James, stand by your principles which have ruled you heretofore, and a happy and prosperous life is before you. This difficulty has proven to you the value of friends who will stand by you when friendship is needed. I have so much I would like to write to you that I haven't time to put it on paper now. But will sum up what I have to say politically in the expression "Down with Boss K. and his allies."

Very truly your friend,

R. BUCKINGHAM

Mr. Weirman, finding himself in the hands of the district attorney with "his disreputable and outrageous methods," came to me, William Krickbaum, and put into my hands the Buckingham letters, one of which is given above, and begged of me money enough to settle the prosecution the district attorney was holding over him. This I finally consented to do; and for the money furnished for that purpose took the following note:

BLOOMSBURG, April 25, 1884

Six months after date I promise to pay William Krickbaum, on order, one hundred and ten dollars, with interest, without defalcation for value received. Witness my hand and seal this 25th day of April, A. D., 1884.

JAMES WEIRMAN. [seal]

So stands the case on the papers, and it seems that Mr. Weirman added to "his disreputable and outrageous methods" the further "disreputable and outrageous methods" of betraying Krickbaum to Buckingham, and Buckingham to Krickbaum. Mr. Weirman, may therefore be dismissed from the controversy as a master of "methods" of which no honest man will desire a part. If, with the above showing, any thing he has said is believed, I make the following explicit denial:

COLUMBIA COUNTY, ss:

I, William Krickbaum, being duly sworn according to law, do depose and say—That I never gave James K. Weirman any money, to be used for any electioneering purpose in any illegal and improper manner, or for any illegal and improper object.—Nor did I ever request or desire him to make such use of money.—Nor did I ever give to him any such sum of money as he claims to have received from me.

WILLIAM KRICKBAUM

Sworn and subscribed before me, August 6th, A. D., 1884
JOHN M. CLARK, J. P.

THAT BARREL OF WHISKEY

COLUMBIA COUNTY, ss:

Before me the undersigned Justice of the Peace in and for said county personally appeared J. M. Long of Benton, who being duly sworn according to law deposeth and saith that in the latter part of March A. D. 1884, he, said Long, used his team to help move Thomas P. Lore to near Pine Summit, said county, from Benton; That on the way back he stopped at Fowler's Distillery and heard Jerre Fowler, the distiller, say, pointing to a barrel of whiskey, "I sold that barrel of whiskey to William Krickbaum; it is to go to the new jail this afternoon; I am going to take it down."

J. M. LONG.

Sworn and subscribed before me this 4th day of August A. D. 1884.
JAMES B. HARMAN, J. P.
The Columbian
August 8, 1884

A CARD

In your last week's issue Mr. Krickbaum charges me with slander for saying that I was informed that he had sent two demijohns of whiskey up in the Benton stage—one to Mr. Karns and the other to Mr. Hartman. I did not say

COLUMBIA COUNTY COURTHOUSE, CIRCA 1923.

that James Weirman received any. I was informed to-day that Mr. Krickbaum failed when up the creek last week to get said parties to make a statement that the report was untrue. Mr. E. P. Albertson does not always drive the stage. Mr. Krickbaum should procure proper affidavits before charging me with slander.

Yours Respectfully,
WM. H. SNYDER
Orangeville, PA.

EDITORIAL

The fight for the Prothonotary was one of the most bitter ever waged in this county over a political office. Every influence was brought to bear on each side, and the interest became so intense that all the other candidates complained that no attention was paid to them, all eyes being centered on Snyder and Krickbaum. All day Sunday it looked as though there would be a tie vote, but on Monday morning this was changed by the report that Krickbaum had two delegates in Sugarloaf. Later in the day Snyder's friends did the smiling when it was found that he had one delegate in Sugarloaf, and one in South Conyngham, giving him two majority.

The Columbian
August 15, 1884

TO THE DEMOCRATIC VOTERS OF COLUMBIA COUNTY

FELLOW CITIZENS:

Permit me to acknowledge the kindness of my many friends in the county, who in spite of misrepresentation, and systematic methods of abuse, have stood by me in the present campaign. It is a source of gratification to me to know, that with all the combination of my personal enemies, who have not hesitated to use means which have disgusted hundreds of democrats and republicans alike, I nevertheless received a popular majority of 175 votes.

To those kind and loyal friends who have stood by

me through this contest, I desire to extend my sincere and hearty appreciation, nor will those grateful feelings be obliterated through life.

Respectfully yours,
WILLIAM KRICKBAUM
The Columbian
August 15, 1884

NEWS ITEM

The chair announced the result in favor of Snyder, and it was received with much applause, and calls for "Snyder," who showed his good sense by keeping his seat. So the smoke of the battle cleared away, leaving the wounded on the field of battle, while the victors had the magnanimity to say nothing of the fallen foes. When the result for Prothonotary was announced, about one-third of those present left the hall.

The Columbian
August 15, 1884

A LETTER

MESSRS. EDITORS:

A few weeks ago no person could have made me believe that there existed in the Democratic Party of Columbia County so much corruption and rottenness as has been shown for the few weeks last past. I say corruption and rottenness, because, if all this scandal (money reports and whiskey reports) which has been flying through our country and other places is untrue and unfounded, the contradictory oaths which have been published in your columns are too abominable to be predicted to persons belonging to the Democratic Party.

What a disagreeable odor a few men can create. All this tends to show that somewhere and by some means a Cassius must have tried to entrap a Brutus and thereby kill a Caesar, or that Caesar was dangerously corrupt himself.

Mark you, the record of this campaign cannot be forgotten for many years; and it now seems but just and right to separate the dross and foreign matter from the purer metal. For many years the constant thunder of Republicanism has awed us, and such blackened clouds as the Electoral Commission have overshadowed us. But, if we cleanse ourselves from all those impurities before November election, the sun will shine brighter than it ever shone in our giving a solid, clean vote to Grover Cleveland.

LITTLE JAY
The Columbian
August 22, 1884

William Krickbaum Dies in 89th Year; Long Political Boss

The death of William Krickbaum removes the most picturesque figure in Columbia County's political life, and for years its most powerful figure as well. For a half century he was a power in the Democratic councils, and for much of that time his word was absolute. His dominance was sometimes questioned, but generally speaking he ruled supreme. He was a man with devoted followers and implacable foes, but his own personality and the power of his publication, the *Democratic Sentinel,* combined for years to make him the outstanding politician of his day—and his day was a long one. "The War Horse of the Democratic Party" was a name he bore, coupled with that of "The Watchdog of the Treasury."

Not only was he able to keep himself continuously in office, but he almost invariably picked the slate that was elected. He elected president judges and associate judges, and controlled the courts; he had his finger on practically every county office for years. During all those stormy years of political supremacy he was frequently threatened physically, but seldom beaten up. But when he was he had the faculty of sooner or later drawing to his side his most bitter enemies.

Columbia County never produced but one "Krickie"; the mould was broken when he passed from the political arena.

The Morning Press
December 20, 1923

Although William H. Snyder goes on to win the November general election for prothonotary, it is a time of great personal tragedy for his family. Between the primary and the general election, three of his six children (Jennie, age sixteen; Charles, age thirteen; and George, not quite two years old) die within three weeks of one another from "the terrible scourge of childhood—diphtheria."

Six months later, on April 12, 1885, William Krickbaum buys the office and plant of the *Democratic Sentinel.* Later, he launches *The Bloomsburg Daily,* which becomes the dominant newspaper in the region for the next three decades. In his new role as a publisher, he consolidates his political power.

Democrat Grover Cleveland is elected president in 1884 for the first of two nonconsecutive terms. In 1888, he wins the popular vote, but loses the presidency to Benjamin Harrison in the Electoral College.

In 1888, William Krickbaum is elected representative to the Pennsylvania General Assembly, where he will serve two terms. He never again loses an election. His political offices in the course of his nearly fifty-year career include: commissioners' clerk, deputy sheriff, deputy county treasurer, prothonotary and clerk of the courts (two terms), county commissioner (two terms), associate judge, county auditor, and school district auditor.

⚞ HAPPY HOLIDAYS ⚟

THE FOURTH OF JULY

Ed. Columbian:

The 4th of July 1898 went off here with some disgraceful peculiarities. There was quite a large attendance in the grove, and many from the country were there who left their fields of harvest to celebrate the day in a becoming manner.

The first disgraceful move was to wrangle an hour to cheat the winner of the bicycle race out of his triumph and give it to the one who came in two or three rods behind him.

The next was as follows: At the beginning of the speaking in the grove, the chairman said, "Let us as we commence these exercises give three cheers for our boys over yonder fighting Spain." And such cheers from that large audience! Weak as chalk and water, fainter than a dying man's last breath. You could have heard a grass hopper leap through the leaves, and this on the 4th of July '98 while America is coping with Spain, light with darkness, liberty with despotism and human weal with human atrocity! Yea, verily, while the Stars and Stripes are shedding their luster on Cuba and the Philip-

pines. Well, such a cheer coming out of the bosom of America all the way from Millville. We shouldn't wonder our soldier boys heard it above the thunders of battle over yonder, and they will write back to their friends about it.

Disgraceful move No. 3: Just as the 3rd and last speaker Rev. Mr. Brouse arose to speak there was a greased pig turned loose outside in a field and a shout went up from the throats of the rabble and about half the audience jumped up and left to see the oiled animal and see someone try to catch it. Wasn't all that polite, sensible and patriotic.

Why was that hog turned loose just then? Why was not that great feature of Millville's celebrating the immortal 4th of 1898, postponed a few minutes till Rev. Brouse had delivered his address? Now, these things are simply a disgrace to any community. It would seem half the people of this mundane sphere would rather go to a fair and see a rotten apple or a pollywog in a mud puddle than hear a sensible address. However, those who went to see the greased hog missed an eloquent speech full of patriotism and truth as delivered by Rev. Mr. Brouse, the Methodist min-

POSTCARD, 1908.

POSTCARD, 1911.

ister of this charge. Those who remained were well paid while they showed good hard common sense.

Anonymous
The Columbian
July 14, 1898

HALLOWEEN

Dear Editor:

Around this time each year we hear the expression "let the kiddies have harmless fun marking windows." I wonder if these persons realize that most housewives have just finished housecleaning and have just washed those windows.

Maybe in the years before autos, youth centers and planned entertainment, this was the only means of making fun for kids—but today parents and non-parents supply plenty of fun and means of entertainment for these so-called "kids," usually high school age. I know my windows were marked by two boys each year until they entered college! They had such fun, Bless 'em.

And I also notice that the fond mamma who stood on her porch and divided the cut-wax between her dear little kiddies, was heard throughout the neighborhood when her window had ONE small circle made by a little guy of pre-school age.

The kids in our neighborhood are too dumb to ring the bell and wait for a treat. They would rather destroy something and run. I know because for the last two years I have purchased candy bars by the box and have had to eat them all myself.

An Irked Window Washer
Berwick Enterprise
October 30, 1954

THANKSGIVING

FRONT OF PETERSBURG, VA.
84TH REGIMENT OF PENNSYLVANIA VOLUNTEERS
Dr. John:

Thanksgiving day is here. The weather is very

much moderated today, as if to make Thanksgiving pleasant. Since the rain, the weather has been very cold. Ice about an inch thick.—Thanksgiving dinner, given by the good people at home, arrived here late in the afternoon, averaging about one pound of turkey to a soldier. But as officers are not supposed ever to get hungry, or to have a taste for turkey, they were omitted in the count, and passed by in the distribution, and so we had to eat potatoes and point. However, the men deserve all they got, and a good deal more, and it helps to cheer them up very much this stormy weather, to know that friends at home entertain some practical anxiety for their comfort. It formed a substantial element of a Thanksgiving day. All is quiet at present, but I have no idea it will long continue so, unless another storm intervenes.

> J. T.
> *The Columbia County Republican*
> December 1, 1864

CHRISTMAS

Dear Editor:

This afternoon (Nov. 27) a number of little children gathered on Main St., Bloomsburg, to see their favorite grown-up arrive in style. Their parents, believing the enclosed ad, clipped from Thursday's *Morning Press,* got them there for 2 p.m.

So where was Santa Claus? In his Candy Cane Cottage—while a mob of kids waited to get in. He had come by fire truck all right, at 1:15 p.m. Many parents wait until later to take the young'un to visit the old gentleman, but with a disappointed kid to please, the mothers made a real crowd.

All I have to say is "Phooey!" to whomever started the parade early—or the dummy who put the wrong time in the paper. You—whoever you are—deserve a stockingful of ashes for Christmas!

> Mrs. George Widger
> (Who borrowed 2 tots to take to see Santa.)
> *The Morning Press*
> December 1, 1970

POSTCARD, 1915.

✠ GUMPTION ✠

DOLLY

Mr. Printer,

Sargeant Loller, with an impudence common to low bred people, has in your paper of July 24, given his advice "to a certain description of females." It is hoped, Mr. Printer, you will permit some of the above described females to inform him, that if ever he dares to poke himself uninvited into their company again, as he did on the island the other day, he will receive not only our refusal to dance with him, but such a correction as a mean spirited pup deserves. So much from

DOLLY
The Oracle of Dauphin and Harrisburgh Advertiser
August 6, 1813

KATE B.

CAMP NEAR BELLE PLAINS, VA.
My Dear Col.:

Allow me to mention an incident, the facts of which I know to be true. Many who were "soldiering" in the spring of 1862 may remember Kate B.—who stopped at the "Clarendon" in Fredericksburg Va. and who sometimes rode a gray horse, and by many was called "Charlie." She had been with McDowell's Corps ever since the organization of the Army of the Potomac and for a long time served as a private in the army. When King's Division left Fredericksburg to reinforce Pope at Culpepper, she made that forced march on foot, carrying her musket, knapsack and equipments. At the Rappahannock Ford, during Pope's retreat she was slightly wounded, and at Bull Run rec'd a severe bayonet wound in the cheek. Since then I had not heard of her until yesterday when behold! "Charlie" in *propie persona* came into my tent. The history of her ramblings in *Secessia* since Bull Run are of the most romantic order. At one time she was in the ———— Pa. Vols. and at another in the ———— N. Y. Cavalry.

Artillerist
Columbia Democrat
April 11, 1863

DELIA

Editors of the American:—

I am not what men call a "woman's rights woman" but yet I do believe that women have some rights which men ought to respect. I have never asked to preach, to lecture or to vote. I am willing to leave those things to the lords of creation. I do not aspire to be a justice of the peace or a school director. I am willing to confine my influence and my enjoyments mainly to my own home. Still I have some rights outside my home. God gives some things to the human family without distinction of age or sex. Among these are pure air and pure water.

I live a short distance from Danville, on a farm, on which there is a spring of pure water. We had quite a basin scooped out and then walled up with stones and there is the living water, as pure as crystal bubbling up and over those stones. Now I think I have a right to that water pure as it is, and no one can rightfully put anything into that spring which will pollute it. The same would apply, even more strongly, to a public fountain. So also God gives us the pure air and fit for breathing and no one has the right to render it impure and unfit for breathing, yet this is done and done in a manner very offensive.

I go to Danville to do shopping and in walking, often get behind two or three men with pipes or cigars in their mouths filling the air with the stench of burning tobacco and making it entirely unfit to breathe. I often turn and cross the street to get rid of the nuisance only to fall into a like snare again. I go into a store and find one or two men smoking there. I go to the post office and generally find it filled with a cloud of smoke which I can scarcely endure long enough to get my mail. At home I am sometimes annoyed by visitors smoking. In carriages and places of amusement, even in the vestibule of the church, everywhere, I am exposed to the nuisance.

The nearest approach to politeness I have witnessed in a smoker is to say, "I suppose smoking is not offensive to you," and then, without waiting for a reply he would light a cigar and puff away. If I say it is offensive, smokers are apt to take it as a joke and light the pipe none the less. Let smokers understand that tobacco smoke is offensive to all but smokers and that very few ladies are smokers. Let common courtesy teach them not to pollute the air on the streets and in places of common resort. Ladies and others who do not smoke have some rights which smokers ought to respect. If they must smoke out of their own house or some room set apart for such a purpose, do let them be on some by-streets and not in the public thoroughfare, and, when they enter the post office or a store or any other place of business, do let them leave their pipe or cigar outside.

I suppose it is your rule that correspondents shall give their names, but, if you can suspend that rule for the present, you will much oblige.

DELIA.
Danville, Pennsylvania
The Montour American
May 31, 1877

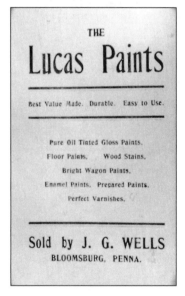

BLOOMSBURG TRADE CARD,
CIRCA 1870 (FRONT).

A CERTAIN WIFE

A certain Mifflinville wife is wondering why her husband thinks she believes him when he tells her he don't know how the lipstick got on his hanky. Says he wasn't drunk coming home at 3 a.m. She is pretty sure she knows where it came from, even if he doesn't. It won't be well if she finds out, that's for sure. The jealous husband wants his wife to be home all alone always. He is heading for an awakening, she says, and so is the owner of the lipstick.

> One Who Knows
> *Berwick Enterprise*
> August 21, 1954

MAMIE

NOTICE!

As my husband, Larue Hess had me advertised in The Argus for leaving his bed and board. It is a mistake. The bed belongs to me and the board we got at my home. But for me to make any bills for him to pay I couldn't expect him to pay any for me now as my folks bought my clothes while we were living together.

> Mamie Hess
> Benton, Pennsylvania
> *The Benton Argus*
> January 6, 1921

JAN

I am appealing to all would-be and current parents, grandparents, or concerned citizens within "ear shot" of this paper to help in a writing campaign.

I recently went to a local convenience store to pick up a few essentials. Upon checking out I noticed a display box on the counter with actual sized plastic guns filled with various juices. The directions on the handle instruct a child to place the barrel of the gun in their mouth, bite off the plastic tip and squeeze the trigger to release the contents of the gun in their mouths. They even go so far as to illustrate the process by showing a child with the barrel of the gun in his mouth and squeezing the trigger. I stood there speechless for a while because I could not ever conceive of ANY company producing such a distasteful, harmful product. I relayed my feelings to the clerk and she stated, "Oh yes, they make grenades too!" What's next—plastic syringes filled with juice? I don't know about you, but the thought of one of my young daughters with one of these "treats" in her mouth is enough to make me become sick.

I am asking two things of you, the readers:

1. If you find a store that carries this particular "treat," please display your disapproval with the manager/owner. Also, for the convenience stores out there that currently carry the product or are thinking to do so, PLEASE DON'T!!! It sends a horribly dangerous message to our children. Remember, this is a society of mimic!

2. Perhaps most importantly, I ask that as many of you as possible send a letter to this company voicing your disgust and disapproval of their products. ONE letter may not make a difference but MANY will certainly get their attention and will surely have some impact. The company is Mackie International Inc.

I will be sending this letter to the editor to all the local papers in the region to aid in responses to this company. We've got to let companies like Mackie International know that everything is NOT ACCEPTABLE today and that we care about our children's moral and mental development.

> Jan Board, Bloomsburg
> *Press Enterprise*
> May 27, 1989

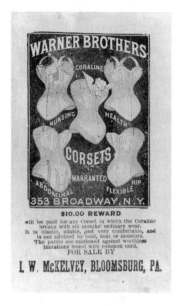

BLOOMSBURG TRADE CARD,
CIRCA 1870 (BACK).

FOURTEEN DAYS LATER . . .

Our voices were heard!

A very special thank you to all those who participated in the fight to remove the product "Chilly Bang! Bang!" from the market. Whether you wrote a letter, made a phone call or networked among your community organizations, it was a combined effort that made our cause victorious!

I truly can't thank you all enough for the support, concern and effort you put forth. It was one of those rare and special times we fought for something we believe in and came away feeling good about ourselves and our future. I know, for me personally, it re-instilled the belief that we do indeed have a voice out there and if we work together, most anything can be accomplished!

> Jan Board, Bloomsburg
> *Press Enterprise*
> June 10, 1989

THE CONSTANT TRAMP OF PROGRESS: 1890–1900

MONEYED TYRANTS

Dear Sentinel:

We have had trembling nerves for the last few years in regards to the safety and perpetuity of the Republic. We have seen millionaires growing up upon every hand, owning hundreds of millions, a thing never known in the history of nations. Trusts, monopolies, syndicates and corporations ruling the destinies of the country and the people. We have been witnessing the rapid departure of the rights and prerogatives of the people. But the strong right arm of public opinion has been stretched out. Plutocracy shall not rule this country; shall not throttle unto death the rights of the 15 millions of people; shall not enslave the hard working classes who run our rolling mills, our furnaces, our foundries, and machine shops, our mines, build our railroads, till the soil, keep our commerce and make us a great and progressive people. They have spoken in our Presidential election in a voice like the thunders of the sea. It was a voice of patriotism and self-preserva-

THE CHANGING ROLE OF NEWSPAPERS

———

The 1890s are a golden age for newspapers. With the technologies of printing and distribution now finely honed, and with the advent of other mass media still decades away, the industry flourishes. Ten daily or weekly newspapers are published in Columbia and Montour Counties; Bloomsburg alone boasts five. Increased competition, and the desire to maximize profits by appealing to as many readers—and advertisers—as possible, lead to an active, lively, crusading press, and tend to diminish but not completely eradicate political bias.

TUSTIN MANSION, BLOOMSBURG.

tion. Moneyed tyrants will take a back seat and the people are still patriotic and potential.

    E. J. Bowman
    Democratic Sentinel
    November 18, 1892

A QUIET DAY

There occurred in our town on Wednesday last two of the greatest possible contrasts. The Christian people of the town were observing a "Quiet Day" of prayer and communion with God. For five hours the people met together, much of the time in absolute quiet, praying the Almighty to send His spirit upon the churches as He promised. It was a most peaceful day and its results will be far-reaching. It was a scene that angels could look upon with pleasure. Christians of all denominations, like the Disciples at Pentecost, meeting together in one place all intent on the same thing. It was a day of Peace and Holy Quiet.

But while this was going on, at a place between the two churches was the wildest confusion. An honored, trusted and influential merchant had failed. Financial stringency, trusting and endorsing had driven him to the wall, and creditors from far and near had come to grasp their portion of the spoils. Because he had magnanimously thrown open his doors and attempted to satisfy his creditors, they flocked in and each tried to secure all his claim whether he needed or not, until the commotion and greed became so great he was obliged to close his doors for self-protection.

Extremes do meet in this world, but when they

come together as in this instance, it shocks us the more and makes one feel, that after all does it pay for a man to live uprightly and honestly? Does it count for nothing that a man has spent his whole life doing an honorable business and helping others? When he fails should he be treated as though he had lived to defraud? A little more of the spirit of "The Quiet Day" in business would give our business men more confidence in the religion of Christ.

An On-looker
The Bloomsburg Daily
January 27, 1894

FIRST PRESBYTERIAN CHURCH,
BLOOMSBURG.

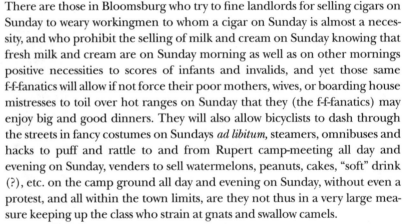

The "honored, trusted and influential merchant" was I. W. McKelvey, who ran a general merchandise business in Bloomsburg. A week earlier, the firm of William Neal & Sons, operators of the Bloomsburg Furnace, also closed shop. The two businesses, twenty years previous, had been joined as McKelvey, Neal & Co. Both families had been active in philanthropic work.

F-F-FANATICS

There are those in Bloomsburg who try to fine landlords for selling cigars on Sunday to weary workingmen to whom a cigar on Sunday is almost a necessity, and who prohibit the selling of milk and cream on Sunday knowing that fresh milk and cream are on Sunday morning as well as on other mornings positive necessities to scores of infants and invalids, and yet those same f-f-fanatics will allow if not force their poor mothers, wives, or boarding house mistresses to toil over hot ranges on Sunday that they (the f-f-fanatics) may enjoy big and good dinners. They will also allow bicyclists to dash through the streets in fancy costumes on Sundays *ad libitum,* steamers, omnibuses and hacks to puff and rattle to and from Rupert camp-meeting all day and evening on Sunday, venders to sell watermelons, peanuts, cakes, "soft" drink (?), etc. on the camp ground all day and evening on Sunday, without even a protest, and all within the town limits, are they not thus in a very large measure keeping up the class who strain at gnats and swallow camels.

Consistency
The Bloomsburg Daily
August 6, 1894

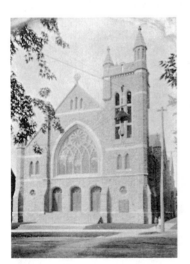

WESLEY UNITED METHODIST CHURCH,
BLOOMSBURG.

SHE SELLS SEA SHELLS

Dear Readers of The Bloomsburg Daily,

Since coming to Florida, this land of alligators, I have received numerous letters of inquiry from home friends asking if I could send them shells from the sea shore. Yes, and now is a good chance to get them for we have just had a heavy storm at sea and the shore is strewn with fine shells, corals, etc., and our editor willing, I will say to one and all that I will pick up and mail a variety of shells to anyone who sends a stamp or two for postage; anyone is welcome to send, and now that the holidays are so near, you may wish to call them a Christmas remembrance from . . .

> Mrs. F. A. Warner
> Jacksonville, Florida
> *The Bloomsburg Daily*
> November 29, 1895

A VARIETY OF SHELLS.

THREE WEEKS LATER . . .

NEWS ITEM

Postmaster-General Wilson has denied the privileges of the mails to Mrs. F. A. Warner of Jacksonville, Florida for conducting a fraudulent business. She advertised in newspapers throughout the country glowing descriptions of flowers, shells, etc., to be obtained in Florida during the winter, and stated that upon receipt of a certain amount in postage stamps she would send these articles. She failed to keep her part of the contract. The advertisement in the shape of a letter appeared in this paper of recent date. The postmaster in Jacksonville reported that her mail averaged a thousand letters a day, each containing

AROUND TOWN

- In 1895, Judge William Elwell dies. He had presided at the Bloomsburg trial of the "Mollie Maguires" in 1877.
- Kee Sing, a "Chinaman" who operated a laundry on Iron Street in Bloomsburg, is arrested in May 1895 for breaking Sabbath laws by working in his garden on a Sunday. He was spotted by J. H. Mercer, who was selling cigars and newspapers in his store, and issued a warrant by Mayor Creasy, who was returning that morning from Magistrates' Court. Mr. Sing was not himself a Christian.
- Corporate mismanagement and thwarted takeover schemes are the alleged motives in an 1896 plot to kill prominent Bloomsburg lawyer Levi E. Waller and his family by bombing their Fifth Street home. Waller, as legal counsel to Mrs. Samuel Knorr (widow of Captain Samuel Knorr), was preventing L. S. Wintersteen from buying out Mrs. Knorr's controlling shares in the Keystone Foundry. Such a buyout, Wintersteen hoped, would conceal his mismanagement of the firm. Wintersteen allegedly hired Mrs. Knorr's dissolute stepson, Clifton Knorr, to plant the dynamite; also to kill Mrs. Knorr, first by poisoning her, then by spreading diphtheria germs on her clothes. Though the bomb damaged the porch of the house, no one was hurt and Clifton bungled all the murder attempts. A mistrial is declared due to witness tampering by the prosecution.

probably from ten to twenty five cents in stamps . . .

The Bloomsburg Daily
December 19, 1895

EIGHT YEARS LATER . . .

Editor Daily and Sentinel:

I want to give housekeepers (who desire it) the seed of a Southern plant that is sure death to that pest of domestic comfort—the house fly—and at the same time harmless to other life. I do not know the name of it other than fly poison. It grows some two feet high, and bears small blue flowers. The leaves are the poisonous parts. Bruise them, put milk or sweetened water on them, and the flies will do the rest, cluster around, eat and die, much to the satisfaction of all concerned. You may say to your readers that I will send anyone the fly poison seed who wishes it, providing they enclose a stamp for reply. It is easily grown and so useful during the fly season that I want to scatter the seed everywhere.

Mrs. F. A. Warner,
Jacksonville, Florida
The Bloomsburg Daily
April 9, 1903

JACKSONVILLE, FLORIDA, CIRCA 1903.

A BENEVOLENT THANKSGIVING

Another year has fled, and we are on the verge of another cold winter, and as the ladies of the Union Benevolent Society find themselves entirely without funds with which to meet the demands that will without a doubt be made upon them in the near future, and as the society has for the last fifteen years depended almost entirely upon the Thanksgiving offering of the good people of Bloomsburg for funds to meet these demands, we, the officers of this society, request that a collection be taken up on Thanksgiving day for that purpose.

Let us mention one case which will serve to show you what the money is used for. This case was reported to the president of the society by a kind-hearted physician of town.

A woman was found in bed in the month of February, with an infant three days old. The only nurse and housekeeper was a little girl eleven years of age. Three other half-clad children were crying on the floor. The only underclothing the woman owned she had on. The only sheet (one) in the house was on the bed. Very worn and thin it was. The only food to be found was buckwheat cakes and molasses and a few potatoes—not a very tempting bill of fare for a sick woman. The husband and father had injured his hand and was unable to work; and as he depended upon his daily toil to support his family, when his work stopped there was no income. He was out gathering coal along the railroad with his well hand, to keep the one fire going.

We could give you many more, but this will suffice. It is for such and kindred cases that the money given us on Thanksgiving day is to be used. For the last twelve years this offering has averaged just $26.69. May we not hope for at least as much this year? While we do not at this writing know of any such necessitous cases, yet if we do not have them before the holidays are over, it will be the first time since the society was organized, and we wish to be ready. Our fund was exhausted last year before the first of April.

Mrs. M. C. Walker
Mrs. Mary L. Neal
Managing Committee
Ladies' Union Benevolent Society
The Columbian
November 29, 1895

⌈ Mrs. Walker, a Quaker, is the wife of the court stenographer. Mrs. Neal, a Presbyterian, is the wife of William Neal, whose business had failed in January 1894. ⌉

THE TRAMP NUISANCE

The tramp nuisance is growing rapidly and Bloomsburg seems specially favored. Two or three years ago the Mayor of a Pennsylvania city told the Mayor of Bloomsburg that among tramps Bloomsburg was considered a tramp paradise. At Bloomsburg they found a lodging place—steam heat, gas lighted, Water Company watered, etc.—and that upon their exit from this jolly lodging place the good, simple Bloomsburg folk gave them breakfasts fit for kings. At one time the Mayor of Bloomsburg asked the Council to instruct the police not to give tramps lodging in the lockup on the grounds that the lockup was for a petty jail, that it was improper to make jails tramp lodging houses, that it was wrong to put our sometimes unfortunate drunks in with a lot of dangerous, dirty, and perhaps infectiously diseased tramps, etc. The Council and police made the cowardly answer: "If we don't give them lodging they will do mischief in the town." The Mayor then refused to let the tramps loose until 9 a.m. This made the tramps swear and complain that after 9 a.m. they could not get good breakfasts. The keeping them in until 9 a.m. system soon about rid the town of tramps. There is no such thing as a deserving tramp.

REICE'S MEAT MARKET AND GUNTON MONUMENTS, MAIN STREET, BLOOMSBURG, CIRCA 1899.

What I have said may be wrong or right, but it is certainly time to call a halt in hospitality to tramps. From 10 to 15 sleep nightly at the lockup now and wander about in the mornings for prey.

A CITIZEN
The Bloomsburg Daily
March 26, 1897

TRAMP, TRAMP, TRAMP

Dear (?) Citizen:

Your little article in the DAILY of the 26th inst. doubtless attracted some attention. When you counsel anyone to refuse a bum (let us call

Mister Editor:

The bum tramp nuisance is one which justifies complaint. No law or custom, human or divine, excuses or palliates it. *"In the sweat of thy face shalt thou eat bread"* is the primal command; and that was followed in due time by another, *"Six days shalt thou labor,"* and another, equal authority affirms the two former, *"He that will not work should not eat."*

But the bum tramp will not work—he will not labor—he will not bring the sweat to his face, to procure his bread. By what right shall he prey upon the community? What claim has he upon tender hearted or the charitable? How has he been exonerated from his share of the labor and sweat and toil which the Creator has pronounced upon His people?

The bum tramp is demanding that we support him in his idleness and vagrancy, in addi-

things by their right names) a little something to eat, you are defying an injunction of Christ himself, *"Whosoever shall break one of the least of these commandments and shall teach men so shall he be called least in the kingdom of heaven,"* and one of Christ's commandments was *"Give unto him that asketh of thee."*

And then another view concerning the lockup. If you were in some of those bum's places, do you know what you would do many a night? I don't believe you do, but I do however. Many a night you would walk the streets from sunset to sunrise not daring to lie down in an alley for fear of freezing to death before morning. You would learn what it is to be hungry and cold with none to pity, none to save. What would your thoughts be then, would you bless or curse the day you were born? Would you think it a sin to be housed overnight and fed? Would you think the policeman undutiful that allowed you to sleep in the station house to prevent you from doing some mischief? Would you think a man or woman a fool that held out to you a piece of bread and a cup of coffee? Ponder over these things, Citizen, and *put yourself in his place.*

ANOTHER CITIZEN
The Bloomsburg Daily
March 31, 1897

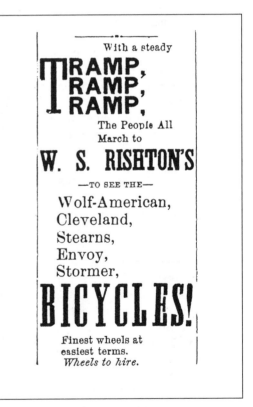

tion to paying our full share of local taxes for the relief of our own poor. Let these bums tramp home and make application to the proper authorities, and if deserving they will be provided for. There is no need of all this whining about cold nights, and lockups, and hot coffee, as matter of charity. Let them work, and they shall eat, let them go home, and they shall be clothed and fed.

> A THIRD CITIZEN
> *The Bloomsburg Daily*
> April 1, 1897

Editor Daily:

The tramp has come to stay. He has come (as a rule) not because he chooses to come, but because he is a victim of circumstances over which he has no control. Twenty five years ago the tramp was seldom seen in this county. During the great panic of 1873 to 1880, industries were closed and hundreds of thousands of industrious men were unable to find employment in the communities where they resided and were too sensitive to become public charges by making applications to the poor authorities for help, but chose rather to start out to some other town in search of employment with the hope of being able to earn a livelihood. In doing this they became what is now designated by some—the bum tramp. The same conditions that put the first army of unfortunates on the road in 1873 have been operating since.

It won't do for us who have been more favorably situated to denounce all men who are homeless and friendless as being entirely bad and undeserving of the ordinary amenities of life.

Again—who was ever made poorer by giving a tramp a meal, a piece of bread or cup of coffee? Who has not felt that he better deserves to belong to the great brotherhood of man after he has relieved the wants of some poor unfortunate? How could a man refuse shelter to one of these in our lockup, where the heat and water must be paid for even though no one occupies its cells, simply because it might interfere with the peaceful slumber of some of "our unfortunate drunks?" Why should a drunken man who has spent his money for drink and as is generally the case, deprived his family of some comfort of life, be treated so much better than an unfortunate tramp? The latter is too often a tramp from necessity, while the former makes a beast of himself because he chooses.

The tramp is not the dangerous criminal of the country. This class of evil doers is too often found among the rich and influential, and not infrequently do we find them connected with our churches. It often happens that the men who would deny a fellow creature food or shelter will be found to belong to some church, and profess to be a follower of Him whose duty on earth seemed to be to administer to wants of the poor.

The tramp is here and we must make the best of him. The evil cannot be cured by refusing them food and shelter. God only knows what might happen if this army of men were driven to deeds of desperation by refusing them a piece of bread and the bare floor of our station houses to sleep upon.

Let us rather find some means to remove the cause and stop compelling men to become tramps. When we have done this we will have done our duty, and not until then.

> FOURTH CITIZEN
> *The Bloomsburg Daily*
> April 2, 1897

Mr. Editor:

I have read in the columns of your paper several articles on the "tramp question," presumably a debate carried on by two citizens. If I might be allowed a word I would say that I think both gentlemen have made a mistake in the premise. The first one asserts that there is not a worthy one in the whole lot, and the second

that they are worthy, worthy as a body, neither of which statement is correct.

I think a person with average sense, and a little knowledge to season it, will admit that there are *some* worthy tramps. Men, who in these hard times are unable to get work at home, and to whom it is a question of work or starve, have left in a vain search for work in other places.

We living in a town of this size, where to one family who has not plenty, there are possibly a hundred who have, know nothing whatever of life in big cities where a man may starve and his neighbor not know it, and for these men it is move or go hungry. I suppose the first gentleman in the above debate would like to know why they don't pay their fare on the cars and travel like decent people.

As for lodging them in the lockup, let them be made to pay in work for their lodging—the unworthy will soon be sifted out. Let him to whom much has been given, give much, and not particularly to build churches or fill up the collection plate, but to alleviate the misery of mankind.

Yours truly,
INTERESTED, OR FIFTH CITIZEN
The Bloomsburg Daily
April 3, 1897

For the benefit of "INTERESTED" we would state that the four articles on "Tramps" were written by four different persons, the name of one not being known to the other.
Editor

THE TRAMP WAGON

An Open Letter to the Town Council:

Before I sit down with my scissors, thimble, needle and thread, like I earn my daily bread, I thought I would plead the tramp question. There was one at our door yesterday morning asking for a cup of coffee, said he was so tired going from house to house; and another great robust man this morning. Some time ago I gave a tramp a lunch, and while preparing it I questioned him and I found out what money he earned he spent for drink and begged his bread. Since then I feed no more tramps, but how to get rid of them I will tell how they do with tramps in the city of Youngstown, Ohio.

Any tramps going from house to house, and if the people notify the policemen they are taken to the lockup and fined a certain amount, and then they must work that amount out in the park.

We went by the park where the tramps were working on a stone pile and they were working like any man must work to earn his daily bread by the sweat of his brow. Just now there is another tramp going from house to house begging for a pair of shoes.

Where I was visiting, the tramp wagon passed, going to and from the park for their dinners. They have three parks, one in particular was a very pretty park— Mill Creek Park—they do not mar the natural scenery. There were two old mills they used for shelter. There were two falls by one mill, one being natural and the upper one artificial.

About a year ago they made an artificial lake, and there was a ramble around the lake on the mountain side. I was told that any men in the city that had not any work they would give them work in the park; sometimes there would be two hundred men working in the park. Any man that has a family and is out of work it is one way to help them.

It is not right to covet, but I wish we could have a pretty park too. I heard a couple ladies speaking on this subject about a year ago. I suppose some may think we do not need a park. I know all the ladies will join with me and say we do. Come, let us reason together why we need one. There are a few who can hire a horse and carriage to go out in the country, but the large majority must work in stores, mills, factories and at other occupations, and this would be a resting place, as well as a pleasure walk for them after their day's work is done, instead of the streets.

I will close, hoping you will give careful consideration. Since writing, there has been another tramp here asking for clothes.

CITIZEN
The Bloomsburg Daily
March 9, 1898

UMBRELLA ROCKS, MILL CREEK PARK, YOUNGSTOWN, OHIO.

TOWN HALL, BLOOMSBURG.
COMPLETED IN 1890.

⚐ CITIZEN ABROAD ⚐

ON BOARD THE TRANSPORT SHERIDAN
NEW YORK CITY
FEBRUARY 17, 1899
To the Bloomsburg Daily:

I will give you a short account of our trip from Fort Riley, Kansas to New York City.

We left Fort Riley, Kansas, on Saturday evening February 11th at half past seven. It was very cold on Saturday; it was twenty degrees below zero. There were three Pullman sleepers to a company and three men to a section; one man slept in the upper berth and two in the lower berth.

Arrived in St. Louis at 7:30 Sunday night and laid there till about ten o'clock. Our next stopping place of importance was at Cleveland, Ohio, arriving there at 12:30 Thursday morning. Arrived at Binghamton, NY, at 4:30. I jumped off there to see Frank Brown at Armour's Beef House but he was not in. We arrived in Scranton at half past eight Tuesday evening. About eight miles from Scranton on Mt. Pocono we got fast in a snow drift and was laid up for about three hours. Arrived at Hoboken, NJ, at five o'clock Wednesday morning.

THE CHANGING ROLE OF NEWSPAPERS

Right through the Second World War, it is standard practice for local newspapers to run regular letters from soldiers in action. Sometimes these are written directly to the paper; often they are personal letters provided to the paper by families with sons far from home. These early "correspondents" are not professional journalists, but merely individuals sharing their experiences with the folks back home.

About eight o'clock two fellows from our company and myself got passes and went over to New York City. At eleven o'clock Thursday morning we were moved from Hoboken to pier

23 Brooklyn where Transport Sheridan was lying, but did not get on board till nearly four o'clock in the afternoon. We intend to sail tomorrow between eleven and one. There were a lot of visitors on board today and I suppose there will be a large crowd here tomorrow morning. I just saw William Samuels and Penman; they are pretty tired out for they were helping to load baggage. Well I must close now. Be sure and send the papers once a week.

> Your Truly,
> Christ. Reice
> Company E, 12th U.S. Infantry
> War Department
> Washington, DC
> *The Bloomsburg Daily*
> February 21, 1899

ON BOARD THE TRANSPORT SHERIDAN
PORT SAID, EGYPT
MARCH 15, 1899
Dear Editor Rutter:

I thought I would write to you and let you know how we are getting along. We left Gibraltar March 4, 1899. They would not let us ashore there because the Spanish quarantine doctors said we had small pox on board, so we took coal and water and started out.

When we woke-up the next morning we were on the blue waters of the Mediterranean Sea. The sea was as smooth as glass and we were very glad of it, for we have had some very rough weather before. The first land we saw was Morocco, then Algeria and the rest we could not find the names of the different countries, but we knew it was all Africa. We passed several funny looking rocks raising straight out of the water, especially two very funny ones and very large, the largest looking like a camel starting up. We passed several pretty and large cities built of stone and painted a light yellow color— they looked very pretty—but the most beautiful things are their churches; they are large with high steeples and round towers.

U.S. TRANSPORT *SHERIDAN*.

We reached Valletta, the capital of Malta, twenty minutes past eleven March 8, 1899. At the entrance to the harbor is a small rocky island with a fort on it that takes up every foot of space. When we were about a mile from the entrance we saw a large battleship come out; she had four smokestacks, and we found out later that it was the new ship *Terrible,* supposed to be the largest vessel of the kind in the world.

On the morning of March 9th we were marched to the parade ground where we lined up and was reviewed by the Governor of the island and British officers. We then marched through the principal streets. When we stopped marching we were down on the Floriana parade ground, and we sat down to eat our lunches. After dinner we drilled a while. We got

VIEW OF GIBRALTAR.

Time Capsule

AROUND THE WORLD

- *The Philippine Incursion.* After a quick victory in the Spanish-American War (April 25–August 13, 1898), the United States finds itself in possession of Puerto Rico, Cuba, Guam, Wake Island and the Philippines. The Americans had found Philippine guerilla leader Emilio Aguinaldo to be helpful—so long as the Spanish were the common enemy. But Aguinaldo's paramount interest is Philippine independence, and he quickly turns against American colonial rule. The Philippine Incursion (1899–1901) is longer and deadlier than the lightning war with the Spanish. And though it ends with an American victory—and nearly fifty years of an uneasy American protectorate over the Philippines—it demonstrates for the first time in the twentieth century the difficulty the American military would face in future encounters with passionate nationalists in their native terrains.

aboard about four o'clock and did full justice to the supper that was placed before us.

The weather is very warm here, and the flowers are in bloom. I saw a field of wheat—at least I thought it was wheat—it was about a foot high. The English men and women are wearing summer clothes and straw hats.

The natives are plenty as fleas with their bum carts loaded with oranges and figs. Oranges are four cents a dozen and are fine large ones.

The native women go around with a black cloth over their faces, so you can not see their faces at all. The milk the people drink here is goats; the milk man drives his goats through the streets and milks them at your door, so the people on the island know there is no water in their milk.

We are the first troops of any nation to land on the island since the English took charge of it, except the English soldiers who treated us fine, showing us around the town and giving us something good to eat. We lost about thirteen of our men out of the regiment; they got left at Malta. We also took away a lot of English soldiers and two sailors that deserted from the English Army and Navy.

They put a big piece in the Malta paper about us, the heading was "American Cousins." I will try and send you one.

> Yours Truly,
> Chris Reice
> *The Bloomsburg Daily*
> April 5, 1899

MALTA HARBOR.

COLOMBO, CEYLON
MARCH 31, 1899
TO: J. C. RUTTER, JR., EDITOR,
THE BLOOMSBURG DAILY
Dear Editor Rutter:

I will now tell you what I have seen since I wrote my last letter. We started to go through the Suez Canal about half-past seven in the evening. The canal is about thirty yards wide, and is eighty four and seven-eighths miles long. We saw thousands of cranes along the banks. It took us about seventeen hours to go through. The Red Sea is a very bad piece of water—

full of rocks. We saw a vessel on a rock but no one was on it and all we could see was the bow and one mast. We only stopped at Aden long enough to put the mail and the Turkish pilot off, then we started for Colombo.

We arrived at Colombo Wednesday morning about nine o'clock, took on the pilot outside the harbor and anchored about one-half a mile from shore. There is a lot of bristle going on in the harbor day and night.

On Wednesday evening about eight o'clock, a man by the name of MacGuire, of Co. F, drowned. He belonged to the same Co. that Samuels and Penman do. Early this morning his body came to the surface.

Yesterday morning at seven o'clock I went ashore on a six hour pass. The natives have rings on their toes, through the nose and ears and have large bracelets on their arms and ankles and have nothing on except a small cloth around their loins. We also visited a cocoanut grove, a cinnamon, a mango, and a banana grove. Monkeys and parrots are plentiful on the island; some of the boys bought a monkey to take along; they paid 25 cents for it. You can buy cocoanut for one cent apiece, pineapples for two cents apiece, a bunch of bananas for a quarter. They also have street cars here and the carriages they use have but two wheels and are pulled by a native who runs nearly all day. They charge twenty-five cents an hour. . . .

We expect to reach Manila in about fifteen days.

Hoping to hear from you soon, I remain,

Yours Truly,
Chris Reice
The Bloomsburg Daily
May 9, 1899

San Pedro, Macati
April 28, '99
To: Mr. William J. Krickbaum, Jr., Editor
The Bloomsburg Daily
Dear Sir:

I received the papers from February 21st to March 18th and was very glad to receive them. We are having some very warm weather down here now and we

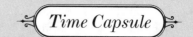

Time Capsule

AROUND THE NATION

- President William McKinley is completing his first term in office.
- Fierce competitors William Randolph Hearst and Joseph Pulitzer dominate the American newspaper industry, building chains of tabloid papers in major cities. In this age of "yellow journalism," the power of print was greater than its accuracy. Many believe their biased reporting pushed McKinley and the United States into the Spanish-American War, and the Philippine Incursion that followed.
- Scott Joplin introduces "The Maple Leaf Rag."

AROUND TOWN

- Bloomsburg is a thriving, growing community. The Proprietor of *The Bloomsburg Daily* is William Krickbaum.
- Private Christian Reice, the son of a prosperous Bloomsburg butcher, is seventeen when he leaves home in the service of his country.

RICKSHAW DRIVER, COLOMBO, CEYLON.

are in the trenches at San Pedro, Macati. Yesterday we had a skirmish with the Insurgents. Three were killed and nine wounded.

A man by the name of Wilson of Company E, 12th Regiment, while marching from our trenches to the scene of the battle, was overcome by the heat and dropped out of the ranks along the Pasig River. Later on his coat and hat were found lying along the banks of the river and it is believed that he went into the water, was taken with the cramps and drowned.

We have been short of rations here for the last few days and have had nothing but hard tack and tea for six meals, but the ration wagon came out yesterday and we are getting enough to eat now. Some of the boys take their guns and go out and shoot pigs and chickens. There are lots of them running wild; nobody owns them. We have all the fruit we want to eat—bananas, pineapples, cocoanuts, oranges, breadfruit and grape-fruit.

Each Company has two Chinamen working for them and a cart with a water-buffalo hitched to it. They are hired by the government at thirty-five cents a day, but are very poor workmen. You have to watch them all the time or they will run off to get something to eat. When they want to eat, which is hourly, they say, "Chow, chow."

I saw Samuels and Penman for a few seconds day before yesterday; they came marching in from the city. They were out in the trenches for over a week. They are in the 1st Battalion.

Well, I must close now, hoping to receive some more papers soon.

> Yours Truly,
> Chris Reice
> *The Bloomsburg Daily*
> June 10, 1899

SUPPLY COMPANY E, MANILA, THE PHILIPPINES.

SAN PEDRO, MACATI
MAY 20, 1899
Dear Sister:

I received your letter yesterday and was very glad to hear from you as I thought you had not received mine. Charles wrote to me the other day but I have not much time for writing and so this one can do for both.

Last night we were ordered to fall in line to listen to a message from President McKinley who sent his compliments to Gen. Lawton and his men. We are in his command. On the night of the 18th of May I was on outpost. It is a very dangerous position for we are within six hundred yards of the Insurgents outpost and they keep firing at us all night. I shot one out of a tree several days ago. He had gone out sharp shooting during the night but was overtaken by the light of day before he could return to camp. As soon as I saw him I took aim and fired. The shot took effect but some of his comrades came and carried him away.

San Pedro, Macati, is on the firing line about six miles from the city of Manila. I haven't much time to go to the city and another reason is that we cannot get excused.

The rainy season is starting and it rains every afternoon between two and three o'clock.

Give my best to Miss Breece, if she is still at school, and to Mrs. Ent, Minnie, Mrs. Kester, and Aunt Annie.

Well, I must close now and hoping to hear from you soon, I remain.

> Your brother,
> Chris Reice
> *The Bloomsburg Daily*
> July 20, 1899

SAN FERNANDO, P.I.
JULY 27, 1899
Dear Father:

I received your letter this morning after breakfast and just got through reading it. I wrote you a letter a few days ago but did not mail it so I destroyed it and wrote this one instead.

We have been having several good scraps here since I wrote you the other letter on June 3rd. Early next morning we started to take the trenches by charge, but we were very much surprised when we were not fired on, and we found out that the Insurgents had run away and left the trenches. They had built some very fine trenches. We found lots of bloody places where the Insurgents had been hit, but we found no bodies, for they are just like Indians, they carry away their dead and wounded. We were then ordered to search the nipa huts and look for arms and other things. We found clothes of all kinds—silk dresses—lots of dishes and the furniture was very fine; most of it was made of ma-hogany inlaid with ivory. We then marched on and started to drive the Insurgents farther away.

We reached Cardona a little before supper time and the first thing I did was go and look for some chickens. I found four in a pen and I took them up to our hut where the boys had a good fire going and we put them on to stew. Shortly after that the hut next to ours caught fire and a little later ours was ablaze. We all had to turn out and tear down the huts to save the town from burning down. The huts are made of bamboo and grass and they just burned like paper. We got the fire out when about twenty-five huts had been burned.

The next morning we started to return to San Pedro, Macati and reached there on June 8th, having been on the march for five days. We now thought we should have a good long rest but the next morning we started for Pasig, near Paraeaque, where there were about five thousand Insurgents. I will send you an account of the battle which the Twelfth Regiment took part in and I was right there too. The account of the fight is taken from the Kansas City *Star*.

The rainy season is pretty bad now. We just had a heavy rain here that lasted over eighty

STEREOPTICON VIEW OF TRENCH WARFARE IN THE PHILIPPINES, CIRCA 1900.

hours. The rivers overflowed their banks and some places the boys were compelled to go around on rafts and we had to wade in water up to our waists for over a mile to get to our out posts. Well I have told you all the news now. I am well so is Willie Samuels and Penman, so good bye,

Your son
Chris Reice
The Bloomsburg Daily
September 5, 1899

ANGELES
SEPTEMBER 5, 1899
Dear Father:

Inasmuch as I have a little time to myself now I will relate to you the recent engagement in which I participated, being the first real hard fight we have indulged in since our arrival in the Philippines in which the Insurgents stood their ground so well. I tell you it was the hottest fire we have yet been under. The 17th Regiment had made two attempts to capture the town but both times were driven back by Insurgents. Our colonel had a bet with an officer in the 17th that we would eat dinner in Angeles and so we did, consequently he won, but only after three hours of hard fighting.

Our killed and wounded in the battle of Angeles numbered five killed and seventeen wounded.

We have been having very poor rations for some time, but are constantly improving and at the present getting fairly good victuals. Yesterday the Insurgents attacked our wagon train but were soon driven off. It keeps us busy watching the railroad.

Well I think I have told you all for this time, so good-bye, your son,

Chris Reice
The Bloomsburg Daily
October 21, 1899

ANGELES
OCTOBER 17, 1899
Dear Father:

I have just recovered from the hard work we underwent yesterday morning. The natives have been attacking us nearly every day, relieving us of what little sleep we have a chance to get. In yesterday's skirmish two men were killed and seven wounded.

I suppose there was an immense crowd at the fair this year and I hope you had a good time.

I can hardly think of anything to write about; everything remains the same, plenty of marching and a number of small fights.

We are now preparing for a three months campaign on the city of Dagipan. To reach the city we have to march from eighty to a hundred miles over rice fields, mountains, and streams.

By the time you receive this letter you will probably have eaten your Thanksgiving turkey while I have mine to get, but I guess from present appearances we will have no turkey in the Philippines.

On October 13th I received the letter written by Helen July 28th. It was very fortunate that I got it at all. The transport *Morgan City* which was carrying the mail across the China Sea sprung a leak and went to the bottom, and of course mail and everything else on board went with it, but divers recovered nearly all the mail. The envelope and paper were very dirty but I managed to read its contents.

Well I must close hoping to hear from you soon, I remain,

Your son,
Chris Reice
The Bloomsburg Daily
November 29, 1899

U.S. ARMY HOSPITAL SHIP MISSOURI
AT SEA
JANUARY 5, 1900
Dear Father:

I suppose that you will be surprised when you

receive this letter and learn that I am on my way back to the States.

We left Manila December 31 and as I am writing this letter we are nearing Nagasaki, Japan.

I have a had a very severe attack of chronic dysentery and have become very much emasculated and weak, but now I have begun to pick up and I think that the sea voyage will go a good ways towards the promotion of my recovery.

We are on our way to San Francisco and expect to reach there by the early part of February.

Give my love to all the folks. . . .

> Your loving son,
> Chris
> *The Bloomsburg Daily*
> February 6, 1900

MANILA.

U.S. ARMY HOSPITAL SHIP MISSOURI
AT SEA
JANUARY 21, 1900
Mr. Chas. H. Reice, Bloomsburg, Pa.
Dear Sir:

Before this reaches you, you will have learned by telegraph of the death of your son Christian on board this ship. Your boy was a good patient and we all took a deep interest in him, I especially, as I am from Pennsylvania myself, and I have often been to Bloomsburg. Christian suffered very little and was always cheerful and hopeful. He was very anxious to see his home and those dear to him again; but at the same time he was resigned to anything. Your boy prayed and I believe he died a Christian. The end came peacefully and painlessly and was no doubt a blessed change for him. May the good Lord comfort the bereaved as only He can.

> Very Sincerely Yours,
> Wm. L. Kneedler
> Captain, Medical Corps USA

Your son's remains were embalmed and placed in a handsome casket. They will be taken to San Francisco from this ship.

> *The Bloomsburg Daily*
> February 19, 1900

NAGASAKI, JAPAN.

Editor Daily:

When a general or some other equally great man dies, not only the community in which he lived, but the whole nation respect and show admiration for his service and his patriotism and it is justly proper to do so, but how often, aye!, almost invariably are the rank and file, those that bear the brunt of the campaign, those that march up to the cannon mouth, carrying the emblem of liberty on to victory and glory, forgotten, and though a fact it should not be so.

No matter if an officer or a private each is as loyal as the other and each should receive the same respect and honor.

Soon there will come to our town the remains of one who, though yet in his teens, when the nation was in danger, responded to

THE FUNERAL PROCESSION FOR PRIVATE CHRISTIAN REICE,
MAIN STREET, BLOOMSBURG, PENNSYLVANIA, MARCH 11, 1900.

her call to arms, and not only gave his service, but his young life in its defense and it is proper (and should be done) that the citizens of his own town, at least, pay fitting tribute to his valor and patriotism.

Too much respect can not be shown a hero, and let it not be said that Bloomsburg failed in her duty to her soldier dead and may garlands be placed on the bier of Christian Reice—Hero.

Citizen
The Bloomsburg Daily
February 23, 1900

Private Christian Reice was not yet eighteen when he died.

The Bloomsburg Daily reported on March 12, 1900, that his funeral cortege was "the largest and one of the most solemn occasions ever witnessed in Bloomsburg. The town presented a holiday appearance, the Silk Mill and other industries having closed in order that their employees might pay their last respects to one who had endeared himself to them. Ed Earnest, known by nearly all our citizens as a man whose mind is somewhat impaired, as a tribute of respect carried a beautiful bouquet of cut flowers from Rupert."

William Penman and William Samuels were both Bloomsburg boys. William Samuels died of dysentery in the Philippines in February 1900.

In the Philippine Incursion, the United States lost 3,493 servicemen; of this, 2,146 were due to disease (mostly dysentery), 918 to combat, and 429 to suicide, homicide, accident, or tainted meat rations.

Christian's father commissioned Bloomsburg artist Mrs. W. A. Evert to paint a portrait of Christian, which he hung in his butcher shop window.

Though reelected in 1900, President William McKinley is assassinated in Buffalo, New York, in the first year of his second term by Leon Czolgosz, an anarchist. Theodore Roosevelt becomes president.

PVT. CHRISTIAN REICE,
BY MRS. W. A. EVERT.

CHAPTER 22

☆ GOD'S ☆
HOUSECLEANING

PRELUDE

Dear Editor,

I am submitting three questions that have puzzled me.

First: How do worms get into chestnuts?

Second: How do squirrels, after cutting off green burrs from the trees and they drop to the ground, open them?

Third: How do squirrels know whether a chestnut is good or not without opening it?

I have tossed many chestnuts to squirrels. All that were good were gathered up and eaten or buried. Others they would not offer to pick up, and to satisfy my curiosity I used my pocket knife to open them and found all bad. To me they looked like good chestnuts. Surely there must be an instinct implanted in them that forbids them from gathering wormy or musty chestnuts.

> W. L. Garrison
> *The Morning Press*
> October 2, 1941

HE STARTS CLEANING

Housecleaning time, you say is here,
And then you say come husband dear,
The heavy things you move away,
We want to clean this very day.
Then all the dirt and dust must go
From attic to the floor below;
Now that is how good housewives do,
And so God's world gets dirty too,
And He starts cleaning just like you.

> Emma Shipe, Pottsville, PA
> World War I
> *The Pottsville Republican*
> July 17, 1917

To The Morning Press, Bloomsburg PA:

The President last night signed an executive order directing that the authorized enlisted strength of the Navy be increased to 87,000. He was authorized by Congress in case of emergency to direct such increases in enlistment. New ships and ships in reserve are being fully

NEWS REPORT

The quota for this county, under the different calls of the government, is 1447. Of this number we have but 595 men in service. This makes it necessary to furnish 852 men by draft. The quota can be made up by voluntary enlistment on or before the 20th inst.

Bloomsburg	*Apportioned*	138	*Sent*	91	*Quota to Furnish*	47
Berwick	*Apportioned*	37	*Sent*	24	*Quota to Furnish*	13
Briar Creek	*Apportioned*	66	*Sent*	12	*Quota to Furnish*	54
Beaver	*Apportioned*	56	*Sent*	7	*Quota to Furnish*	49
Benton	*Apportioned*	54	*Sent*	21	*Quota to Furnish*	33
Conyngham	*Apportioned*	120	*Sent*	30	*Quota to Furnish*	90

The Civil War
The Star of the North
September 17, 1862

commissioned as rapidly as possible and the need is imperative for a larger enlistment to man them.

Will you not emphasize this need by giving special prominence on the first page of your paper to President Wilson's order, and also by making an editorial appeal for new recruits for the Navy?

The Navy offers exceptional advantages to young men of stuff and ambition to serve in the first line for a national defense. In this emergency you have the opportunity and privilege of supporting this public service and I am confidently appealing to you for your cordial and helpful cooperation.

Josephus Daniels,
Secretary of the Navy
World War I
The Morning Press
March 25, 1917

Our Country has a big job ahead. The uncertainty is cleared. Patriotic citizens cannot waste time. Each one must apply himself to the task at hand and make our armed forces as efficient as possible. Shall we be unwise and allow the liquor traffic to have its way in making beer easily available to our boys in service? Would you want your son to have a big percentage of beer drinkers in his division?

Mrs. F. T. Kocher
World War II
The Morning Press
December 12, 1941

We left the harbor of New York with bands playing, guns firing, banners flying and the officers making speeches and all of us singing patriotic songs. A great many of us are getting seasick now.

W. J. Lanyon
The Philippine Incursion
The Bloomsburg Daily
March 24, 1899

To Our Friends in Bloom:

We were once jolly good fellows like the rest of the young, free and pleasure seeking of your community, but on account of an extra outburst of patriotic enthusiasm we, like more of our comrades at Fort Slocum and elsewhere, enlisted in the army of Uncle Sam for a period of three short years.

We are making all the necessary preparations to sail, about the beginning of next month, for the Philippines. There, no doubt, we will be able to expend all of our patriotism, and, besides, expend all the reserve money and health, too, very easily. The question confronting us is, what can the far off Filipinos do?

Time, as folks do say, will tell,
In this case, a well directed shell,
Followed by a good victorious
    yell,
May drive the Filipinos pall-mall.
Whatever, then, may be our fate,
We will tell e'er it is too late,
How all things are in the
    Philippines,

Besides picturing some lively
    scenes.
From two soldiers who enlisted in Bloom,

Wm. B. Irving and Albert Stonge
The Philippine Incursion
The Bloomsburg Daily
October 23, 1900

It was with a heavy heart that some of us embarked on board the canal boat *Rolling Wave,* and gave our farewells to the assembled hundreds at Port Noble. It was not regret for what we had done that saddened our thoughts, but the reflection that some and perhaps all of us were bidding final adieus to weeping friends and that many of us were beholding the spires of Bloomsburg for the last time.

We stopped for a short time at Catawissa Bridge where a number of citizens had assembled. Our next stopping place was Danville, where notwithstanding the rain a large crowd assembled. A multitude also greeted us at Northumberland, among which was a sprinkling of the fair sex. The Collector was kind enough to pass us free of toll. Our excellent band played them a few choice tunes after which we turned our attention to the larder, which we found plentifully stored with the ne-

WORLD WAR I RECRUITING.

WILLIAM LUDWIG, BLOOMSBURG BUTCHER,
TRADE CARD—CLOSED,
1918.

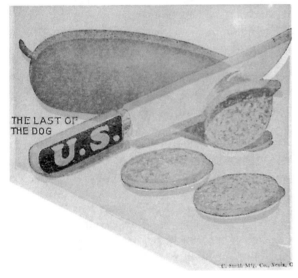

WILLIAM LUDWIG, BLOOMSBURG BUTCHER,
TRADE CARD—OPEN,
1918.

cessities of life. Our beds consisted of straw strewn along the bottom of the boat. This was comfortable enough had there been room; but experience showed us that 100 men more than filled it; hence many slept on deck.

We were all routed up at Selinsgrove, where we were met by the brass band. We reached Harrisburg about three o'clock. Capt. Ricketts immediately formed the company and marched us through the principal streets of the City and Capitol grounds. On the route the constant inquiry was, "Where are you from?" As praise after praise fell from the lips of the spectators, we began to conceive a better opinion of ourselves and bear ourselves as soldiers indeed.

> C. B. Brockway
> The Civil War
> *Columbia Democrat*
> May 11, 1861

The kindness and attention the ladies of Danville manifested toward the members of the Volunteer Company which left Danville this morning has been of the most agreeable and considerate kind. They presented each member of the Company with a copy of the New Testament, for which may they be rewarded by Heaven's richest blessings. And notwithstanding the morning was of the most disagreeable kind when the Volunteers started on their journey, the doors, windows, and even many parts of the street were filled with them. And the expression "God bless you," and "God Almighty protect you," fell from the lips of many, while others filled with tender emotions, and their eyes swimming with tears, waved their handkerchiefs in token of respect. And surely, if the prayers and tears of such angelic creatures will be regarded by the God of battles, our arms cannot be otherwise than victorious.

> Charles W. Fortner
> The Mexican War
> *Columbia Democrat*
> January 9, 1847

I was a young man clerking in Bloomsburg when the war with Mexico began in 1846. I walked to Danville to see the Columbia Guards leave for Mexico, and if my memory is not at fault, I think the company numbered 110, and when they returned in 1848, I again went down to see 47 celebrate their return. Many widows and orphans sat in their homes in sadness that day.

> I. W. Hartman
> Remembering the Mexican War
> *The Morning Press*
> June 28, 1916

While we have lots of large motor trucks, we have not quite discarded the proverbial Army mule, which seldom misses on any cylinder. Each company is allowed eight teams of four head each. Generally speaking camp life and drilling are certainly great as well as invigorating but doing the same drill over time becomes monotonous and makes the boys all want to be on the march for "over there."

A few miles of trench system takes a vast amount of work to build, as the dugouts are numerous and from twenty to thirty feet underground. Their draining must be reckoned with as it would not do to drown your own soldiers out while it works fine on the enemy.

> Pvt. William B. Wilson
> Co. 9, 204th Engineers
> World War I
> *The Morning Press*
> May 22, 1918

I am doing ward duty, and although I have long hours the work is very pleasant. We have a fine dining room and good eats. I would like to tell you what we had for Thanksgiving Dinner. We were allowed 19 ounces of turkey apiece, and apart from that I won't mention any more as paper is scarce and it would be a letter of itself. I have gained only 17 pounds in the past five

JUST THINK

I WALK ONLY 100 MILES A WEEK

POSTCARD, 1918.

months so I won't tell you any more about the eats. You can imagine the rest.

You folks back home may ask yourselves the question of what impresses me the most in army life. The first thing I would say is that I like it here. Secondly the bigness of the system of everything which makes us proud we are Americans.

> Harold L. Ledyard
> World War I
> *The Morning Press*
> December 13, 1917

It is my opinion that 85 percent of the people of Bloomsburg hardly realize our country is at War. We grumble and growl if we can't get all the sugar and tires, pineapple and silks that we think we must have, but what we do not think of is that Bloomsburg is only about seventeen minutes from the coast by fast bomber. Of course,

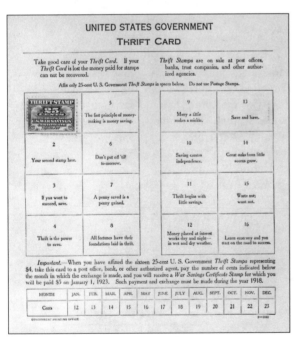

most of us think the idea is quite remote, but the possibility is there.

We do know the Axis powers have struck in some very unexpected points and that they are known for their surprise attacks. The idea that "it just can't happen here" is past. We just hope and pray that it won't happen here. Now there is a group of men in Bloomsburg who do realize the seriousness of this possibility, and they are your Air Wardens. There are 120 Air Wardens in Bloomsburg, plus the Special Police, the firemen, and the First Aid Detachments. Their only duty is to help protect you. It is your duty to cooperate with them, because they are not looking for medals or honor. So, if the alarm sounds, black out completely, stay off the street, do not use the phone except for emergency calls, don't turn in the fire alarm, don't call your Air Warden off the street, and above all try to keep calm! Try to set an example for your family.

R. P. Kashner
World War II
The Morning Press
February 23, 1942

Am sending you a few lines from the biggest lot of disappointed boys in America. We had expected to spend Christmas in Bloomsburg this year and most of us had been promised passes, when along came an order last night from Washington that no passes would be granted for Christmas except for those who can get home by trolley. This naturally cuts out everyone in this camp except those from Washington and Baltimore. Therefore there is gloom in the camp. It was thick last night, you could have cut it with a knife.

Corporal F. D. Hughes,
Camp Meade, Maryland
World War I
The Morning Press
December 18, 1917

Well, I am somewhere in France at last and I will tell you I am glad that I am here. My trip across was great

HE STARTS ACROSS THE SEA

So God sat yonder on His throne,
Looked down to earth—the world
    bemoan,
He said, old world, you're choked with
    dust,
And rum and filth houseclean I must.
And so He starts across the sea,
The attic first, this had to be.
There filth and dirt had piled for years,
It cost the Belgiums blood and tears;
The "housecleaning" all lands fear.
       Emma Shipe, Pottsville, PA
       World War I
       The Pottsville Republican
       July 17, 1917

IF WISHES CAME TRUE

POSTCARD, 1918.

and I am having the time of my life. The novelty of the whole thing surely pleases me because it is so different from civil life. Brother Herbert, I think, is just ahead of me for I am sure that he passed thru this camp and also slept in the same building I was quartered in last night. I am living in hopes of meeting him some day soon.

This country is so different from the old USA. Everything seems so queer. Unable to understand or speak their language I don't think I will talk very much to the people over here. This is surely a great country. I am feeling fine and am the happiest boy in the army. I will tell you about a lot of things but wait until I come back, so don't ask me where I am or what I am doing for I cannot say. Be of good cheer and all will be well for God is with us.

The people dress very queerly, even to their wooden shoes. As we entered their land a French woman immediately swung to the breeze an American flag and we sure did make it ring with cheer.

Well, Mother, write me often and I will write whenever I can. My best to you and Father and all others and God bless you.
       Your faithful son in arms,
       John R. Bisset, Jr.
       World War I
       The Morning Press
       June 22, 1918

The rainy season is here and it has rained every day for over a week. It began raining and blowing yesterday afternoon and up to five o'clock this evening it has not subsided. We have just finished supper.
       Christian Reice
       The Philippine Incursion
       The Bloomsburg Daily
       April 5, 1899

We have been in Saudi Arabia since 18 Aug. 90. These guys and myself endure the harsh conditions of the desert and the time away from our families day by day. When we first got here the temperatures reached 120 degrees during the day with almost no wind. Now temperatures run about 80 degrees during the day and can drop to the upper 30s at night. Also the wind blows a lot of sand and dust now at times making it almost impossible to see fifty yards. Another thing that is hard to get used to is the flies, they seem to be everywhere.

SSG Jack Rowlands
Desert Storm
Press Enterprise
January 11, 1991

Our regiment was again paid off on Tuesday evening and Wednesday morning. The boys obey no command with more promptness than the one "fall in for pay." After pay come the camp followers. These are too numerous and various to describe. Perhaps the most useful is the book peddlers having a few volumes of good tactics and any amount of trashy novels. Next appears the stationery peddlers, with all sorts of fancy patriotic paper and envelopes which he sells very cheap (about six times the ordinary rates) considering "the purty pictures on 'em."

Samuel Knorr
The Civil War
The Star of the North
October 3, 1861

YOU'LL HEAR FROM ME SOON

I PROMISE TO WAKE UP AND WRITE

POSTCARD, 1942.

They are cutting hay in France now and they have some pretty crude methods. The women take a large part in the haying and farming of all kinds. They follow the men with the scythe and spread it to dry, afterwards raking it together in heaps. The women don't look very good or pretty in working clothes but when they get dressed for church Sunday it makes all the difference in the world in their looks and the way they act. But they are robust and husky. Perhaps it would do some of our girls good to go into the fields and build themselves up.

Private Otto Lynn
World War I
The Morning Press
August 15, 1918

This is a beautiful country and this part is especially pretty. It is near a river quite as large as the Susquehanna at home perhaps even larger. The roads here are the best I have ever seen, especially the roads between the large cities which are quite like our state roads only much prettier. They are almost straight and lined the entire length on both side with large trees. Any road that has been in use any length of time is lined with trees while the very old roads dating back to the time of Caesar have magnificent trees along their edge. France is almost a toy country and this idea is increased when seen from an aeroplane.

Cadet Ralph Harriman
World War I
The Morning Press
January 4, 1918

Hello Bob,

It was certainly a pleasant surprise when I received a copy of "The Argus" in the mail last week. It is the first copy I have seen in months. The hometown paper sort of fills in the news gaps that personal letters can't take care of.

And we fellows over here are just as interested in knowing how things are going at home as the home folks are in receiving the war news.

After our setback a few weeks ago, the news now seems to be very favorable. And I hope it continues to be that way. Sorry I can't say more but a new set of very rigid censorship regulations have just been published which prevents us from mentioning any thing regarding the progress of the war.

I'm still busy doing my part to help arrange that day the soldiers all like, "pay day." It's a non-combatant job but still lets us in for an occasional bit of excitement.

April 22nd the army will be starting a new battle. The battle against malaria. On that date we start taking the new substitute for quinine, knows as atebrin. We get two tablets a week, which is supposed to build up a resistance to the disease. It has been reported by the medical department that malaria is so prevalent in North Africa that from 90 to 100 percent of the population in some areas are infected. The disease is in full swing from April until November, the mosquito season. The army is certainly taking all precautions against it and we will probably win the battle against the mosquito as we hope to win all the rest of the battles in this war.

Yours for victory,
Ira R. McHenry, in North Africa
World War II
The Benton Argus
April 15, 1943

Last week we escorted 35 B52's bombing the daylights out of the Republican Guard and other front line positions in Kuwait. That guy can't have a whole lot left.

It's sad that we killed some of our own Marines, but that happens in every war I guess and I just hope it doesn't happen too often. We are still flying just as much, 20 sorties a day, but our pilots tell us that they aren't even encountering much radar anymore. I think we just have

Saddam whipped! This has to be one of the finest displays of military might ever used and I just hope that the rest of the radical countries in the world take heed! There is no match for us!

Terry Liddick
Desert Storm
Press Enterprise
March 12, 1991

We have at present about a mile of different trenches. Are now digging a slope 90 feet long on a 30 degree angle which will meet another shaft and tunnel from that shaft under the trenches we are supposed to blow up. The reconnaissance section does all the scouting and map drawing of the land around and in our lines and enemy's lines if possible for one to steal in. I have been put on the last named section. This is a fine life but awful hard. Up at 5:45 a.m. and continually going until 5:45 p.m.

We are getting food and plenty of it. They have fixed us up with straw ticks, wooden floors, wooden sides and a wood stove. So all the rumors to the effect that we lack a whole bunch of comforts are untrue. We have been a little short in clothes and shoes and blankets until we were issued another blanket the other day making three in all.

L. C. Thompson
World War I
The Morning Press
November 19, 1917

I had to swallow hard to keep that lump down, no not of homesickness—a lump of happiness which one can only experience when they are really truly happy and you know when one receives fourteen letters and then one has them topped off with eight or ten individually wrapped newspapers of the best class and containing everything of interest to everybody he is really made happy and if you were never made happy and proud of your home town come "over here" and go without a word from home or people you know for a period of several weeks and then get a bunch of letters from friends and family and after reading each one, read *The Morning Press* and then re-read the whole lot again and you will feel as I do now. Happy? Proud? Anyone who wants to do a bit of encouragement to a Bloomsburg boy who is "over here" just find out whether he gets *The Morning Press* or not and if not, subscribe to it for him!

The service I am connected with does not give a man a chance to fight for his country or his life. The ambulance driver, knowing that every trip he makes is going to be a possible suicide has no chance to fight to save that life which is so dear to him and his. But! He must go on that open road where even fighting units are forbidden to travel and he must drive back his car to the post and bring back wounded over that same road. He cannot, if his engine fails, coast to safety and make a clean landing either inside or outside of enemy lines. He gets out amid the shells and machine gun shower of bullets and makes the adjustment or crawls under cover and awaits a time he can. But the adjustment must be made sooner or later amid that storm of steel but he is only a part of the machinery which restores the morale of our armies.

Smooth tongued orators can not in any way picture to you people at home the suffering or the fighting spirit of these soldiers.

Irvin A. Robinson
World War I
The Morning Press
June 17, 1918

PLACE: WHO CARES
DATE: DITTO
Greetings:

After leaving where we were before we left for here, not knowing we were coming here from there, we could not tell if we would arrive here or not. Nevertheless, we are now here and not there.

The weather here is just as it is at this season, but, of course, quite unlike the weather where we were before we came here. After leaving by what we came by, we had a good trip.

The people here are just like they look, but do not look to be like they were where we came from. From there to here is just as far as it is from here to there.

The way we came here is just like everyone comes from there to here. Of course we had to bring everything we had with us, for we wear what we would wear here, which is not like what we would wear there. The whole thing is quite a new experience here, because it isn't like what it was like where we were before we left there for here.

It is now time, in all probability, to stop this somewhat too newsy letter before I give away too much information, as the censor is likely to be a spy.

Love,
Uno Hoo
"Bill"
World War II
The Benton Argus
April 15, 1943

SACRIFICE WE MUST

Housecleaning, then, stirs up the dust,
And sacrifice we surely must.
Our boys are called across the sea,
Housecleaning implements to be.
They would some heavy burdens bear,
So we must help and do our share
To clean the world and make it new:
He calls to me and you and you,
Let's help God's Housecleaning
 through and through.
Emma Shipe, Pottsville, PA
World War I
The Pottsville Republican
July 17, 1917

While lying close to a piece of woods waiting to be placed in position, the enemy again opened on us. A surgeon rode up hastily and told us the rebels were moving up large forces of infantry—that his wounded had been captured—and that our Division would have to repel the enemy alone, as the others had expended their ammunition. He was evidently *scared*. But such news and the enemy's fire had the effect of causing a disgraceful stampede of ambulances, battery wagons, forges and of many of the troops engaged in the day's action. Although the rebels fired uncomfortably close, they did not damage us. Our line was then formed; and the artillery and infantry put in appropriate positions.—Scarcely had we attained them, when the enemy brought a battery out of the woods and opened a terrible fire on our force, and for a time the scene was terrible though animated. We soon silenced them, and uncertain quiet again resumed its way. We could see the lights of the enemy, hear the rumbling of their artillery, but of their movements knew nothing. It was a night of terrible suspense.

About 3 o'clock in the morning the forces on the right fell back, and took up a new position. Daylight showed us numbers of the enemy on the mountain to the front, but our force was not large enough to warrant us in attacking them in so strong a position.

A visit to our impromptu hospitals revealed all the horrors of war. Some 600 lay scattered around with all imaginable wounds in the limbs, body, head and face. Some quiet as death, perhaps dead; others cursing horribly, and others bearing their suffering like heroes. Sunday evening I rode over part of the battleground. On the ground where the enemy's battery had been placed the night before, lay thirteen dead horses, three men, two of them being officers, pieces of harness, cut traces, and fragments of clothing. One of the officers had his head shot completely off, and it was nowhere to be seen, and the other was shot in the breast, and his face so begrimed with pow-

der as to be unrecognizable. Further along in the woods were dead men, horses, ruins of wagons, etc. The enemy at the foot of the mountain prevented us from inspecting further.

Yesterday (Monday) we were engaged in burying our dead and taking care of the wounded. Our total loss is about 1500. Gen. Geary and Col. Knipe, 46th Pa., and many other distinguished officers have been wounded. Crawford's Brigade lost the most as it was not supported till late in the afternoon. I can make no estimate of the enemy's loss. Prisoners say that after we silenced their battery the Brigade supporting it fell back in confusion, and the Battery was left on the field till near daylight. The rebels have been reinforced, and now have with them Generals Hill, Ewell and Longstreet. We have been reinforced by Generals Sigel, King and Burnside. The grand battle is yet to come off, and we are momentarily expecting it. I will write you more particulars here after.

ARTILLERIST
The Civil War
Columbia Democrat
August 23, 1862

H. B. M. Ship *Poietiers* (74) At Sea.

The fortune of war has placed us in the hands of the enemy. We have been captured by this ship after having ourselves captured his Britannic majesty's brig *Frolic*.

The *Frolic* was superior in force to us—she mounted eighteen 32 pound caronades, and two long 9's. *The Wasp,* you know has only 16 caronades. The action lasted 43 minutes—we had five killed, and the slaughter on board the *Frolic* was dreadful. We are bound into Bermuda. I am quite unhurt.

In great haste,
J. Biddle
The War of 1812
The Oracle of Dauphin and Harrisburgh Advertiser
November 7, 1812

FRANCE, 1918.

At that moment a soldier cried out, "There are the Indians now," and sure enough they were jumping from tree to tree endeavoring to surround the party—the Indians were about 40 in number. The Lady was immediately dismounted and placed in a wagon, Lieut. S. then tried to arrange his men so as to give them a fight—when, I am sorry to say, the men behaved badly, four took flight, and he was left with but 6 to defend the woman. The Sergeant Major being one of the six, he was shot thr'o the heart the first fire—the horses broke loose and came flying back to this post.

In ten minutes a reinforcement was on its way from here but alas! it arrived too late. Lieut. Montgomery the husband of the lady was first on the ground, the Indians were gone, and there lay his young bride dead and stripped of her clothing, a ball having been shot through her breast; by her side lay a soldier yet living, but wounded in the breast and naked; his words to Lieut. M. were, "your wife,—I fought to the last, but it was no use." He is since dead.

> Lieut. Arthur T. Lee
> Lewisburg *People's Advocate*
> The Florida War
> January 30, 1841

They all say it is a great life if you don't weaken. (Physically) (Morally) (Mentally) which?

> Harold L. Ledyard
> World War I
> *The Morning Press*
> December 13, 1917

I will tell you how I celebrated my 22nd birthday. I secured a pass from the Captain and went to Manila. There I went to the hotel and enjoyed a good square meal. I spent the balance of the day looking at the many interesting sights, such as buildings blown to pieces by Dewey's big guns. I returned to camp about nine o'clock in the evening and on my way I met a Filipino who had been hiding in the bushes. He made a dash at me with a big knife. I raised my gun and shot

FRANCE, 1918.

at him. He dropped over and died almost instantly.

William Lanyon
The Philippine Incursion
The Morning Press
July 21, 1899

He fell during operations against the enemy in
northern Luxembourg. The heavy machine
gun platoon of which he was a member was attached to a rifle company to lend support in an
attack upon the high ground near a small town.
He was advancing with his platoon when he was
killed instantly by an enemy rifleman. He was
buried in a United States Military Cemetery in
Luxembourg. A Protestant chaplain officiated
at the service when he was laid to rest. There is
nothing that I might say that can in the least
measure ease your irreparable bereavement. Yet
there is pride in his contribution to the cause of
freedom. Our ultimate victory will provide a
symbolic monument to augment the white
wooden cross which now adorns his grave.

Roy G. Mosher, Capt. 357th Infantry
Asst. Adjutant
World War II
The Morning Press
April 11, 1945

Sir: the following is a correct list of the casual-
ties of Company D, 84th Regiment, Pennsylvania Volunteers in the engagement near
Winchester on Sunday March 23rd, 1862:

Killed—William R. Fowler
Wounded —
Sergeant H. Funk, Thigh
Corporal J. M. Price, Ankle
Corporal C. Mummy, Hand
Corporal T. C. Fowler, Shoulder
Private C. D. Bowers, Knee
Private M. Fitzharris, Head

Private G. Holcomb, Head
Private Wm. Prosser, Arm
Private J. C. Tesler, Abdomen
Private J. S. Wheeler, Groin
Private J. Prosser, Breast, mortally
Very Respectfully,
Alex J. Frick, Capt.
Commanding Co. D., 84th Regiment,
Pennsylvania Volunteers
The Civil War
Columbia Democrat
March 30, 1862

Sir: Corporal Reman D. Lee of Co. H 1st Cavalry was killed in battle with Indians on the
morning of June 17, 1877. When I last saw him
he was mortally wounded. We were forced to retreat leaving our wounded in the hands of the
enemy who dispatched them. The bodies were
found about ten days after the battle and found
just where they fell. Corporal Lee received your
newspaper through his friends who reside in
your vicinity, and I take this means of acquaint-
ing them with his death. He has money in the
hands of the government, clothing money, pay,
&c., which they can get by applying to proper
authorities.

Yours, &c.
M. McCarty, 1st Sergeant
Company H-1 Cavalry
Fort Walla Walla, Washington
Territory
The Indian Wars
The Columbian
August 17, 1877

What about the heroines who gave up husbands, fathers, sons and lovers and gave them
courage to go forth to battle for their country;
heroines who made heroes and whose words
were heard above the roar of battle and the

storm of the conflict? Will they not live in history? Then we must remember that bandages and cordials were just as essential as bullets and bayonets, and they come from woman's hands.

E. J. Bowman
The Bloomsburg Daily
July 28, 1898

SOLDIERS' AND SAILORS' MONUMENT,
MARKET SQUARE,   BLOOMSBURG, PA.
COMPLIMENTS OF THE BIJOU,
BELOW THE SQUARE.

GIVE MY ALL

God's housecleaning we call war,
Come, do your bit, close not your door!
To Uncle Sam, but say now here,
I'll give my all, my boy so dear.
At first, dear Lord, I could not see
That he was more to You than me.
Just use him, then, where he may be
A soldier best on land or sea
To help bring peace and liberty.

Emma Shipe, Pottsville, PA
World War I
The Pottsville Republican
July 17, 1917

And now we have it that the widow of the soldier can draw no pension if she has any means of living without it. She gave her husband in the hour of peril for her country's defense. He was the head of the family, the family's support, her only support and defense. She bid him farewell with the prospects of never seeing him again, to die upon the battlefield, in the hospital or starve to death on Belle Island or in Andersonville. He left the children with her to be clothed and fed perhaps with meager menus, if any to support herself and them. She gave up all in defense of her country. It was not considered whether this husband and father left a livelihood for his family or not. He was wanted in the army, and his wife had to yield up her welfare in his, make a full and complete surrender of his care, protection, sustenance. And now she must prove herself a pauper to get a pension. It is blood money.

Penholder
The Bloomsburg Daily
January 24, 1895

As a Korean vet I know how they feel. But when in the hell are we going to get any credit? No one gave anything to our families. If you borrow from a bank, you have to pay it back.

Robert DeShon
Press Enterprise
March 2, 1991

Do you think God promotes war and the killing of human beings and were you in Vietnam? I think not. I was. Do you know what the hell went on there and what it was all about and

how the vets were treated when they got back?
What about those that were left behind?

> Bloomsburg Woman
> 30 Seconds
> *Press Enterprise*
> October 12, 1992

Did you know that in Washington, D.C., there is
no monument dedicated to the troops of WWII?

> Chic Thackara
> *Press Enterprise*
> March 13, 1991

I'm a veteran of World War I, and a confirmed
pacifist ever since, I would like to express. . . .
How long, how long, before people will learn
that war is the real enemy, not our brothers and
sisters of different nations?

> The PA Veteran
> *The Morning Press*
> November 11, 1974

GOD'S HOUSECLEANING

For God will not forsake His own,
He watches them from yonder throne,
Then when this sin-cursed world is free
Glad hands will clasp across the sea
In peace and love and harmony.

> Emma Shipe, Pottsville, PA
> World War I
> *The Pottsville Republican*
> July 17, 1917

⚔ THE ⚔
PRESIDENT IS . . .

PREAMBLE

I just want to know if anybody knows how a common citizen can run for the President of the United States, if you have to have a party endorsement or several hundred signatures. Or doesn't it work that way? Do you have to be a member of a certain organization? Please, if anybody knows if a common citizen can apply to be voted on the ballot to be President of the United States, please call in with the information. I would appreciate it very much. Thank you.

> Anonymous Caller
> 30 Seconds
> *Press Enterprise*
> May 11, 1995

GEORGE WASHINGTON

It is true, President Washington has issued his proclamation of strict neutrality in the efforts of the brave defenders of French liberty. But what does it signify? The supreme power is vested in the people. We have never been consulted in the business. We have the right to give away our money as we think fit.

> One of the People
> *The Oracle of Dauphin and Harrisburgh Advertiser*
> May 22, 1793

JOHN ADAMS

Some men, like Duane, thought Mr. Adams a FOOL.

> The Man in the Woods
> *The Republican Argus*
> July 20, 1804

THOMAS JEFFERSON

IMPORTANT INFORMATION! I have lately been informed from *high authority* that Thomas Jefferson is now plotting against the United

States, to turn congress neck and heels out of doors. I was also very credibly informed that on Wednesday evening last, in one of his diurnal reveries he took his own nose for an apple dumpling and absolutely bit it off!

Tom Thumb
Dauphin Guardian
April 7, 1807

JAMES MADISON

Our situation is exactly that of a besieged city. Nothing doing, all business at a stand, nothing thought or talked of but the enemy and the war. The expectation here is that we shall not be attacked until our army re-enters Canada, when the enemy will give reins to his resentment and do all the damage he can. Why will Mr. Madison tempt the vengeance of the enemy? It is cruel, inhuman. The blame will be thrown upon him, and not upon the provoked enemy.

Baltimore Correspondent.
The Oracle of Dauphin and Harrisburgh Advertiser
May 22, 1813

JAMES MONROE

Mr. Monroe has been frequently spoken of as the most suitable candidate for *president.* His services, talents, integrity, and patriotism are acknowledged by all republicans. The flimsy and factious objection that he is a *Virginian,* needs no other weapons than ridicule and contempt.

New England.
Pennsylvania Republican
February 27, 1816

JOHN QUINCY ADAMS

Christians of America! Ye who have been brought up to abhor this practice of duelling; will you suffer the only candidate before you who has not dipped his hands in the blood of another human being to go unrewarded? No! Mr. Adams is the only one before you who has done nothing to create your displeasure.

Baltimore Correspondent.
The Oracle of Dauphin and Harrisburgh Advertiser
August 7, 1824

ANDREW JACKSON

I was once an ardent advocate of Gen. Jackson. I have been disappointed. Politicians are now enjoying the sunshine of Executive favor and living on public bounty, fattening in the "spoils of victory" and receiving the rewards of their intemperate zeal.

Snyder
The Berwick Gazette
July 19, 1834

MARTIN VAN BUREN

Martin Van Buren has justly earned the title of a "Magician." I look forward with confidence to the time when Martin Van Buren will be seen in all his "native ugliness—a serpent with an Angel's tongue."

Columbia
The Berwick Gazette
May 23, 1835

JOHN TYLER

Tylerism seems to create many bitter feelings. If every person who gets drawn into the vortex of contention only knew how effectual *Sherman's Camphor Lozenges* were in keeping down bad blood and maintaining a proper degree of decency in their behavior, especially as it is feared that such hot-headed conduct will only hasten the overthrow which is sure to overtake a bad cause.

John Moyer
Advertisement in the
Columbia Democrat
August 23, 1845

WILLIAM HENRY HARRISON

Poor old Gen. Harrison is a besotted guzzler of hard cider.

A Democrat
Columbia Democrat
August 22, 1840

JAMES K. POLK

Almost every day brings forth new men who avow themselves against Polk, a man who is in favor of the pauper labor of England, the slave labor of the South, and against the labor of the honest farmer, mechanic, and laborer of this country. I assure you that the rottenness of the party has become apparent. The spirit is with us, the hurrah is with us, and the ladies, God ever bless them, are with us.

Catawissa Correspondent
The Old Warrior
August 17, 1844

ZACHARY TAYLOR

"Old Zack" appears to possess the rare merit of keeping his political friends in utter ignorance—not to say total darkness.

Observer
Columbia Democrat
January 6, 1849

MILLARD FILLMORE

Mr. Fillmore blushes with maiden modesty as often as the Presidency is mentioned in his presence.

Observer.
The Star of the North
November 6, 1851

FRANKLIN PIERCE

Mr. Editor: Having heard it reported that a personal indignity of the grossest character was inflicted upon Gen. Franklin Pierce, over a "game of cards," I write this to enquire whether you have any information upon the subject.

> J. R. B.
> *The Whig State Journal*
> September 16, 1852

We have taken some pains to inform ourselves of its truth, and have not the slightest doubt. On the night before Gen. Pierce left the city of Mexico, HIS FACE WAS SLAPPED at a game of cards, which insult WAS NOT RESENTED by him. A friend apologizes for Pierce's non-resentment of the insult by saying that when the officer slapped his face, Pierce fainted!

> Editor

JAMES BUCHANAN

On election day when James Buchanan was elected President of the U.S., Peter Eveland went and voted for Buchanan, and the next day he dropped dead on the wood pile. The shock to the neighborhood may well be imagined.

> John C. Wenner
> *The Columbian*
> March 16, 1894

ABRAHAM LINCOLN

Let the people in the County demand that these troops be removed from our midst. 'Twas an act similar to this which caused our forefathers to rebel against King George, and we advise King Lincoln to take warning.

> Sassycus
> *The Star of the North*
> August 24, 1864

ANDREW JOHNSON

I made my way up Main Street, when much to my surprise I found squads of gentry flying in numerous directions. I stood for some moments wild with amazement. Has President Johnson been assassinated?

> Spectator
> *The Star of the North*
> May 17, 1865

ULYSSES S. GRANT

Human idolatry never reached a more beastly depth than in its worship of Grant. The country does not owe as much to him as it does to hundreds of others. But because he has lost his ill gotten fortune through stupidity and fraud, and his wonderful health through prolonged dissipation, the Senate, a portion of the press, and a herd of millionaires dissolve in maudlin pity over an example of spurious greatness to which history furnishes no parallel.

> Regular Correspondent
> *Democratic Sentinel*
> January 23, 1885

RUTHERFORD B. HAYES

Whether by oversight or design, Congress removed the limit to the number of Notaries Public that may be appointed for the District of Columbia. Here is the opportunity of Mr.

Hayes' lifetime. A few citizens of Ohio have not been appointed to office. A few Louisiana thieves have not received reward for stealing the Presidency for Mr. Hayes. Let it be the boast of his Administration—it will have nothing else to boast of—that under it every citizen held office. Let us be a nation of Notaries.

Seminole
The Columbian
August 16, 1878

JAMES A. GARFIELD

Some of my opponents are circulating a base falsehood accusing me of voting for Garfield in 1880. Such a foolish idea. I never voted for Garfield or any Republican in my life.

Alex Kanouse
The Columbian & Democrat
August 10, 1888

CHESTER A. ARTHUR

President Arthur's recent invitation to Mrs. Blaine (whose husband lost the election to Mr. Cleveland) to assist him at his New Year's reception was resented by that woman in a discourteous note giving as her reason that the President had not assisted Mr. Blaine in the late campaign.

Washington Correspondent
The Danville Intelligencer
January 9, 1885

GROVER CLEVELAND

I have endured frontier life and drought and grasshoppers and am now suffering from the affects of the Cleveland administration, the hardest of all. We cannot borrow one dollar, la-

boring men are in want, our crops are dried up the worst in 27 years, and now the small pensions secured under the Harrison administration are being taken from us by rebel brigadiers. God help us to live through it. The Soldier boys will know better next time. I hope you in the east may all be happy. I remain

Wm. Hohnbaum
The Columbia County Republican
August 31, 1893

BENJAMIN HARRISON

President Harrison introduced an innovation in White House customs this week that is deeply regretted by conservative people, who believe that the dignity of the Presidential office should be increased instead of decreased. It was a positive shock to find that the President had had himself interviewed by a newspaper.

Jay Eye See
Democratic Sentinel
November 15, 1889

WILLIAM MCKINLEY

If McKinley wins hell will be on top and it will rain ashes in this country for four years to come.

G. M. L.
Democratic Sentinel
October 29, 1896

THEODORE ROOSEVELT

The whole trend of the Roosevelt administration has been along the line of concentration of power in the White House. It is generally believed, however, that the American people are too shrewd to be misled and that they will recognize that the present incumbent of the White House, even if he be himself honest, is a menace to American ideals and to liberty and that he is being made the tool of men who are far his superiors in forecast and sagacity.

Regular Correspondent
The Columbian
September 4, 1902

WILLIAM H. TAFT

Secretary of War Taft, whose nomination for the presidency is now looked upon as assured, will take up residence with his multi-millionaire brother in Cincinnati. This brother, it is understood, has been financing his campaign and is ready to finance it further and to almost any extent.

Regular Correspondent
Catawissa News Item
June 4, 1908

WOODROW WILSON

There is a great deal of dissatisfaction among voters in the Democratic and Republican parties. They cancel each other's votes. If they will vote the prohibition party they could kill the liquor traffic. Will the voters of the Nation keep the Anti-Prohibition party in power by re-electing Wilson?

Thomas C. Wilson
The Morning Press
November 2, 1916

OUR CHOICE

WARREN G. HARDING

Citizens of Montour County who desire to make a contribution to the Harding Memorial Fund can mail or bring their contributions to Frank Peters, Mahoning Street. There are scores of good folks in Montour County, maybe hundreds of them, regardless of whether they are Republicans, Democrats, or other party affiliations, who look upon the death of Mr. Harding as one of the outstanding calamities of our nation's history. Mr. Harding, dead, they regard as a great man who actually laid down his life in the service of his country. Contributions should be voluntary, an outpouring from the people to express their sense of personal loss in the removal of a great, sincere, upright servant. The memorial must ever remain an impressive reminder and an inspiration to coming generations of Americans.

> F. G. Peters, Chairman
> *The Danville Evening News*
> December 13, 1923

CALVIN COOLIDGE

Despite his approval of fraternal orders, President Coolidge is not a "joiner." He belongs to no lodges, societies, or similar organizations and knows no secret grip, passwords, or incantations. The oath of office is declared to be the only oath ever indulged in by the president.

> Harry B. Hunt
> "Hunt's Washington Letter"
> *The Danville Morning News*
> September 15, 1924

HERBERT HOOVER

At different times we hear our President call on the people for more law observance and more law enforcement, while the privilege and pillage boys get their millions regardless of Federal law, God's law, or the laws of humanity. I believe in the doctrines of Washington, of John Adams, of Jefferson, of Lincoln, that these United States are for all the inhabitants thereof, and not for the few thousand money changers that appeal most to the Hoover regime.

> James A. Rodgers
> *The Benton Argus*
> July 9, 1931

FRANKLIN D. ROOSEVELT

When Roosevelt first gained office, it is a fact that all over Russia banners were displayed proclaiming the first Communistic President of the United States.

    Glenn Letterman
    The Morning Press
    September 21, 1941

HARRY S. TRUMAN

I don't wish to criticize the President, but think he made a great mistake. He advocated an advance in wages which immediately gave backbone to the Union. This had the effect of other unions to follow suit and this has demoralized the whole country and caused a feeling of unrest and uncertainty all over the country. What do we tell our war veterans returning home when there are no jobs awaiting them? We ought to hide our faces in shame whenever we meet them.

    H. B. Low
    The Morning Press
    March 11, 1946

DWIGHT D. EISENHOWER

It is amazing how many columnists and commentators have soft-pedalled the impending visit of Nikita Khrushchev. It is equally amazing how President Eisenhower proceeded to give out with the soft sell by telling us some good will come of this visit. What good can we do by consorting with this butcher?

    Frank Buffone
    Berwick Enterprise
    September 1, 1959

JOHN F. KENNEDY

Since nearly half of Columbia County Democrats did not vote for Kennedy, the following will be of much interest to not only these Democrats, but to

FOR BEST RESULTS have plenty of light, either artificial or sunlight. Look intently at small star on nose for sixty seconds (or count to sixty slowly)
THEN
look intently at a light wall, the sky or any other light flat surface and you will see

OUR NEXT PRESIDENT

WELCOME...
VICE PRESIDENT NIXON
TODAY NOV. 1st 11 A.M.
at the
BERWICK DL & W RAILROAD STATION

"DICK" NIXON

Perhaps the greatest testimony to Nixon's character was Dwight Eisenhower's selection of him as his running mate in 1952, for General Eisenhower had spent his life judging the character and quality of men. And since he took office as Vice President January 20, 1953, Nixon has been charged with precedent-breaking responsibilities, including presiding over the Cabinet and the National Security Council, and consulting with the President on such matters as internal security, political timing

THE MORNING PRESS, NOVEMBER 1, 1956.

all Republicans who did not buy the Kennedy promise of something for nothing and all for no cost. Keynoting the first White House Regional Conference, Bobby Kennedy told of dreaming of a meeting with Saint Peter. He was handed a piece of chalk and told he could enter Heaven only if he wrote down every broken promise on the rungs of the ladder. Someone passed him coming down. It was the President. "What are you doing up here?" Bobby asked. "I'm going down for more chalk," the President replied. In joking about the broken pledges, Bobby admits the Kennedys squeezed by on the basis of a fraudulent campaign made up of statements they never intended to keep. Bobby should leave the laughs to the professional comedians.

> Boyd H. Kline
> Publicity Chairman
> Columbia County Republican
> Committee
> *The Morning Press*
> November 18, 1961

LYNDON B. JOHNSON

I see that President Johnson's "proposed creation of a cabinet level department of housing and urban development" has been passed by the House. Also that "a program to continue public housing and urban renewal programs" has been passed by the House. If our President, who surely is a well educated and far-seeing man, approves these things, why should the C.O.G.D.—Citizens of Greater Danville—oppose them?

> Name Withheld
> *The Danville News*
> July 28, 1965

RICHARD M. NIXON

One of the most vehement anti-communists who ever waved a flag, Richard Nixon wines and dines with Brezhnev and Chairman Mao.

> John A. Sturgin
> *The Morning Press*
> January 15, 1973

GERALD R. FORD

I don't know where this depression started and under what President but I do know it took years to get us in this shape and it'll take years 'til we see daylight again. We're in a rut that only seems to run down hill and the only solution is a slow climb back and we'll all have to help in doing that. All I can say is President Ford cut himself a pretty big piece of cake, any man willing to take on this mess sure needs help slicing it.

> Barbara Davis
> *The Morning Press*
> November 20, 1974

JIMMY CARTER

If Mr. Carter gets in the White house, will we all be working for peanuts?

Clyde C. Bauman
The Morning Press
October 30, 1976

RONALD REAGAN

Throughout this campaign, Reagan has consistently quoted Democratic presidents, naming such luminaries as Roosevelt, Truman, and Kennedy. I have yet to hear him make such glowing references to Eisenhower, Nixon and Ford. He hasn't held up Hoover as a shining example. I ask if memory has failed you, Mr. President. Have you forgotten what party you belong to?

Dana Eugene Creasy
Press Enterprise
October 30, 1984

GEORGE BUSH

Some people says George Bush don't know what poverty is. This is not true. As a young man he grew up during the Great Depression of the 20s and 30s. Now his family had to lay off two of the maids and one chauffeur. This created a hardship on his family. When you have a depression this is what you have to do. I'm 85 years old and I lived through the Great Depression. So I can sympathize with George Bush.

Charlie Karns
Press Enterprise
October 28, 1992

BILL CLINTON

I'd like to respond to Cal Thomas' statement that Democrats are unfit to rule because of their fornication. He should know that fornicators built this country. Ben Franklin was a big orgy meister and still did good service for the country. In addition, Presidents Jefferson, Franklin Roosevelt, Eisenhower, Harding, all had mistresses. Some were good, some were bad. So let's talk issues, not BS. By the way, I'm not calling to defend Clinton, I'm calling to defend fornication.

Benton Man
30 Seconds
Press Enterprise
September 18, 1995

A SILENT MESSAGE

Let us send a silent message to the Supreme Court.
Let us send a message to those who burn our Flag.
Let us help our Flag defend itself.
Let us construct our Flag with fire-resistant material.
Think about it.

    Charles Evans,
    Shickshinny
    Press Enterprise
    June 29, 1989

CHAPTER 25

STANDARDS OF BEHAVIOR: THE 1920S

TIE US DOWN

We all say when we come home we are going to tear things up for fifteen miles around, so you want to catch us in time and tie us down before we get in trouble.

> Private Alfred Bowe
> Company K, U.S. Infantry
> American Force, Paris
> World War I
> *The Pottsville Republican*
> November 23, 1917

NEWS ITEM

PASTORS URGE THE WOMEN OF TOWN TO GO TO THE POLLS

AND MAKE CERTAIN THEY REGISTER FOR THE NOVEMBER ELECTION

AN IMPORTANT DUTY

Bloomsburg women were urged to register Tuesday and Wednesday by Dr. A. Lawrence Miller, pastor of the First Methodist Church, in the prelude to his sermon in the church yesterday morning.

Attention was called to the fact that equal suffrage was now part of the law of our country, and that the women had often expressed the hope before the eighteenth amendment became effective that they would like the ballot to vote against the liquor traffic. The speaker declared that to be one of the big items in the congressional elections this fall, and that every woman should take the steps necessary to insure her getting the ballot in November so she could cast her vote against any candidate who had allied himself with the liquor traffic.

At yesterday morning's service in the Reformed Church, Rev. P. H. Hoover called attention of the women in his congregation to the importance of their registering for the November election Tuesday or Wednesday.

Some of the women declared they were going to register, and others said they did not know how to go about it. To all such Mr. Hoover stated he was ready to lend his aid.

"I only went so far as to tell the women it was their duty to register," the Rev. Mr. Hoover explained. "How they vote is a matter that rests with them."

The Morning Press
August 30, 1920

TO THOSE WHO MOTOR

Just why most motorists have two standards of behavior, one for the town or city and one for the country, is hard to understand, yet such must be the case from the evidence one sees any day when passing thru the country.

If any flowers or fruit, especially wild strawberries or apples, are discovered in any seemingly unlikely place, they at once think they belong to them or at least to anyone who can get away with them without being caught in the act and proceed to gather them. Every field belongs to some one, therefore, someone expects to gather and enjoy the fruits and flowers although they may not at the moment a motorist appears be there to claim them.

THE CHANGING ROLE OF NEWSPAPERS

The advent of radio, and of national radio networks, brings a new set of rivals to the daily paper for the attention of the news hungry. Newspapers are now competitive commercial operations, and competition leads to consolidation. By the dawn of the 1920s, Columbia and Montour counties have just six newspapers. *The Morning Press* is the only one in Bloomsburg. Concepts of journalistic impartiality supersede the overt political partisanship that ruled the day through the nineteenth century.

ADVERTISEMENT IN *THE MORNING PRESS*,
MAY 20, 1916.

Just how the people in a town or city would feel if motorists drove up and gathered any flowers, fruit or anything that belonged to them is not hard to imagine. Neither is it hard to imagine how they would proceed to get retribution. Yet they commit the same offense in the country time and time again without any pangs of conscience.

Strewing the highways and pleasure places with papers and refuse from lunches is another offense committed endlessly by many many motorists. Wherever another one has lunched, paper plates, napkins, egg shells or some unsightly refuse is sure to be found. If there should be a sign forbidding such litter being left and a guard to enforce the order they often are peeved and throw it out along the road as soon as they think it safe to do so. How thoughtless and unkind it is. If everyone did so and no one gathered up the refuse, the places would soon become so filthy and unsightly no one would want to travel there. How easy it would be to place the rubbish back in the lunch basket in the tool box, or some niche in the car and burning it at home thereby saving work that is thankless and unpaid for those who care enough to gather up the rubbish that beauty may reign. Again turning the tables, how would town dwellers enjoy cleaning up the lunch rubbish after motorists driving in town?

Since seemingly nice, respectable people commit these depredations, it must be through thoughtlessness on their part. They have never stopped to consider the result of their action or how selfish and unkind it seems to others, or they could not retain their self respect and continue to despoil the beauty of our highways and pleasure places.

This is an appeal to all motorists to be just and honest in the country and to help and keep our country beautiful.

One who suffers by living by a Watering Trough.

> Mrs. Alfred N. Keller
> *The Benton Argus*
> September 16, 1920

MAIN STREET LOOKING WEST, CIRCA 1925.

NEWS ITEM

THE QUIETEST AND MOST PEACEABLE WAY

AMAZING CLAIMS OF STRENGTH OF HOODED ORGANIZATION

Has the Ku Klux Klan in Northumberland County gathered sufficient strength numerically to sweep everything before it?

Does it control the sheriff's office, the county detective's office, and the district attorney's office at Sunbury?

Does it have Northumberland county, including the territory lying just across the river at Danville, under its thumb?

These astounding claims are made in a letter sent by the Kleagle of Northumberland County, Knights of the Ku Klux Klan, from Sunbury to Grant Huber of Riverside, urging him as a trustee of the Patriotic Order of the Sons of America (P.O.S.A.) to use his influence in having the dance held weekly in the P.O.S.A. hall at Riverside brought to a stop.

Hitherto unrevealed activities of the Klan in

this section, indicated numerical strength undreamed of by local citizens, are made plain in the letter if the statements it contain can be relied upon.

"Dated at the Klavern
Send Reply to Invisible Empire
March 23rd, 1924
Mr. Grant Huber, Esq.
Riverside, Penna.
"Dear Sir:

"We are informed that you are one of the trustees of the Riverside Camp P.O.S.A. The attention of Sunbury Headquarters Klan No. 1 has been called to certain occurrences connected with the weekly rental of your lodge building for public dances. Your name has been suggested to us by one of your own lodge brothers, who is also a member of our noble order, as one of the three trustees who is opposed to the rental of the hall for dance purposes.

"This organization, as you know, stands for the active principles of patriotism, clean morals, good government, and the protection of our young womanhood from the many evils which are prevailing today. We have gained sufficient strength numerically in this community to sweep everything before us. We are therefore in a position to undertake and carry out the many needed local reforms for which our order stands.

"With control of the sheriff's office, the county detectives and the district attorney's office, we can do much to bring about desired conditions. We are inaugurating a clean-up of all questionable places of amusement, dance halls, saloons and gambling joints. We are prepared to carry on this crusade actively from now on to a successful conclusion.

"This clean-up will proceed from now on throughout the entire Northumberland County.

"Contrary to popular opinion, we are not lawbreakers, cut-throats and villains. We do not use brute force and always feel the quietest and most peaceable way of handling situations is the best. We are therefore writing to you with the desire and hope of interesting you in our cause.

"We are given to understand that you alone, of the three trustees, are opposed to those weekly public dances in the above mentioned hall. Can you not lend us your aid and assistance in winning over Mr. Vastine to your and our way of thinking and thereby close up your hall to such affairs? We believe you can. Will you try?

"This we feel is the quietest way of settling the matter and getting rid of a very objectionable feature in the life of the young people of your community. We are aware that this dance is supported almost exclusively by the younger set. We are also aware of every occurrence at every dance. The state requires a license for the operation of a regular public dance. You will realize that the law is being broken in this respect. A license is also required for the dispensing of candies, cigarettes, and other refreshments. Cigarettes are also being sold to minors. In addition to the above, the place is a nuisance to the community at large by virtue of the noise which is being made during and after each dance.

"All these facts we are familiar with by reasons of the reports made by our investigators who are always in attendance at these affairs. We have the evidence and are prepared to use it immediately for prosecution if no other means of stoppage is to be had.

"Aside from this the moral effect upon the community is tremendously negative. We are sure that you as a patriotic, law-abiding, Christian gentleman would not desire your daughter to attend these or like functions. Do you not feel it your duty to co-operate with us in making Northumberland county a better place to live in?

"In closing may we reiterate again our previous sentiments and say that the quietest way out of these affairs is the best. Numerically we have Northumberland County under our thumb and we mean business. However, we do not wish to use the above stated evidence unless it is absolutely the last resource. The publicity attached to the prosecution of such a case would be tremendous, and make many people very uncomfortable. It is therefore not to be desired, but will only be used as a final resort.

BLOOMSBURG KLAVERN
K. K. K.
ATTENTION
U. B. THERE   1t

THE MORNING PRESS, FEBRUARY 2, 1927.

"We deem two weeks to be sufficient time to close the matter and will take no further steps till that time.

"Yours very respectfully,
S'bury 496
Kleagle of Northumberland Co.
Knights of the Ku Klux Klan"

The Danville Morning News
April 18, 1924

Grant Huber, upon receipt of this letter, and in defiance of its dictates, turns it over to the press. In the weeks and months following publication of this letter, the Klan denies its authenticity, the mentioned public officials deny Klan connections, and the dances in Riverside continue.

NEWS ITEM

THE OLD-TIME TRAMP
IS PASSING

D. A. Macklin, superintendent of the Luzerne County poor farm at Retreat for twenty-five years, is authority for this statement. He has been in a position to know.

"The character of our population has changed in the last twenty-five years," he explained in commenting on the situation. "The old-time tramp or vagrant is passing out of exis-

BLOOMSBURG FAIR
October 6-7-8-9-10
1925
Automobile Races Saturday

tence, at least insofar as the alms house is concerned. This type represents an ever decreasing element with which we have to contend.

"The eighteenth amendment has been in a large measure responsible for this, but more so the organization of charitable agencies and social service workers which make life more and more disagreeable for this type of unworthy, then, too industrial conditions have so changed that there is little chance for the failure of the mentally and physically fit to find remunerative employment."

The Morning Press
October 14, 1925

NEWS ITEM

TO ACCEPT GIFTS OF KU KLUX KLAN

After receipt of the following letter, the Berwick school board decided to accept the Bibles and flags offered:

"THOMAS BUCK,
PRES. OF THE BERWICK SCHOOL BOARD.
"My dear Mr. Buck:

"The women and the men of the Ku Klux Klan desire to present to the Market street new building a Holy Bible, also an American flag to each of the thirteen rooms. We would like to present them on Thanksgiving Day. Will the board be present at a public meeting and accept the Bible and flags? We are to have two bands and a large delegation from the northern part of the state.

"The Burgess has granted a permit for a robed parade in the afternoon. National and state speakers will be here. May I hear from you if the board will accept the challenge? I am,

"Post Office Box No. 125
Berwick, Pa."

The Morning Press
October 14, 1925

STRIKE

Dear Editor:

Conditions in the Anthracite Coal Fields remains unchanged. This little article which I would like you to find room in your paper for is very interesting, as I see very little in the papers which favors the miners. The following editorial under the heading "The Wages of Death" recently appeared in the Indianapolis (Ind.) *Times*:

If all the aviators in the U.S. Army, Navy, Marine and commercial were to go on strike, demanding a 10 per cent wage increase, the sympathy of the whole country would be with them.

They are entitled to any pay they may ask, we would say, because of the dangerous nature of their work.

There is another class of workers who daily risk their lives. Great numbers of them are killed at their work and much greater numbers are maimed for life. The last official monthly report of the Bureau of Mines, U.S. Dept. of Commerce, concerning them told that 195 were killed during August this year, a smaller number than the average for August in the past ten years.

The workers referred to are coal miners. Forty-six of those killed in August worked in the Anthracite field of Penna. That was an average of about 2 miners a day killed there, considering the number of days worked.

But there is nothing spectacular or thrilling about an anthracite miner. He doesn't go up into the air to get killed; he goes down into the ground. He doesn't meet his Maker filled with zest of high adventure and the swift romance of modern existence. He meets death in a musky pit out of the sight of those he serves. And unless a dozen or more of his kind is obliterated at the same time, his death is not a matter even for newspaper notice.

P. S.—Everyone around us is enjoying prosperity. Why not the men whose work is hazardous, who give us our winter comforts, who digs the coal from the depths of the earth the same right to enjoy life as the other fellow.

An even break is all the miner wants. If the people

BREAKER BOYS IN THE PENNSYLVANIA ANTHRACITE MINES.

who are against the miner would dig up the real truths of what is causing the price of anthracite to advance and not so much cost of production, I think it would be a different story.

Waldo Bucher
Wilburton, Pa.
The Morning Press
December 2, 1925

ARBITRATION

Dear Editor:

Thanking you kindly for printing my last contribution, hope you will do the same with this little article, which is my views of the anthracite strike:

The coal operators still hang to the idea that the men should go back to work and agree to arbitration. The miners got bit before on arbitration and no one can blame them for not getting bit again. Every one knows the operators have more money than the United Mine Workers of America and could easily win out. A few years ago the miners agreed to arbitrate and President Wilson picked a man by the name of Thompson and he agreed to give the men 27 percent increase at 9 o'clock that day, and at 10 o'clock the next day he gives the men 17 percent. Who made him change his decision? Surely not the miners.

I would like to ask why the operators don't agree with Governor Pinchot's plans, which the miners accepted, the miners would gladly arbitrate on higher wages but not on lower. The Operators would like to arbitrate up and down, and every one knows it wouldn't be up but down.

The Operators are spending thousands of dollars sending men and circulars throughout the region and country telling people their side of the story. I say here and now that the Operators have lost enough money since the suspension started to pay the men a 10 percent increase for the next three years.

The Operators know when they break up the union they are breaking up one of the strongest unions in the United States. And I would like to know who would like to work in the mines without a union for protection.

The latest Pennsylvania state figures show that the anthracite miners lost over 2 days a month from accident. Such is the terrific toll which the anthracite industry levies upon its workers. Every fourth man killed at work in the whole state of Pennsylvania with its 3,000,000 male wage earners is an anthracite miner.

This industry is not keeping pace with others where protection of life and health is enforced as a natural thing. Our industry is not even standing still. It is dropping behind.

Sent in by
Waldo Bucher
Wilburton, Pa.
The Morning Press
December 30, 1925

CONSTANT DANGER

Dear Editor:

While reading last Saturday's paper I took particular notice that forty-six more helpless unfortunate men lost their lives in a mine explosion. And I dare say all of them worked in a non-union coal mine.

Within the last two months more than 200 men have been killed in soft coal non-union mines. The scene of last Saturday's disaster and horror was laid in Alabama where the miners' union is barred out and not allowed to do anything for the protection of the men. Experienced and inexperienced men are obliged to work together, thus placing the real miners in constant danger because of the lack of knowledge on the part of the green man. This may be hard to believe, but the state of Alabama even works convicts in its mines while they serve their prison sentences. Many of these men never saw a coal mine until forced in one to work not for the state but for some private corporation under lease. So you can see why disasters happen in Alabama. The only wonder is that they are not more numerous.

Human life is the cheapest thing there is in the non-union coal fields of Alabama. The condition of these men is pitiable indeed. But as long as these non-union miners resist the helping hand of the U.M.W. of A., just so long will present conditions continue.

And I say that conditions in the hard coal fields would be bad if some of "those wise doctors" from Philadelphia could have their say and abolish the mine certificate law of Pennsylvania. I really believe the men who are fighting it never saw the hazards of a coal mine.

Yours truly,
Waldo Bucher
The Morning Press
February 5, 1926

Seven days after the publication of this letter, the longest strike in the history of the anthracite region and one of the greatest industrial struggles in the world's history of labor ends. Ten counties in northeastern Pennsylvania, a total of 272 collieries serving 828 mines, and 158,000 workers are affected. The miners had walked out on September 1, 1925.

EDITORIAL

COUNTING THE TOLL

Three persons were killed and two more are in the hospital. Newspaper reports have it that the driver was drinking.

A man was frozen to death in a field.

A man shockingly injured himself in colliding with a building corner.

That's the toll in which booze played a part over one week-end in this section.

The amazing fact is, that this is a condition of

ARE YOU WET OR DRY?

Copyright By Charles B. Meekins
The Paramount Question of The Day

PROHIBITION POSTCARD.

affairs against which altogether too few voices are raised.

It's not a condition due to Prohibition, but a condition that exists in spite of Prohibition because the voice of the public isn't raised.

In the old days when staggering men were a common sight, when the saloons—with which every town and village was dotted, spewed out their derelicts—a stench in the face of mankind and an insult to womanhood, conditions were infinitely worse. You haven't forgotten them, have you?

But the fact remains that many who ought to be outspokenly against the evil remain complacently silent, and, in some instances, aid and abet the violation of the law.

If a man were robbed or a woman attacked, there would be a hue and a cry, but that which robs man of his manhood and woman of her womanhood exists only because of the indifference of the public.

That's a fact that cannot be gainsaid.
The Morning Press
March 9, 1926

BLOOMSBURG TROLLEY BARN.

NEWS ITEM

LAST TROLLEY CAR

When the Danville trolley car pulled into Bloomsburg shortly before midnight last night, there was marked the end of 22 years of operations of the line between Bloomsburg and Danville.

This morning Douglas Ford will begin operation of a bus line between the two towns.

The Morning Press
March 3, 1926

THE NEEDS OF THE HOUR

I was pleased to read your editorial in The Morning Press of Tuesday, March 9th, on the booze question under the heading "Counting the Toll."

It is true that public opinion is entirely too slow in arising to the needs of the hour on this question. I believe if the thousands of right thinking people in Columbia County would assert their feelings on this question, the violators would soon quit or hie themselves to a more comfortable location.

Some try to excuse their indifference by criticizing constituted authority. It is a known and proven fact that officers follow their own tendencies in such matters only so far as public opinion will allow.

I believe that most thinking people feel that right must and will overcome. "Why not now" while it can be done within the domain of the courts in a bloodless conflict?

Do the fathers and mothers of this county and commonwealth wish their children to face lawless conditions similar to the days of the Molly Maguires or worse?

"The mills of the gods grind slowly but they grind exceeding small." Let us hope that public opinion is growing stronger in this period of seeming quietness to the extent that it will soon arise and sweep everything before it.

In the meantime we hope to see many such editorials as the one above mentioned.

Sincerely yours,
Mrs. F. T. Kocher
The Morning Press
March 22, 1926

NEWS ITEM

EXCITING SCENES IN HUNTINGTON

Postponement of the Huntington Mills school dedication announced for Saturday brought exciting scenes in the community that had its climax when the president of the School board declared his opinion that the Bible had no place in the schools.

The directors had previously voted to accept Bible and flag from the Ku Klux Klan for the various rooms. The Klan announced a big demonstration in connection with the presentation.

The crowds arrived and with them the Klan and the Bibles and word was given of the postponement. The reason cited was the fact the building was not ready, while members of the board who were in sympathy with the demonstration give the reason as the fact that the Klan was considered by the others to be taking too prominent a part in a school affair. The crowds were soon on edge.

The Klan removed from the school and proceeded to hold speech-making. One of the speakers stated that things had come to a pretty pass when the Bible was refused from the schools. He quoted a remark from the wife of the president of the board to the effect that she did not believe the Bible had any place in the school room.

President Bittenbender took the floor and declared he was the one who made the remark, and believed the Bible should not be in the schools as the schools were for Protestant, Catholic, Jew and Mohammedan alike.

"So is the Bible, Mister," was the call of an aged woman from the rear of the crowd, and the conviction in the tone set off the crowd afresh.

Bittenbender was hooted down and could not continue his address.

The Klan continued its celebration, heard several speakers and burned a cross during the exercises.

The Morning Press
September 8, 1926

ANY PARTICULAR CREED

To correct any misunderstanding or misinterpretation of my statement publicly delivered on Saturday, Sept. 4th, I wish to submit the following explanation:

To quote the great American, Abraham Lincoln, "Four score and seven years ago our fathers brought forth upon this continent a new nation conceived in liberty and dedicated to the proposition that all men are created free and equal."

By that simple straightforward declaration, the immortal Lincoln stated the fundamental principles of our government. If these then are the fundamental principles of our government they should be the fundamental principles underlying all governmental activities and enterprises, one of the greatest of which is our public school system. And since our public schools are maintained by universal taxation of our cosmopolitan population in direct proportion to their wealth, and without regard to race, color, or creed; and, since by law, every child is compelled to attend school until they reach the age of sixteen, I believe that the reading or teaching of any particular creed or dogma should be left strictly to the homes and churches or such schools as are conducted by the followers of those creeds without any support from public funds; and in as much as in a cosmopolitan community such as ours, where we have Jews and Gentiles, Protestants and Catholics, and followers of other beliefs, and where those in the minority have neither the means nor the facilities to maintain schools in support of their particular beliefs, and should use special care that nothing of a religious nature is read or taught that is objectionable to the least of these.

I was born in a Christian home, raised in a Christian community, and thoroughly believe in the teachings of the Bible and the principles of Christianity.

I am also thoroughly convinced that better citizens can be made of the youth of this country if the parents would use the same care and effort to teach their children these wonderful truths and principles by example and precept as they wish to have it done for them by teachers in the public schools.

However, regardless of my personal opinions, the law of this great commonwealth provides that the Bible be read in our public schools and I firmly believe in obeying and respecting the law regardless of personal opinion. For this reason as long as I have a voice in the conduct of school affairs and the law stands as it is, I will endeavor to see that its provisions are fully complied with.

F. E. Bittenbender
The Morning Press
September 16, 1926

OUT OF THE STATIC

We have been very much interested in Bloomsburg's broadcasting and this evening were able to get them for about 20 minutes between 8 and 8:30 P.M. Please let us hear oftener from Bloomsburg.

Mrs. Anna Alpaugh
Oldwick, New Jersey
The Morning Press
February 18, 1927

FOUR WINDS

NEWS ITEM

MAKES AFFIDAVIT TROUPE WAS NOT LIVING AT THEATRE

A. Lychos, owner of the Martha Washington Hotel, on Saturday made affidavit that the Hopi Indian troupe has been living at his hotel, con-tradicting the rumor that gained wide circulation that they had been sleeping and cooking their meals at the Victoria theatre. His statement follows:

"BLOOMSBURG, PA.
MARCH 12, 1927
"To whom it may concern:

"This is to certify that Mrs. Billingsley and her entire Hopi Snake Dancer Troupe registered at the Martha Washington Hotel on Wednesday of last week. They not only slept here but had their meals as well. At the time of the discovery of the fire at the Victoria Theatre, they were all in bed and I had my girls awaken them so they could try and save some of their effects.

"I give this information that it may prove statements to the contrary untrue.
"Signed,
A. Lychos
"Sworn to and subscribed, before me this 12th day of March, 1927, W. Warren Shutt, Justice of the Peace. My commission expires first Monday in January, 1930."

The Morning Press
March 14, 1927

NEWS ITEM

WEIRD HOPI RIGHTS HELD IN THEATRE RUINS IN DRAB DAWN

As the first streaks of a drab, gray dawn appeared in the east, two figures made their way into the ruins of the Victoria Theatre yesterday. A moment later came the weird chant of the Hopi Indian tribe as Chief Soloftochee performed the last rites on the property of the Indians which had been destroyed in the fire seven days before.

The Ceremony was the climax to the ceremonies which had been held nightly during the entire week. The Saturday night before the ceremonies had lasted from 7 p.m. until 7 a.m.

The chief snake priest of the Hopi, and M. W. Billingsley, custodian of the Indians on their tour, and himself an adopted Hopi, performed the last rites of the Indians yesterday morning.

As the weird chant proceeded for some minutes, Chief Soloftochee scattered corn meal to the four winds, and the Great Spirit then was satisfied that there had been done everything that was possible under the religious ceremony of the tribe.

One o'clock yesterday morning saw the beginning of the rites—probably the first in Bloomsburg in more than a century and a quarter. They were the rites of the red man, performed usually in his dances in the wigwam of years and years ago, when Indian villages dotted this part of the country.

There were no witnesses to the ceremonies. The Great Spirit was pleased with their rites, for the three insignia on their kachina heads represent clouds, rain and the skies, and the rain that followed during the day was evidence of the Spirit's pleasure.

Facing the east, and in his weird monotone, the chief chanted the last rites amid the ruins of the theatre. The police had been told in advance that the ceremonies would take place at dawn and they agreed not to interfere since they knew what was taking place.

For the Indians, Mr. Billingsley yesterday thanked the people of Bloomsburg who had assisted them following the loss of their possessions in the fire:

"My Hopi brothers cannot express to the white man their heartfelt gratitude, and in days to come, back in the Hopi villages of Walpi, Mosagavi, Shomokiano, Toreva and Phoenix, all in Arizona, from whence we came, the legend will be told for centuries of the white man's

city of Bloomsburg, of the great fire and of the greater love and hospitality these Indian chieftains received in their time of distress from Bloomsburg's inhabitants."

In holding the last Hopi rites which were held in the Victoria Theatre ruins on Sunday morning as the day was breaking, mention was made how well a city was named "Bloomsburg." A kind prayer went up for those who are lost among us: "May the Great Father of all bring to every heart blessings of peace, of prosperity, and may Bloomsburg be blessed eternal."

The Morning Press
March 21, 1927

VICTORIA THEATRE,
BLOOMSBURG.

A TOWN TOUR:
THE 1930s

PARADE ON MAIN STREET

Editor Bloomsburg *Morning Press*:

It often seems funny to me concerning the judges of masquerade parades that they do not take into consideration the clown when awarding the prizes, so I am writing you this letter sincerely hoping that you will print it in your newspaper so the judges in your recent parade can peruse same and probably next time they will take into consideration the lowly clown and at least award them something.

I was in Bloomsburg on Friday night and attended your parade, marching just advance of section bearer No. 3 and there was a clown dressed in checkered suit with a long nose and light in end of same and I took particular notice that he received oh's and ah's from one end of your town to the other; he wore no cheap false face and had his face painted, which probably took 30 or 40 minutes to put on and about an hour to get off—and besides he came 20 some odd miles to attend your parade: went to great pains to have something original (the light on the end of his nose) and yet he received no award, while some other individuals with age worn out costumes and ideas with cheap false faces received prizes.

Understand me right it is not the value of the award but I think at least one prize should go to best clown in parade, for who is it, and who has it been for ages past but the clown who makes people laugh.

Yours in fairness and justice.

A. MUMMER
The Morning Press
October 31, 1929

THE BANK

The Editor of *The Morning Press*
Dear Sir:

Last week your news article about the "Use of Scrip is Extending" contained two very interesting paragraphs that might be applicable to Bloomsburg. The city of Charleston, S.C., had a deficit of $90,000 when it issued scrip in denominations of $1, $5 and $10, which was made legal tender in payment of taxes and water bills. The businessmen of the community agreed to accept this money and it was paid out to the city employees on a basis of 50% national currency and 50% scrip. Before many months had passed a quarter of a million dollars in delin-

MARTHA WASHINGTON HOTEL,
MAIN AND CENTER STREETS, BLOOMSBURG.

quent taxes had been collected and now Charleston has a surplus in its treasury. It is my understanding that the scrip has been redeemed.

This experience of Charleston, as well as that of many other communities which have made good use of scrip with a great resultant good, is clear evidence that this country is suffering from a money famine brought on by the throttling curtailment of credit by the banks following the panic of 1929. If business is not permitted to operate with credit then it should be given sufficient cash to permit it to develop and flourish on a cash basis. This is what is accomplished by the use of scrip. Of course it would be far better for the federal government to control this scrip money rather than the individual communities just as it is better to have the federal government handle the mail. But it is sadly true today as in the past that the federal government usually lags far behind in meeting the needs of the people, that the state and communities must lead the way.

Therefore let us not simply mark time waiting for the federal government to cure the causes of the depression. Let us do what other communities have done: remove the chief cause of depression by issuing scrip money. This money could be paid out as it was in Charleston to the town employees and to the teachers. It could be used in financing our employment relief on much more equitable and extensive scale, giving sufficient work to all to enable them to support themselves and their families on a standard comparable to that of their more fortunate towns-

AROUND THE WORLD

- The New York Stock Exchange takes a dive beginning on Black Friday, October 29, 1929, when it loses 11.7 percent of its value. (It had dropped 12.8 percent the previous day.) By some estimates, within a week, $30 billion have "vanished from the economy." By 1931, some 2,300 banks have failed in the United States alone, and the world is in a full-blown and protracted Depression.
- In November 1931, Ivar Kreuger, the "Swedish match king" and one of the richest industrialists, purchases the holdings of the Federal Match Company (gaining control of the former Fred Fear match plant in Bloomsburg). Four months later, in ill health and financial straits, he commits suicide in Paris. History has exposed him as a crook and a con man.
- Swiss physicist Auguste Piccard ascends by balloon into the stratosphere in 1931. Two years later, U.S. aviator Wiley Post makes the first solo round-the-world flight in seven days, eighteen hours, and forty-nine minutes.
- In 1932, Aldous Huxley writes *Brave New World*.
- In 1934, German president Paul von Hindenburg dies and Adolf Hitler is given dictatorial powers as "der Führer."
- In Spain, a bloody civil war erupts in 1936 when the right-wing army revolt led by Emilio Mola and Francisco Franco challenges the left-wing Popular Front. An "axis" alliance is formed between dictators Hitler and Mussolini.

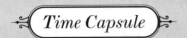
people. Our Welfare Association has done a remarkably fine piece of work, considering its financial difficulties. Now let us enable it to give 100% relief to the unemployed. Of course the taxes will have to be raised to meet this expenditure for welfare work, but by the issuance of scrip money the people will be able to pay their taxes just as they did in Charleston S.C. There will simply be a more Christian distribution of the wealth of Bloomsburg. There will not be a large number of people more prosperous than they ever were before, while an equally large number are suffering from privation, hunger, and cold, and perhaps worst of all, loss of self-respect.

Very truly yours,
C. HOMER ARTMAN
The Morning Press
February 9, 1933

HOTEL MAGEE AND LEADER STORE,
MAIN STREET, BLOOMSBURG.

THE HOSPITAL

Dear Editor:

I have read the report of our President's speech in behalf of the infantile paralysis victims with much interest and enthusiasm. I think it is a project that deserves the support of the American People. I believe all right thinking citizens could grow enthusiastic over the slogan—"every person who is restored to useful citizenship is an asset to the country."

I hope that slogan sinks deep into the hearts of a large majority of our people. Let it sink so deep that they will observe other liabilities about us caused by strong drink. We can see many who are total liabilities and others who are half disabled. They are not useful citizens and, what is more important, are preventing the best physical, intellectual, and moral development of their children. The liquor business causes thousands of times more blasted lives than infantile paralysis does. Were we wise, we might know how many of the infantile paralysis cases are due to strong drink. Only God above knows that.

Sincerely yours,
Mrs. F. T. Kocher, Espy
The Morning Press
February 3, 1934

THE FAIR

The Bloomsburg Fair is advertised as a state and county attraction. The Schools are closed for it, and the papers herald it, but what do you see when you arrive there? We admit the exhibits of the schools and local people are excellent, but on what grounds can you defend burlesque shows that publicize small children doing dances that made grown people turn away in disgust; the songs and the motions that were gone through closed the show in Reading after just one showing. Today—the show is still on in Bloomsburg. Bloomsburg frowns upon obscene actions of its young, but gives it plenty of examples to follow in their fair carnival.

Gambling is not allowed in the state and arrests are made in the community for people who allow you to gamble nickles on a punch board or petty gambling game. Just take a walk through the Fair midway. We saw one fellow robbed in a gambling game of $90, another of $40 and one of $50. They were just three out of many. We called the State Police and he immediately jumped on the loser. Would he make an arrest? Not if he could help it. He says, "Give me evidence" and when you offer it to him, he finds an excuse or takes the gambler up and fines him a few dollars. Two minutes later, the stand is running full sway. If you think, well, it serves him right for gambling: just see how quickly you are roped in. They won't even bother to give you the change that belongs to you.

Don't worry. We are not preaching because we got

AROUND TOWN

- When the Depression strikes, Bloomsburg has its share of misery. However, this area escapes the collapse of banks and savings and loans groups, and by 1932, the town has eliminated its debt by slashing expenses, and has cash to meet some months of future obligations.
- In April 1930, the dirigible *Los Angeles* leaves Lakehurst, New Jersey, and cruises over Bloomsburg at a low altitude. Schools are dismissed and a crowd of thousands enjoys a good view. Seven years later, the German dirigible *Hindenburg* is destroyed by fire at Lakehurst.
- On January 14, 1932, the official temperature reaches 75 degrees in the shade with an unofficial 104 degrees in the sun. The first robins appear, flowers bloom, and two people go swimming. Two months later, accumulated snowfall topples miles of power lines.
- On the night of March 1, 1932, the infant son of Charles A. Lindbergh is kidnapped in New Jersey. America shifts its attention away from economic crisis and toward the mysterious stories of ransoms, hoaxes, and mobsters offering aid. Detectives visit Columbia County several times to investigate a claim by a Danville man that a midnight caller may have had a baby in his car. These rumors, like many others across the nation, lead nowhere. Two months later, the murdered child is found near the Lindbergh home.

caught in the game—we didn't: we went to find out what it was all about.

A pick pocket doesn't quibble—he gets you—so will the Fair's gambling games with their cappers leaning on the counter controlling the wheel.

We want a clean town—we need as clean a Fair. We need to live up to the beauty of the flowers exhibited and hand work, and the labor in raising fine stock.

A READER
The Independent
September 27, 1935

With the Depression, the coal mines in southern Columbia and Schuylkill counties shut down. Miners, unemployed like most of America, independently and illegally dig small new mines on the coal companies' property. Called "bootleg operations," these hand-hewn mines help to keep the miners' families warm, and to provide an income.

THE COLLIERY

I wish to take this means of commending you on your stand against the Bootleg coal business. We as taxpayers and citizens of this country would do well by giving more thought to things of welfare to our communities.

I have marveled at the stand people, and people whom you would think should do differently, take when it comes to deciding about the purchase of merchandise. We are too often narrow and selfish and think only of our own personal welfare and buy coal that is stolen property. If each one of us would give the same thought to this problem as we would to the matter of purchasing a stolen automobile, horse or fur coat, then many of our local problems would be solved.

I cannot understand why a man has any more right to dig coal from another man's property and we any more right to buy it than one man has a right to dig

CALDWELL CONSISTORY, MARKET SQUARE, BLOOMSBURG.

THE MORNING PRESS AND THE MOOSE,
MARKET SQUARE, BLOOMSBURG.

potatoes from another man's field and we buy them as bootleg potatoes.

Very truly yours,
NEIL S. HARRISON
The Morning Press
January 9, 1937

THE GROCERS

The past few days there have been considerable mention of the State Tax on Chain Store systems. In their statements appearing in the daily newspapers concerning and criticizing this tax, the home-owned grocer has been led to believe that his support to a community has been naught.

However, the home-owned grocer does not approve of the higher cost of living, but the price of the local grocer's merchandise must be sold a few cents more than the chain store because they do not have the buying power of the chain store system.

FIFTH STREET, BLOOMSBURG.

The home-owned grocer in a community supports the community affairs; he pays his school, personal and property tax to the government of that community and often times gives of his time and service to any project that will be a betterment to the community of which he is a part. The home-owned grocer feels justly proud that in time of need he has done far more than the chain store system in helping the people of his community by extending to

them credit whereby they themselves and their children need not go hungry or unclothed due to the shortage of money which of course is the sole buying power in the chain store system.

If, however, the prices of merchandise would be equal among the local grocer's stock and that of the chain store the former would be certain that he, too, could give the same service, as far as existing prices are concerned, to the people of the community. Again the home-owned grocer does not wish the cost of living to increase but does object to the situation as now existing. If prices were brought on even basis for both, then, too, the home-owned grocer could be sure of an income from the community of which he is a part, and which he justly deserves.

H. A. Van Horn
The Morning Press
March 23, 1937

THE GARDEN

I noticed in *The Morning Press* that Bloomsburg's Easter flower business had been the best in a number of years, and that Bloomsburg is recognized as probably the most flower minded town of its size in the country.

I wonder if the reason for being flower minded is that we have so many flowers around us and that the town's name is Blooms-burg.

There are flowers that bloom every day of the year and yet many people never see their beauty.

Our churches are blooming every week and they are the most beautiful flowers in life. Many never see the beauty of a church for the sake of their souls and the satisfaction a church can give.

Our fraternal and civic organizations blossom forth with service and good deeds for the town as a whole and also for individuals who do appreciate their beauty and help.

The industries of our town are a special flower these days when many of the town's flowers of industry have wilted and died, or have been translated to a garden in another state. Our leaders of industry are certainly good gardeners and still there are many people who instead of trying to help cultivate these plants are making it tough for the gardener.

The youth movement supported in Bloomsburg is one of the best variety, and the most beautiful to look upon anywhere in the world today. The Boy and Girl Scout movements are the buds of today that will certainly bloom tomorrow into flowers that will make any community beautiful and proud.

Our public school system is much like a garden of rose bushes. They always bloomed very nicely until a few years ago they were blighted and the gardeners had quite a job cultivating

COBBLESTONE TEA ROOM,
BERWICK ROAD, BLOOMSBURG.

them into thriving bushes again. But today they are doing very nicely and the roses are just as beautiful as ever. We see the athletic bush producing champion roses again and they are the kind that we can be and are proud to have. The music bush, especially the high school band variety, is gorgeous this season.

The stores in Bloomsburg are of the variety that are pleasing to everyone. There are few if any wilted flowers in the town's stores and other places of business. They are always well cultivated by their gardeners and have an inviting appearance.

Bloomsburg, the gateway to scenic Pennsylvania, certainly is a beautiful flower garden and we should all appreciate and help cultivate the flowers for the years to come.

The gardeners of the community have a real

job cultivating and keeping the flowers for the years to come.

L. E. Bason
The Morning Press
April 17, 1939

THE SALON

HERE'S NEW YORK'S MOST EXCITING STYLE NEWS

New York, the fashion center of the world, is humming with Spring Styles these days. Here in the Hotel Pennsylvania, where I have been attending the INTERNATIONAL Beauty Show, models of all ages have been showing the latest in coiffures and costume ensembles.

I know you will be particularly pleased to hear about the new trends in hair styles. Everywhere I look . . . here at the Show, on Fifth Avenue, and in the theatre . . . I see shorter hair that is always arranged in smart, harmonious lines with a definite feeling for the practical. Fresh flowers are worn in the coiffures for evening, and orchids have moved from the shoulder to the head.

The Fifth Avenue windows are so appealing it's hard to pass them by. They're alive with color, and I have selected several new shades for street and evening makeup which will blend with these costume colors. Sailor hats are worn down over the eyes thus revealing most of the coiffure, and dainty, white dimity blouses of all kinds are the perfect compliment to the new rich shades in nail enamels.

I returned from New York today, March 23rd, and I would like to show you several coiffures which I have selected especially for you and which I believe you'll really enjoy wearing. Won't you drop into my salon sometime soon?

Cordially,
Helen Harrison
The Benton Argus
March 23, 1939

THE OUT-OF-TOWNER VS. THE FARMER

Dear Sir:

I am writing this letter in the form of three questions:

First, why is it necessary for three or four peddlers to stop the automobile traffic on North Market Street to peddle their produce?

Secondly: If they must use North Market Street as a free marketplace for their produce and flowers why can't they park parallel to the curb so that traffic can still move on the street?

Thirdly: Why shouldn't they have to purchase a permit like any other peddler, or persons soliciting in town limits?

An Out-of-Towner
who pays taxes in Bloomsburg
The Morning Press
July 7, 1971

Dear Sir:

I hope I can answer the three questions the out-of-towner asks about the curb market. First could it be she was the one that near run a woman down on Tuesday morning when she went down Market St. against the sign DO NOT ENTER?

We are not peddlers, better look up what a peddler is.

We pay our meters as well as any other "cars" that park on that street.

I am afraid that there wouldn't be a need for sewers if the farmers did not sell the food, and I know most of the town people appreciate the fresh home-grown produce.

I do hope if this out-of-towner don't like it, they will pay their taxes and go where they don't need food and flowers.

NOT A HAWKER
Madge Dietterick
The Morning Press
July 10, 1971

Dear Sir:

To the Bloomsburg taxpayer who lives out of town:

If you live out of town, why are you picking on the farmer who works from dawn till dusk

raising fresh produce and flowers for us town folks!

They get up at the peak of dawn to get to town with a very attractive display of fruits, vegetables and flowers for us town people who do not have time or space to raise them. They then sell them for almost nothing.

Do you not love fresh flowers and vegetables enough to drive out of your way so these very nice people can have a safe and pleasant spot to sell their wares?

I would not call them peddlers and if I'm not mistaken they do pay for their space. I'd be ashamed! I'm not one of your so-called peddlers, but I sure do like their fruits, vegetables and flowers.

Also a Bloomsburg taxpayer
The Morning Press
July 9, 1971

Dear Sir:

Now I notice that the "Curb Stone Merchants" are forcing the school buses to use other streets rather than park their three or four vehicles on one side of North Market so that the buses can pass through. They stagger their "Stores" all over the street as though they were attempting to halt a Panzer Division.

Seeing that Market Street is the connecting street between the three in-town schools, they could show a little consideration by using one side only.

The Out-of-Towner
The Morning Press
September 15, 1971

THE OLD JOB

Mr. Printer,

In my travels through our county, I have often been surprised to see so few Sheep in the fields, and those I do see, only of a very inferior kind. The keeping of Sheep is important, not merely in a national point of view, but also, when rightly managed, profitable to the farmer. Your correspondent, "Confucius," in your last week's paper has proved conclusively the necessity of fixing our domestic manufactures upon a permanent basis; permit me, then, through your columns, to call upon the farmer to enter more largely into the Sheep business.

The manure of sheep is very grateful to the soil, and I have known fields which were considered incapable of producing grain, being laid down in grass and cropped for a few years by a flock of sheep, were again rich and fertile. In Dutchess County, New York, and in the eastern States generally, the farmers have realized many advantages in raising sheep. Now if it is profitable to keep sheep in Dutchess county, then it must assuredly be more so in Columbia County where the land is so much cheaper.

The quality of our sheep must, however, be first improved, before we can go into the sheep business with profit. The Marino breed is very small, but has the best wool: the Saxon breed is larger, but on the other hand the wool is not so fine. In the eastern States these two breeds are generally crossed, and by this method the wool of the Saxon is improved, and the carcass of the Marino made more strong and healthy. I think that either the Marino or Saxon crossed with our common sheep would improve our stock very much.

If men of talents and influence would take hold of the matter, I can assure you that lasting and beneficial results will be the consequence.

W. J. E.
Columbia Democrat
November 3, 1838

To the caller who talked about workers crossing the picket line with no backbone: Maybe they have families to feed.

Berwick
30 Seconds
Press Enterprise
January 20, 1992

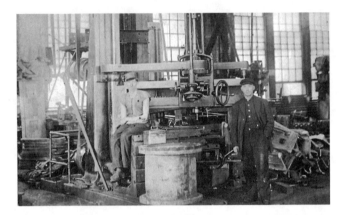

Well, for news of the Forges, we are running on six-and-two-eighths tube iron, and have plenty of work. Besides the mill, we have eight Knobbling fires running steady on iron for the finishing mill. The blooms are hammered and then rolled into boiler plates, so you can see we are running steady, with no slack of orders. The mill and forges employ about one hundred and twenty men and boys. Quite a number of Danville boys are employed here.

> Theophilus J. Foley
> *The Gem*, Danville
> March 20, 1886

I'd like to thank all the employers in the Bloomsburg area as well as Danville and Berwick. I moved here to Bloomsburg in October. I have looked for work endlessly and can't seem to get a job anywhere because I'm not a college student and I'm not 18 years old. I think it really stinks. Because I'm a single mother trying to get off welfare. And after putting so many applications in, I don't even get a call. This is really disgusting. I think I'm out of here.

> Bloomsburg Woman
> 30 Seconds
> *Press Enterprise*
> July 24, 1997

News Item

Narrowly Escaped Death

Daniel Pifer Pitches Down an Elevator Shaft from the Second Floor to the Basement

Wednesday evening Daniel Pifer, who is a loom fixer at the Bloomsburg Carpet Mill in company with the other employees, quit work when the whistle blew and started for the stairs leading to the lower floor. The building is lighted by electric lights and it is said that sometimes in cutting up pranks the boys turn on and off the lights, and at about the same time Pifer reached the door, which is along side the elevator, the light went out and in mistake he ran into the elevator entrance and down he plunged head-fore-most from the second floor to the basement, a distance of over thirty feet. Few, if any one, was close enough to give a clear and intelligent account of how the unfortunate accident happened. Had the guard been down probably Daniel would have been prevented from falling, but some one had raised the guard and it failed to come down. Fortunately however, the elevator was above the second floor or Pifer would have fallen on the frame of it and probably had every bone in his body broken.

As it was he fell into the pit on a cement bottom. When picked up he was unconscious and remained in that condition a number of hours after he was carried home. Dr. Bruner was called and assisted by Dr. Bierman made a thorough examination and found that the right leg was broken at the thigh and the leg jammed up into the body several inches, a long gash was cut in his forehead, nose badly cut both inside and out and the lower lip cut and bruised, besides several bruises elsewhere on the body. The fracture was reduced, the cuts stitched and the patient made as comfortable as one could be expected to be under the circumstances.

This morning when a representative of *The Daily* called at Mr. Pifer's home on Barton street he found him resting easy and conscious of all that was going on about him, and as the reporter stepped to the bedside Dan recognized him and called him by name. Dr. Bruner who was there stated that his condition was greatly improved and very favorable, and that unless something unforeseen set in his recovery was only a matter of time.

The unfortunate man is a son of John Pifer, is married to a daughter of James Lanyon and has three small children. He is an industrious young man and was one of the best workmen in the Carpet Mill.

His friends wish him a speedy recovery and that he may yet have a long and prosperous life before him.

> *The Bloomsburg Daily*
> June 16, 1896

ABOUT THE PIFER ACCIDENT

We are in receipt of a letter from Jas. Magee 2nd in which he says (in relation to the accident at the Carpet Mill by which Daniel Pifer was se-

WHEN JAMES MAGEE II MOVES HIS SMALL INGRAIN CARPET MANUFACTURING OPERATION TO BLOOMSBURG IN 1891, HE BEGINS WHAT IS TO BECOME BLOOMSBURG'S MOST SUCCESSFUL INDUSTRIAL CONCERN. THE MAGEE CARPET COMPANY, UNDER THE LEADERSHIP OF HIS SON, HARRY L. MAGEE, BECOMES ONE OF THE WORLD'S LARGEST PRODUCERS OF CARPET, AND IS FOR MOST OF THE TWENTIETH CENTURY BLOOMSBURG'S LARGEST EMPLOYER, KNOWN FOR A TIME AS "THE MILL OF TWO THOUSAND DINNER PAILS." THE LEADER STORE, THE HOTEL MAGEE, AND WHLM RADIO (NAMED AFTER THE INITIALS OF HARRY L. MAGEE) WERE OR ARE AMONG THE MAGEE FAMILY'S MANY HOLDINGS. AFTER THE AGNES FLOOD OF 1972 AND THE DEATH OF HARRY L. MAGEE, THE COMPANY RETRENCHES AND REFOCUSES UNDER THE LEADERSHIP OF A THIRD GENERATION. UNDER HARRY'S SON JAMES, MAGEE INDUSTRIAL ENTERPRISES FOCUSES ON CARPET FOR AUTOMOBILES, BUT REMAINS INVOLVED IN MANY OTHER VENTURES.

riously injured) that "the electric lights were burning, for the unfortunate man was seen to go down by Mrs. Patterson and it was she who gave the alarm." He further says: "the safety gate at the elevator opening was down, was in perfect order, was not broken as some one else has stated, and after the fall of Pifer the weaver working nearest the opening looked over the gate in search of his vest. We sympathize with the wounded man and his family and without venturing an opinion as to how it happened, we can say that it was due to no carelessness on our part, or want of any precaution which we take to prevent any accidents to our employees. It is probably one of those things which happened and for which the injured party can hardly give an explanation. All that is right and proper will be done for the comfort of Mr. Pifer, but we dislike to be accused of carelessness."

> James Magee, 2nd
> *The Bloomsburg Daily*
> June 17, 1896

Some people say that laughter is the best medicine. Well, I have to agree. Since last week I was in the Bloomsburg Hospital. The person who brought me up on the floor was caring, nice and brought a smile to my face throughout my stay. I just wanted to call and say thank you to that young man. I'm not sure what his name was, but he had a little green dot on his ID badge. Thank you very much, sir, and I hope you bring smiles to as many peoples faces as you did mine.

Bloomsburg Man

30 Seconds

Press Enterprise

November 16, 1993

Dear Sirs:

Two and two make four—not always; depends upon what "two and two" are. Two gallons of water and two gallons of milk don't make four gallons of milk. Neither does four gallons of paint that's half lime, whiting, clay and kerosene oil make four gallons of real paint.

That's what we mean by saying "Fewer gallons, wear longer," It takes fewer gallons of Devoe Lead and Zinc than of mixed paint to paint a house, and it wears twice or three times as long as lead and oil mixed by hand.

Mr. Chas. Avery, of Herkimer, bought 51 gallons of Devoe Lead and Zinc to paint his five houses, his painter having figured that it would require at least that amount; 36 gallons did the work and he returned 15 gallons.

Yours truly,

F. W. Devoe and Co.

New York

P.S.: J. G. Wells sells our paint.

The Bloomsburg Daily

May 4, 1903

I resent the whole concept of tipping. Why should the public be obligated to supplement an underpaid employee? I've waited tables and felt like giving service was begging for a tip, which it wasn't. I hated it. I was a hair stylist and I found tipping degrading. It's a profession. Like any other service no different and like any other profession. When I was in aerospace, I received raises when my work was exceptional. Many employees work above and beyond their job and no tipping is expected. Tipping is a money-saving perk for the employer.

Bloomsburg Woman

30 Seconds

Press Enterprise

November 2, 1993

Dear Sir:

The clerk at the Exchange Hotel told me to go and see the Ostrich Farm. "It will be the most remarkable thing you ever saw," he advised. Curiosity and a very lazy afternoon made me go. What I saw there was truly remarkable. I imagined myself in the wilds of Africa. The hot September sun added color to the illusion. They told me there what a powerful influence for progress and advertisement the farm was for Bloomsburg. They told me many things there. Then I returned home wondering.

The car bounding over the up and down grades, whisked by a big foundry and plant. I looked at it and wondered too. All around it were weeds and brush. The panes of the windows were smashed in. The wooden fence around it broken and falling. Here and there through the tall weedy growth, the top of a flask or a pattern was just visible. The big smoke stack stood staring at the blue skies without a wisp of smoke to show that there were fires of activity and manufacture beneath. And all around it was wrapped the shrouds of a deathlike stillness. The hum of the carwheels seemed to break out fearfully on the silence. Then my wonderment came to an end. My meditation became a mass of firmly formed conclusions.

If Ostrich Farms were a success and a drawing influence for Bloomsburg, how much so too, would be the starting up of a big plant—one that would employ hundreds of men at fair wages. Prosperity is beckoning to you. Will you go to her outstretched arms and partake of her blessings, or will you merely sit silent and staring, just wondering and dreaming as you are doing now?

Answer,
Yours respectfully,
S. A. De Witt
Democratic Sentinel
September 22, 1911

IN 1909, WILLIAM H. HILE RAISES A MILLION DOLLARS FROM INVESTORS TO OPEN AN OSTRICH FARM IN ESPY, JUST OUTSIDE BLOOMSBURG. OSTRICH FEATHERS ARE THE FASHION RAGE OF THE TIME, THE MEAT AND EGGS CAN BE SOLD FOR PROFIT, AND THE FARM IS EXPECTED TO ATTRACT TOURISTS. ALTHOUGH TOURISTS DO INDEED COME, THE OSTRICHES DO NOT FARE WELL IN THE PENNSYLVANIA WINTERS, AND THE RAGE FOR OSTRICH PLUMES WANES. THE AFRICAN OSTRICH FARM AND FEATHER COMPANY CLOSES ITS DOORS IN 1915.

In regard to the woman from Bloomsburg who did not agree with tipping. I understand that you waited tables in a restaurant and did not like it. Maybe if you did not like it, you couldn't do a good job. So you

didn't make any money. I'm a very good wait-ress. I've done it for many years. I work hard to wait on my customers. It's not my fault the wages are low. It's not the fault of the employ-ees that work with me. It's no one's fault but management and the business owners that we only make $2.34 an hour. So please, when you come into our restaurant, tell us who you are and we'll make you go to the kitchen and pick up your own food, clean off your own tables and get your own drinks. Also, I hope you never waitress again.

> Waitress, Bloomsburg
> 30 Seconds
> *Press Enterprise*
> November 16, 1993

Communicated:—

Some farmers are cutting wheat; more will be at the same work soon. I see by your paper that the Farm Bureau, Food Administrator, dog catcher and someone is to come out and see that we farmers cut and haul in our wheat at the right time. If such is the case, the expert ought to be on the job soon. No one is more anxious to save this enormous amount of wheat wasted than the farmer, who gets his living from the crop. If we have been farming all these years and do not know when to cut and haul in our wheat, it is high time we learn. Sure thing we do not want to poison anyone with our wheat or the dust from it. The farmer and his family would likely get the worst of it, as they are bound to be in it.

If we could fix our wheat in a way that would put these self-appointed advisors off until the war is over it might be a blessing to our country. There is no mistake that we farmers are getting tired of the tommyrot we read and hear nearly every day.

On Monday morning I drove into town to get an article I needed. It was about 8 o'clock when I reached the place of business. It was locked up. Someone told me the man usually

got around by 8 o'clock or 8:30. As it was the only place of its kind in town I concluded to wait a spell. As the carrier dropped the morn-ing paper at the door I picked it up and the first thing I noticed was the "Appeal to the Farmers to Prevent Wheat Wastage." Reading on I saw the danger of cutting when the dew is on.

It struck me then that I had ordered the man to get out our three binders and start cutting wheat. Well, it nearly made the cold chills run over me to think what had happened, so I hur-ried home to see that they did not get started before the dew was all off. To be sure, we do our own threshing, but it is a public place and all kinds of people come around and I might poi-son the Food Administrator, the Board of Health or the Public Safety Committee and a lot lesser lights.

I had to make another trip to town to get what I wanted, but I suppose that it was my fault. We farmers ought to know enough to lie in bed until 8 o'clock in the morning: then by the time we get to town everyone would be on the job. If we would allow our help to sleep un-til 6:30 or 7 o'clock, by the time they ate their breakfast and got into the fields there would be no dew to poison anyone.

Most of the advice and criticism the farmers get comes from the people who never farmed an acre and don't know whether to sow clover in the fall or spring or put a horse's collar on over the head or the tail. It grinds on our nerves. The most of these advisors remind me of the serpent in the spring or the year before it has lost its scarf pin and with the scales from its eyes. Being partly blind it doesn't see any-thing clearly and has its tongue out hissing and blowing at everything moving. It is a bigger nuisance than when it can see clearly. But I suppose such persons have greater claims to a farmer's pity than his contempt and we should be patient with him: but there comes a time when forbearance ceases to be a virtue. In these war times when farmers are asked to dou-ble their crops with less fertilizer, less help and other drawbacks, we would like these smart

guys to either come out and show us in some practical way how to do it or shut up and go to work at some job that nature fitted them for and that may be a job that takes less brains than making two ears of corn grow where one grew before.

> FARMER
> *The Morning Press*
> July 13, 1918

This is to the management of Heinz Pet Products. We the people that work for Heinz would like to know why all the salaried people get 6 percent raises, and we, the workers that have to sweat in the heat, get nothing except hamburgers and hot dogs on a grill. That's our appreciation.

> Heinz Employee
> 30 Seconds
> *Press Enterprise*
> August 4, 1995

Gentlemen:

The writer has been advised that you published an item concerning the recent fire at the McDonald Service Station, at West main and Railroad streets, stating that the fire was caused by defective wiring.

Whoever the person was who furnished you with the information, he had no authority or any grounds in the least for making such a statement. The building was rewired several years ago by R. H. Joy, an electrical contractor in Bloomsburg, and fortunately the writer is in a position to know that Mr. Joy made an excellent installation. If defective wiring was installed then it was installed without the knowledge of the proper authorities.

To the electrical industry, fires caused by defective wiring have become more or less of a joke. An electrical installation made by a competent contractor in accordance with the National Electrical Code is practically fireproof and foolproof. It is only when this is added to, subtracted from, divided by, multiplied by or subjected to any other mathematical process by incompetent persons that it becomes dangerous.

Will you please publish this in all fairness to everyone concerned, and for the benefit of your readers.

> Very truly yours,
> Albert O. Emig
> Electrical Inspector.
> *The Morning Press*
> March 31, 1932

I'm just calling to say about the paper boy getting a Christmas gift. I gave my paper boy a Christmas gift and I'm very thankful that I did. I have a wonderful paper boy. I appreciate his wonderful care so very much. He is very particular and takes care of the papers. I expect to give him an Easter gift, also. Those who think they can't afford a little gift for their paper boy, why, I feel sorry for them.

> Millville Woman
> 30 Seconds
> *Press Enterprise*
> November 16, 1993

The strikes are not helping to ease the situation at all. Who can figure any gain when the loss of

FROM 1830 UNTIL 1900, WHEN IT IS COMPLETELY SUPPLANTED BY THE RAILROADS, THE
NORTH BRANCH CANAL MOVES GOODS AND PEOPLE ALONG THE SUSQUEHANNA.

wages and production are counted? A radio voice said recently that the
whole country is united in this fight against the corporations which is not
true. However that seems to be the main goal of the strike leaders. That is a
blow to the roots of our economic system.

We must produce, and produce some more to conquer our huge debt. Is
it not better to have our millions in the hands of industrialists who use it to
produce than in the hands of political party leaders and the P.A.C. who use
it to corrupt elections?

Only one kind of industrialist should be curbed in their production,
those who manufacture harmful products. The manufacturers of alcoholic
beverages loom highest in that group. How can the liquor industry help
pull us out of debt with its 3 billion revenue when their business costs the
American people over 11 billions? That includes the 7 billion drink bill plus
the cost of crime, relief, and allied expenses to our government, the taxpayers. It is never possible to count the complete cost in cash to say nothing of
the heavier burden on society in the form of broken lives, broken homes,
under-privileged children, and the rest of the injuries too numerous to
mention.

> Mrs. F. T. Kocher
> *The Morning Press*
> February 14, 1946

To the Public of Danville:

Do you think it right to put a man in care of the public men's and
women's toilet in the Old City Hall?

I think it's a woman's job to oversee a place like that and would like to see
what the Public thinks about such a move.

The Board of Health has praised the work done there so far. Now it's to be done for less money by a man.

Mrs. Elizabeth Reedy
The Danville News
June 26, 1957

I'm just in the area looking for work and I'm from Northumberland. I used to work at Dorsey Trailers. I'd like to say that the union told us that if we stuck together, we could get some changes made. And I thought myself that the job wasn't really too bad, you know, that I had. They said if we stuck together then we could make out okay. So I realize some of it was my own fault, but they kept saying stick together. The old job kind of looks good right now.

Anonymous Caller
30 Seconds
Press Enterprise
February 17, 1996

We here at Magee's Main Street Inn have once again suffered a devastating loss with the passing of Larry Klinger. Even though we're a business, we're also a family, and when something happens to one of us, it affects all of us.

To you, the general public, this probably won't mean very much. After all, Larry wasn't someone you would have seen when you visited our establishment. But, he was an important part of our organization. The cog in the wheel, so to speak.

He was just an ordinary guy who happened to cook breakfast for the last 20 some years. He was always at work by 3:30 a.m. before most people knew the world was waking up.

He made the best Eggs Benedict and even had an entree named after him—Eggs Larry Klinger. The customers who did know him always requested something special, which usually he'd make.

Larry could always keep the orders coming out and even had time to keep us in stitches. Always kidding. That sense of humor is what kept us going through many difficult days.

They say, you can always be replaced. That's true to a point. But our business is difficult at best and to have a reliable, loyal employee is a very rare commodity today!

He was my close friend and I know that everyone who knew him will miss him. But one thing, he used to tell me was that he'd "never be as old as I am."

Yeah, Lar, you were right about that one.

Ruth Ann Krum
Press Enterprise
July 29, 1994

AT&T/COMSAT ROARING CREEK SATELLITE EARTH STATION.

ACF PLANT, BERWICK.

WOMEN AND MEN: SEX IN SOCIETY

WHERE IS THY BLUSH?

Dear Colonel,

There is an evil in the community which cries aloud for redress. It is a most vile fashion some old men, heads of families, have of telling smutty stories, and cracking obscene jokes, in the presence of their grown up Daughters, and often too, when young men, strangers, are in the company.

Now in my opinion, any Father of a Family, who will be guilty of such a breach of decency, deserves to be kicked out of the room. What for an opinion can young gentlemen entertain of the purity of young ladies, who are thus, every hour of the day, subjected to the vile language and outrageous behavior, of the Father. I have seen many old men who seemed to delight in detailing such stories, and committing such actions. I have not the language to express my feelings, at the grossness of such an outrage, in the presence of unmarried Daughters—

If it were a stranger, the recurrence could be prevented by forbidding him in the house. Shall a Father be licensed to behave worse? Is it possible, that he who should protect them from even the suspicion of contamination, should be the first to dull the moral perceptions of his Daughters, and destroy that innate feeling of modesty, which is natural to every woman?

You have many subscribers, heads of families, old men who are guilty of the gross and outrageous practice, to which I have alluded. What would you think of a stranger; who should do or say in the presence of your family, what you, yourself, have done and said? Would he dare to insult them as you consider yourself privileged to do? Have you not often caused your Wife or Daughters to blush, for your want of decency? For shame! Oh! for shame, heads of families!—

If there is any place which should be sacred to moral and mental purity, it is the social circle; where the child is ready to watch and imitate every word and action—the stripling girl, just awakening to a sense of womanhood, hears allusions but half understood and piqueing curiosity—the full blown maiden, in the very heyday of her young blood, is prepared for corruption, by a Father's brutality, obscenity and indecency. Shame, where is thy blush?

Madame Nemesis
Democratic Investigator
January 12, 1854

NEWS ITEM

LETTER IN A BOTTLE

JUST WHO ARE THESE LOVE LORN TOWN GIRLS

The Sunbury Daily Item of Thursday evening had the following:

John B. Martin picked up a bottle along the river bank at the foot of Market street yesterday which contained the names of six young ladies residing in Bloomsburg, who wrote a letter in which they declared that the young men of that village "were slow," and declared that they were anxious to meet some real "live wires." In describing themselves they declared "they could cook and sew and did not care to attend the movies more than twice each week."

Martin has not the courage to face the six young ladies single-handed and is now looking for five volunteers who will aid him in storming the stronghold of love.

> *The Morning Press*
> January 15, 1916

SIX TOWN GIRLS WANT "FAST" MEN

NAMES OF THE SIX WHO WROTE LETTER AND PLACED IT IN SUSQUEHANNA RIVER

The letter of the six Bloomsburg girls written and placed in a bottle in the Susquehanna River, and found by George Martin, of Sunbury, and was published in yesterday's *North American*. The letter follows:

"We are all good looking and industrious young women, but the boys of our town are too slow. We want husbands. They must be good to look at and strictly temperate and above all they must not be slow. Bloomsburg girls like the dashing kind of men. Our subject is matrimony. Now if you mean business please write, finder of this bottle, and we will be glad to tell of our abilities and exchange photographs.

> Freda West, 447 West Street.
> Marie Rhodes, 247 East Fourth Street.
> Ella Barnes, box 63, East Bloomsburg.
> Elsie Broadt, East Bloomsburg.
> Erath Werkheiser, 119 East Main Street.
> Margaret Kline, 419 West Street."

> *The Morning Press*
> January 17, 1916

GOING TOO FAR?

Dear Editor:

Our family has the privilege of having *The Morning Press* delivered at our doorsteps. Never in all the years that we have been faithful readers did we look forward to six a.m. with such eagerness as we have been lately. Children and adults try to beat each other to the front door. The resulting scramble beats the best eggs you can imagine for a hearty breakfast.

Would you like to know the reason? Well, our children love to put us on the spot. If we don't beat them to the paper, they will confront us, at the breakfast table and when we are least prepared, with such instant questions as: "Do you agree with Ann Landers that masturbation does not kill virginity? Do you ever dream about perfect love affairs with faceless men? What do they look like? Are both of you 'Pooped in California Not in the Mood in the A.M.'? Hey, this gay tells Ann Landers that he absolutely refuses to have sex with members of his own sex. Can you tell us why?" And on and on it has been going for some time now, morning after morning.

This morning we finally ran out of answers. We just don't know for sure which is better: 30-year-old Alice sleeping with her 15-year-old male pupil, or a 30-year-old Alex sleeping with his 15-year-old female pupil. (See Ann Landers, April 23, 1979.)

I suspected for some time that age has endowed Ann Landers with more than a leathery grin. She has become an expert on masturbation, homosexuality, rape, and other assorted sexual phenomena, if not on virginity. It wasn't until last week, though, that I got really frightened. Reading your report on "Sex Researchers Probe Daydreams" (April 18), I realized that I could be one of those Americans who are plagued with "cross-reference phantasies." I am going to tell you something I never told to anyone. I am having a terrible, erratic nightmare you wouldn't believe. Instead of all the cross-referenced beautiful or handsome movie stars others dream about, who do I keep seeing in my fitful sleep but columnist Ann Landers. Erect as a column, she is standing on a throne, head high up despite the weight of a golden crown. A true Queen Victoria. Except that for regalia she is wearing nothing but a bikini. Now, that is nightmarish enough, but what makes me wake up in cold sweat is the horrible suspicion that something is wrong with me. For much as I stare and stare, I cannot tell for the world of me if my Virgin Queen is a tired old man or simply a dirty old woman. Once awake, though, I soon relax for I know that the real-life columnist is nothing more than an expert businessperson who knows that sex helps sales.

As for the *Press,* I truly wish it left Annie's column and all other dabbling in morning porno to the professional candy-store sex mags. Instant coffee is bad enough and expensive enough. Served with a dish of instant smut education it is apt to make some pooped parents finally pop and upchuck one of these mornings. And guess what expensive family paper they are going to wipe up the mess with.

Because of the delicate nature of this matter, please sign me simply as

RUDE PRUDE PA
The Morning Press
April 26, 1979

THE RIGHTS OF DANCERS

Once again the *Press Enterprise* shows how news-worthy and up to date they are. September 1 they ran a story about some girls who received citations for nude dancing a whole six weeks ago.

It is amazing that a story one-and-a-half months old gets front page and a major hurri-cane gets page 16.

I certainly hope they sold some extra papers because the girls have nothing to be ashamed of. The people that should be ashamed of this story is the supervisors, police and the media because they have to exploit these girls in an at-tempt to make a few extra bucks.

What the story did not say was these girls were arrested only because when the supervi-sors could not find any other way to close the club, they passed a law that allowed them to go after the dancers.

One of the supervisors thought the girls were being exploited because of their dancing. No, the girls were exploited by the supervisors be-cause they are using them in an attempt to close the club. And the media certainly ex-ploited the girls in an attempt to add a little sensationalism to their stories.

Jeff Long even called me to get the girls' side of the story. What I didn't see in his story is how the girls feel they were used and harassed by the police in their so-called investigation.

To take pictures of them on stage for evi-dence is one thing, to take their cameras into the dressing room and watch the girls change into street clothes is quite another.

To haul them off to a magistrate's office to write summary tickets just so the reporters see them is another. And then to fine them $600 plus costs, give me a break.

The *Press Enterprise* also reported on Septem-ber 1 that a person was fined $379 for having drugs and another was fined $129 for theft. I guess having drugs or being a thief is better than being a dancer. There are a lot of things

that were done by the police that some of the dancers and myself feel violated their rights. We will have to wait for the court to decide.

Jeff Long also seemed to make a big deal of the fact that some of the dancers have children. There are a lot of moms out there dancing, at least they are not sitting at home collecting wel-fare. They are also not the women who go out on the weekend, get all drunked up and then go home with just about anybody that asks. This is a job, just like any other.

Now I am not asking you to find a place in your heart for dancers, and I am not asking you to approve of them or like them.

What I am asking is, if you don't like them or approve of them, which is certainly your choice, then don't go where they are dancing and leave them alone. But don't condemn them because they are doing their job and they are not doing anything to you.

If you do like them, go out and see a show sometime, and if you have the looks and the in-terest, call me, I'll give you a good job.

Thomas A. Bodman
TAB Enterprises, Bloomsburg
Press Enterprise
September 3, 1993

A PREGNANT TEEN

This letter is in response to the November 13 edition of the *Press Enterprise* on teen preg-nancy.

I was recently a pregnant teen until my son was born on September 7, 1993. Unlike most teen-age fathers, my boyfriend stayed with me. We've been together for over a year now. He lives with me at my parents' home. He was with me through my rough pregnancy, long labor, and after my son was born, he was there through my strenuous recovery. I had my family and friends to lean on. It's been so hard. I won-der how girls get by without support. I wonder why some teen-age fathers think that they don't

LORI L. HALTEMAN.

have to take responsibility for their actions. I believe both parties consent to sex, unless it is rape. I also believe that if guys didn't pressure girls, girls would wait a long time for sex. It's a known fact that a woman's sex drive isn't nearly as high as a man's.

Many guys don't feel that they pressure girls into sex. Asking for sex or suggesting it is pressure. It's not fair that most of the blame is on the pregnant teen. It's not fair that guys don't have to deal with responsibility if they don't want to. Pregnant teens get all the recognition and blame. I know for a fact that many girls would take back their sexual encounters if they could. Why is it that unwed mothers get looked down upon, and most unwed fathers don't even get acknowledged?

I am asking that mothers of daughters get them on birth control. Don't think they will rush out and have sex because they are protected. It's not always the girl's decision.

Most guys have sex for pleasure and fun. They make themselves believe that the girl they had sex with liked it as much as they did, when actually the girl is home regretting that she even consented to such an act. At least that's how it is in most cases.

Please, girls, there is no reason to listen to me, but please take what I say into consideration. If you have sex with your boyfriend or any guy, you're not likely to keep them for too long afterward. The thrill will be over. They will probably move on to other girls. If you don't have sex, you will keep them wanting. If they break up with you for not having sex, then they probably did not care too much for you anyway. It's as much your decision as it is his. You have a mouth. If you feel you're not ready, say "no." Tell him that you're sure about your decision and that he need not ask again. Don't wait to think about birth control until after you're pregnant. I know it's hard to get a guy to wear a condom. Don't rely on the guy to have protection. Protect yourself now, and please don't forget about AIDS.

I say we forget about telling kids not to have sex, because if they're going to, they're going to. No one can stop it.

Parents, talk to your children, no matter if you think they're having sex or not. My parents never talked to me the way they should about sex. I feel that if they did, I would have waited. I was scared to go on birth control. I wish someone would have told me. I love my son, but now I have to miss out on so much.

I'm hoping that if I talk about my experience that people will learn from it. If I can stop one girl from making a mistake, it will mean a lot to me.

To explain why I feel that unwed mothers get most of the recognition and the fathers don't, I'll tell you a story. Someone said that I was the talk of the town; a seventeen-year-old girl with a baby. And do you know what? They didn't even know my boyfriend's name.

> Lori L. Halteman
> Berwick
> *Press Enterprise*
> November 19, 1993

⚲ THE GAME ⚲

I hereby challenge Silas Hendershott, the well known farmer from Berwick, to a match race of 100 yards—Hendershott to have one yard start. B. F. Sponenbenberg to hold stakes; Si Perkins, pistol firer; Alvyn Joelyn, referee. Jonas Crispin to absorb all unnecessary aurora borealis, for $100 a side, open for $1000—money to be placed at once—race to come off (dead or alive) on the 17th day of March.

(signed) S. J. BARBER
The Bloomsburg Daily
March 10, 1894

Seven Innings

Dear Editor,

In reading your paper, lately, have noticed from time to time, articles printed of some of the old ball games played. Now, I distinctly remember one game that was played at Benton several years before the B. & S. was built. It was played, if my memory is correct, either in the first or second week of October, I have forgotten the year. But seeing an account of the death of Boyd McHenry reminded me of this game, as it was thru him, that three of us from Bloomsburg played with Benton that day. . . .

BLOOMSBURG, PENNA, FEB. 29, 1896.
TO MESSRS. GRIER MATTHEW QUICK AND
FRED TAYLOR IKELER:—
Sirs:—

We, the undersigned, hereby challenge you to shoot against us in a pigeon match, at any time and place named by you and under the following conditions:—

1st. Each man to shoot at ten live, sound and healthy birds.

2nd. American Association rules to govern said contest.

3rd. The losing side to pay for all birds trapped.

This challenge must be accepted within five days or the match will be declared off for the reason that our time is entirely too valuable to be wasted in waiting for the acceptance of a challenge from second class shooters.

Respectfully,

Wm. H. Snyder

Frank Ikeler

BLOOMSBURG, PA., MARCH 2ND, 1896

TO WM. H. SNYDER AND FRANK IKELER:

Dear Little Boys:

After considering your mental infirmity and weakness of intellect we have decided to kindly pardon the presumption which prompted your challenge of the 29th.; and believing that you ought to receive the benefit of an exhibition of our superior skill and marksmanship, and thus learn your real insignificance as shooters, we have concluded to accept your challenge in a spirit of charity and benevolence toward you. Of course you must not begrudge the expenses of the birds, remembering that you will reap untold profit from being thus kindly permitted to witness our skill. If after the shoot you haven't the necessary money to defray expenses Mr. Snyder can obtain from Oliver Wilson, Poor Director, an order for "outside relief." Let us advise you not to be "puffed up with pride" because we have accepted your challenge but receive the same with all due thanks and humiliation, remembering that we only grant you this unusual privilege that you may be benefited thereby.

Very truly yours,

Fred Ikeler

G. M. Quick

NEWS ITEM

The match took place and here is the score. The team of Frank Ikeler and Wm. H. Snyder won the challenge with a score of 13 Kills to Fred Ikeler and G. M. Quick's 11 Kills. Referee—Clark Hagenbuch. Scorer and Trapper—W. S. Rishton.

The Columbian
March 12, 1896

EDITOR OF DAILY:—

The management of the base ball club were very much surprised at the last game by seeing several of the prominent business men of our town driving up to the fence of the Base Ball Park on Decoration Day and standing in their buggies witnessing the game. The management do not object to persons who are unable to pay the entrance fee witnessing the games, provided they come to the ticket office and make the same known, but they do object, most positively, to the business men of town who should assist in supporting the team repeating the work of last Tuesday. If they haven't the quarter and will come to the gate, they will be given a pass.

S. H. Harman, Manager
The Bloomsburg Daily
June 5, 1893

. . . The arrangement for us to come to Benton was made while sitting in the grandstand watching the races at the Fair. Boyd McHenry spoke to me about their having a game with Laporte, Sullivan County, and asked me if I could get a pitcher and another man to come to Benton and play with them the following week. I told him I thought I could. He left me to make the arrangements with the two other men, so I secured Colonel Rhodomoyer and W. H. Eyer. They agreed to go along, so wrote him the arrangements were then made to play on Thursday of the following week. . . .

I feel my experience last year on the first day of trout season would be to the benefit of your readers. My friend Bill Longenberger and I have been fishing in Mountain Springs Lake since its opening approximately 12 years ago, sleeping at the Lake in the parking area in a station wagon.

Last year we decided to take our sons, ages eight and twelve, with us. I fixed up my FWD to sleep four. Off we went for the kids' first day of trout fishing, which to me was always like Christmas Eve.

To make a long story short, we got arrested at approximately 11:30 p.m. the night before the opening day of trout season by the Sweet Valley Waterways Patrolman, and his deputy for camping on an access area. Having $27 between us, we paid the $25 field fine. Needless to say, that ended the fishing trip for all of us. We came home.

I realize we broke the law. We paid the fine. I hope this letter saves someone the hurt and disappointment we all shared. We are not bitter. We will have a go at it this year somewhere.

I sincerely hope you print this. When the law, right or wrong, arrests someone for sleeping with his son in the wilderness in his sleeping bag and ignores, for example, streakers, who are obviously breaking the law (indecent exposure), it's pretty much of a letdown for everyone. Incidentally, this past opening day of trout season was the first day I missed since I was nine years old, except for two years in the U.S. Army in France.

Sincerely,
Ned L. Derr

P.S. To everyone, good luck and good fishing. I love it, fortunately, my son does too.

The Morning Press
March 28, 1974

. . . When the day for the game came, it was raining in the early morning and kept up until about eight thirty, when the wind changed and the sky cleared off. I looked up the others and they did not want to go. I told them that they would surely depend on us, and I did not want to disappoint them, so at last they agreed. We went to the livery stable, operated at that time by John W. Gibbs, underneath the rear of the old Shives block, now occupied by the building of Moore, Keller and Moyer, corner of Iron and Main Streets, secured a team and rode to Benton, arriving at the Hess Hotel in time for dinner. Found the Laporte team players on hand. . . .

I wish to echo your commendation of Senator Sones for voting right on Sunday Sports. Columbia County may well take pride in the voting record of its legislators. If the people back home do as well, we need not have saloons return to Columbia County. Now is the time to think and not be fooled by the wets. Don't let them tell you there is no harm in 3 or 4% beer. There is enough alcoholic content to create the alcoholic thirst.

It is the nose of the camel which is easier excluded than to put the beast out after it has become entrenched. Legislators and high officials refuse to see that day when each succeeding generation will have less alcoholic thirst under Prohibition properly enforced.

Booze has no argument for itself. It destroys all that is good in the man or woman who indulges. Just make it quite clear, it's liquor that must not return.

Sincerely yours,
Mrs. F. T. Kocher
The Morning Press
March 21, 1933

OPEN LETTER

To the Coaches and Board of Directors of Bloomsburg Little League:

What do you say and how do you comfort an 11-year-old boy who has just learned that he can't play baseball with all his friends anymore; because a bunch of grown men have gotten together and have decided he isn't good enough to play Little League?

Of course he may play on the Minor League again, if he really wants to play bad enough, and if he doesn't mind being teased and ridiculed by the other children and parents for doing so; after all, everyone knows an 11-year-old wouldn't be there, if he were a good player; so therefore, he's the object of everyone's laughter and ridicule.

Do you men ever stop to think how these boys feel, or don't you think an 11-year-old has any feelings? Well let me tell you, when a boy that rarely cries; cries himself to sleep, after being teased the entire day at school, for not making Little League: I can assure you they do have feelings.

The object of Little League is supposed to be good sportsmanship, but in

Bloomsburg, it's pick the best, and win, win, win. Perhaps it's time that someone considers the boys; and put a little less emphasis on which coach has the best team.

Maybe someday I'll thank you for teaching my son, at an early age, that life is full of disappointments and he has to learn to cope with them, perhaps: God willing, he'll turn out to be the better citizen and adult for it, but right now, it's hard to tell an 11-year-old that someday, he'll benefit from this experience.

A Concerned Parent
The Morning Press
April 28, 1972

. . . After dinner went out to the field owned by Daniel Hartman, and with the tape, the two teams measured off the diamond, placed a small board for home plate, marked a pitcher's box, and the bases with stakes driven in the ground in grass almost to your knees. I do not remember the names of the Laporte players as they were all entire strangers to me, except a young man by the name of Ingram, son of the former Judge of Sullivan County. The members of the Benton team consisted of the following: Boyd McHenry of Benton; Marve McHenry, Joe Connelly, of Stillwater; Harry Low, Harry Harman, and Bill Fleckenstine, of Orangeville; Colonel Rhodomoyer, Warren Eyer and myself, B. W. Hagenbuch, of Bloomsburg. . . .

Snowmobiling in this part of the country is a weekend recreation, for 99 per cent of the riders. There may be wrong do'ers. You will find them, wherever you find human beings, 1/4 or 1/2 or 1 per cent. I do not know, time will tell.

Yes, they make noise, so do cars, trucks, motorcycles, airplanes, etc.

How many weekends so far this winter have we had snow?

Citizens working in stuffy offices, cow barns, loud and noisy factories, doctors in hospitals and sick rooms, lawyers, or lawmen, housewives caring for their families 24 hours a day, students striving to become worthy citizens, and many other strenuous jobs to make a living, why shouldn't the human being be considered?

I have had the pleasure of seeing the exultant look on the riders' faces after a brisk ride, at a temperature of 2 above zero. Young and old enjoy this sport.

I too love most animals, and I'm happy they have a place to live on the gamelands and enjoy their lives.

Deer do not consider my feelings or my needs, when they uproot and eat and destroy my vegetable and flower gardens. Animals do more injury to human beings than snowmobiles do to them. They have thousands of acres to live on game lands. Why get upset because a few roads, through the gamelands, especially the mountains are being used once in a while, according to the amount of snow, and in good condition for riding.

Why not consider the human being, his money purchased these game lands, let him too, enjoy our hills and valleys.

I'm over 60 years old. I love animals, but I also enjoy a snowmobile ride.

Grandma Sutliff
Jamison City
The Morning Press
January 27, 1972

We love you, Berwick Bulldogs. Don't you ever forget that. We love you and Coach Curry. Berwick Bulldog Football has put Berwick on the map. You have done more for Berwick than anybody has ever done for Berwick since Berwick was created. Don't you ever forget that we love you. The whole town loves you and will never stop loving you. God bless you.

Anonymous Caller
Noise from the Bleachers/30 Seconds
Press Enterprise
December 16, 1993

As my Olympic experience comes to an end, I'd like to take this opportunity to thank the many fans from the Bloomsburg area. Your support throughout my gymnastic career has been wonderful.

Since making the Olympic Team in Boston in June, I have had many memorable experiences. But ten years from now, when I look back at this summer, my fondest memory will be Aug. 24, 1996, the day I was honored by my hometown community.

I would like to thank all the volunteers who planned and orchestrated the events of that day. Your efforts were worthy of a gold medal.

Kip Simons
Olympian
Press Enterprise
September 22, 1996

. . . We played seven innings, and if I remember correctly the score was 24–6 in favor of Benton. The home plate was situated near where the B. & S. depot is now situated. We batted toward the creek. It was a long game and after securing an early supper we all from down the creek, (eight of us) left Boyd McHenry, the only member from Benton, alone with the team. Boyd told me afterwards that they razzed him and made an awful "kick." Then for the first I found out that we had been playing for the price of the suppers. I think Boyd McHenry was the

oldest ball player of Benton. There is some few people in Benton, I suppose who will remember this game.

        "Pop" Hagenbuch
        The Benton Argus
        July 2, 1925

I would like to take this opportunity to congratulate everyone who played a part in the recent Bloomsburg Renaissance street festival. It provided an opportunity for thousands of people to enjoy themselves throughout the day. At the same time, many charitable organizations were able to raise money for their programs.

I especially want to congratulate Lisa Basci for her role in bringing "Jello Wrestling" to Bloomsburg. Lisa conceived the idea and worked with all phases of the project until it was completed. Without her, this event would not have taken place.

This is just one more example of the many ways in which the community and the college work together in creating a better place in which to live.

        John Trathen, Director
        Student Activities and Kehr College Union
        Press Enterprise
        May 10, 1983

⊿ HAPPY DAYS: ⊾
THE 1950s

THE FLUORINE SOLUTION

To The Editor:

I have been the examining dentist in the Danville Public and Parochial Schools for several years. Having worked in that capacity, besides being a general practitioner in dentistry, in Danville, I have had the opportunity of examining the teeth of all the children in our community. These experiences have led me to believe our children are suffering needlessly from tooth decay.

I have followed with great interest the scientific research that has been made with fluoridation and the wonderful results accomplished. It is not now in the experimental stage. Fluoridation is a scientifically proven method of reducing cavities in children.

The United States Public Health Service and the American Dental Association have endorsed the principle of fluoridation of public water supplies.

In January 1945, Grand Rapids, Mich., became the first city in the world to put a fluoride compound in the water supply to prevent tooth decay. Hundreds of cities followed suit. Now it is the concern of the officials of thousands of towns and villages.

I firmly believe fluoridation is a scientifically

THE CHANGING ROLE OF NEWSPAPERS

———

Television, now appearing in nearly every living room, is the latest technological rival to compete with newspapers as a primary information source. Local Columbia and Montour County newspapers, now down to four published by three concerns, are commercial operations that seek profit even as they define themselves as community crusaders. While studiously avoiding the cast of political bias, some editors encourage Letters to the Editor, others run very few, while others seem to be very selective in running those that are "for the good of the community."

---

proven method of reducing teeth cavities in children.

MAIN STREET, BLOOMSBURG, CIRCA 1958.

The value of such a program far outweighs the cost of equipment and fluorine solution.

I am convinced the children of our community are in need of such a program. It will eliminate much dental work and make for healthier and happier children.

For these reasons I heartily endorse the proposal of fluoridation for Danville water supply.

J. C. Blackburn, DDS
The Danville News
May 4, 1957

SENATOR JOSEPH MCCARTHY

Dear Sir:

The Enterprise has clouded the issues many times in the past concerning Senator Joseph McCarthy. In the issue of Nov. 8, left hand brevitorial stated, quote: "McCarthy appears to be the 'lame duck' as Senate convenes on censure."

Friends of McCarthy believe that is hitting below the belt.

What is a lame duck? Webster's says, "A senator or Congressman who has failed to be re-elected and who is approaching the end of his term of office."

First, McCarthy was not up for re-election.

Second, McCarthy's political influence is not becoming less but on the contrary the recent election proved beyond doubt that his following is tremendous.

We shall try to prove who is a lame duck.

In my book a lame duck . . . or a dead duck is a person who tries to minimize the part McCarthy played in ridding the country of Communist agents.

Is there one person who McCarthy accused of being a Communist agent who proved to be not? Name one.

Who are the lame ducks or dead ducks who hold Senator McCarthy more odious than the quisling Alger Hiss?

Mrs. Roosevelt . . . who said, McCarthy is another Hitler. But also said . . . Dictator Tito . . . is a great man . . . youthful . . . whimsy . . . This man who butchered American airmen in 1946.

Clement Attlee . . . comforter of tyrant Mao who is responsible for the slaughter of thousands of American youths.

I could go on and on, but space is lacking.

A recent Gallup poll showed that the American people support McCarthy five to three. He ranks seventh among the 10 persons Americans most admire.

Many, many of our writers, have been taken in ridiculously by the Reds. They consider Marxism progressive, even now after a dozen of our planes on peaceful patrol have been savagely cruelly shot down. They grudgingly concede the diabolical nature of the Red record.

These pathetic dupes do not want to face facts.

They do not want to admit their monstrous mistake.

Hence, their annoyance at Senator McCarthy, but history will prove him to be one of the greatest Americans.

Thanking you very much for allowing me to express my thoughts on this matter.

Orterio Villa
Berwick Enterprise
November 12, 1954

TWO DISEASES

Dear Editor:

Just a few lines to advise the readers of this paper that there are two VERY contagious diseases going around. One is the lack of sympathy and the other is viciousness. It seems that the night air and late hours are very good for both diseases.

A Berwick RD 2 Reader
Berwick Enterprise
January 29, 1955

MEDDLING

Dear Editor:

We have had occasion to travel a good bit in the south, over the years, and we had sincerely believed the two races were getting along well. Like in so many other situations, when the "outsiders" begin meddling, and certain the National Association for the Advancement of Colored People is meddling in the

AROUND THE WORLD

- In 1950, North Korea invades South Korea, setting off the Korean War, which continues until 1953. That same year, the U.S. sends military advisers to Vietnam.
- In 1952, the U.S. explodes the first hydrogen bomb in the Pacific. The Soviet Union explodes one ten months later. *Waiting for Godot* is published.
- In the summer of 1954, Vietnam is divided into North and South at the Seventeenth Parallel.
- In October 1957, the Soviet Union launches *Sputnik 1*. The USA joins the space race by creating NASA, which launches *Explorer 1* in 1958.
- In 1958, an international symbol for nuclear disarmament is created. It becomes better known as "the peace symbol."
- In 1959, Fidel Castro leads a revolution in Cuba, introducing Communism to the Western Hemisphere.

POST OFFICE, BLOOMSBURG, CIRCA 1959.

south these days, trouble begins. Each area understands its own problems so much better than those from other sections.

Anonymous
Berwick Enterprise
September 18, 1957

AN UNWANTED RACE

Dear Sir:

Regarding the integration and segregation crisis enveloping our country today, I feel that we are on the threshold of a very grave situation. I further feel that we are in need of a law of assurance to all citizens, interested or disinterested, involved or otherwise and who isn't?

Integration under the Constitution is the law. From this we can neither deter or by-pass.

The law of assurance I speak of would guarantee, under law, to preserve the dignities, rights and privileges to all citizens, with one exception, the right to mix blood.

To ignore the issue entirely would allow its poisons to eat into our very established way of life and create hatred never heretofore experienced. This is now taking form, as I see it, to the glory of our enemies.

Creation of an unwanted race within our confines is certainly not desired by any right thinking American, regardless of color and I feel that it is not desired by the Almighty, himself.

Fear is definitely one ingredient in this present turmoil. To remove this fear would install a medium of confidence for the future. You no doubt are amazed by this letter directed to you but here in your field of readers the topic is quite rampant, especially the present contempt for the federal government, as shown by one particular state. This startling stand could readily be taken up by many more.

Sincerely,
Raymond H. Koepke
Berwick Enterprise
September 18, 1957

HOT AND HEAVY

To the Editor:

In the past few weeks the newspaper headlines have read the same—"Racial riot—Negro children not allowed into white schools" or "Negro children are allowed into school only because of National Guard or area policemen standing by." After seeing these articles, I simply nodded my head and said too bad. However, another attitude some people get is against the Negro, while others defend the Negro. Finally this all leads up to arguments which sometime become "hot and heavy."

This has happened at my house. My father and I argue pro and con about what is happening to the Negro today. Our arguments are not entirely one-sided respectively. We both try to be broad-minded enough to see the other's point of view. However, there are times that we do get pretty "hot and heavy." During our last argument we confronted each other with some questions—Why are the races fighting like this? Why does the white want to keep the Negro out? Why does the Negro want in? Why all these fights? What are we to gain?

Dad and I finally hit upon a possible solution—take it for what it is worth. We wonder (and think it highly possible) that the Communists in America have been known for these types of tactics—arouse the Americans to blind frenzy and then hit them hard. Dad and I looked at each other and said, "How stupid we are, here we are arguing and fighting with each other as the Communists want us to."

If all the people could understand this and reason it out, we could all become better Americans. Internal pressure defeated Rome; let's not set ourselves up the same way. The Communist knows by past history, that the Negro-White problem is one of long standing. He is like a parasite who feeds off the bleeding wound.

Don't be a blind follower of the Communist;

think over this problem wisely. We all want to be worthwhile citizens and Americans. Don't be grilled to the venom of the Communists' leech.

All men are created equal—don't let the Communist take away our precious rights. What do you think? Are we being blinded by the Communists or do we just take our rights for granted? Citizens of Danville: Let us not be led into a Red trap.

> John and Robert Thomas
> *The Danville News*
> September 14, 1957

GOOD OLD U.S.A.

To the Editor of the *Berwick Enterprise*:

I was a bit confused when the newsboy brought our paper on Saturday. After reading your editorial on school integration in Little Rock, I had to check the front page to make sure there wasn't some mistake. At first I thought perhaps someone had made an error and delivered a paper from Biloxi, Mississippi, instead of Berwick, Pa. But, sure enough, there it was, *Berwick Enterprise,* and there it was, too, an editorial denying everything this country is trying to build.

Of course, your editorial didn't exactly say that Negroes should be relegated to second-class status and denied equal rights with other American citizens, but that was the exact intent and effect of your editorial. Why don't you just say right out that you believe in Totalitarianism and segregation just like they have in the good old U. S. A. (Union of South Africa, that is)? Instead, you have to hide behind a smokescreen of charges about communism and quotations from a Negro who happens to hold views that perhaps one in a thousand Negroes hold.

First of all, it is ridiculous to hint, as you do, that Communists support school integration and therefore, ipso facto, integration is a bad thing and everyone who supports it is a Communist. I am quite sure that President Eisenhower and the Supreme Court could hardly be called card-carrying Communists.

Rather, it is people like you who are intentionally, or unintentionally, playing into the hands of the Communists by keeping the whole situation stirred up. No one has any right to keep Negroes from public schools of their choosing if you believe in the principles of democracy. Let's admit it, if Communists are in favor of school integration, they happen to be on the right side. We should do what is right by Negroes or any other group of people who are discriminated against through hate, fear, and ignorance. If that were the case, the Communists would have no issue to exploit.

I'm sure there was much joy in Moscow when Orval Faubus, for his own political advantage, stood up on his hind legs and defied the federal government. Let's cause a little sorrow in Moscow and for Communists in general and give an equal chance to all Americans.

> Herbert Rosen
> *Berwick Enterprise*
> August 7, 1958

CARVER HALL,
BLOOMSBURG STATE TEACHERS COLLEGE.

FLUORINE

To The Editor:

Looking at fluoridation from the standpoint of the physician and also the father of four children, I readily agree on the immediate introduction of fluorine into Danville's water supply.

The benefits have been described over and over again in medical and dental journals and repeatedly brought to the attention of the public.

For the future protection of our children, Danville should have fluoridation now or just as soon as it is physically possible.

> William O. Curry, Jr., M.D.
> *The Danville News*
> May 3, 1957

A LITTLE ARTICLE

I once wrote a little article to the Tunkhannock paper and he published it and a woman in Pittsburgh read the lines and thought them good and clipped them out and sent them to her sister in Philadelphia and she liked them so much she pasted them inside her Bible cover and sent me a letter of appreciation. I sent the same article to you at the *Berwick Enterprise* and it went into the waste basket.

> Mrs. M. R.
> *Berwick Enterprise*
> February 26, 1955

FLUORIDATION

To the editor:

The Women's Society of Christian Service of St. Paul's M.E. Church by a vote of its members present would like to go on record as being in favor of the fluoridation of Danville's Water supply.

> St. Paul's Church
> W S C S
> *The Danville News*
> March 15,1957

COMMUNISM

The danger of atheistic materialism becomes magnified with each atom blast, and each headline forever reminding the public of the cold war that exists. With the spiritual dignity of man threatened, once more divine providence is called on to stop this wave of godless tyranny which is known as communism.

The American public can no longer remain complacent. We must stand up and be counted, we must manifest our loyalty and allegiance to the United States, and make the American way of life a full time job instead of recognizing only the few days set aside each year, to make our patriotism known. The whole world must know how we feel, and we cannot deceive them, since they look to us for leadership in this renewed battle of "isms" where brain washings, kangaroo courts, self-appointed liberals, and one-worlders have found a place in our vocabulary during this modern version of communism which is trying to enslave the world.

How can we become casual with our way of life and have no regard toward our duties to combat this false philosophy? What more must happen to arouse the patriotic temperament that has long been traditionally American, when our liberty is in jeopardy?

Talk is cheap. It is already too late. This cancer called communism does exist. It is real and revolving around our every day life. It is up to us. Do we cope with the situation by appeasement or do we strengthen ourselves for that sweet day when the world shall know liberation to be a reality and to work with the free world to bring an end to all "isms" and prove to ourselves that we can live within the brotherhood of man under the Fatherhood of God.

Louis Jordan, Chairman
American Legion
Committee On Un-American
Activities
Berwick Enterprise
March 30, 1955

Time Capsule

AROUND TOWN

- Bloomsburg celebrates its Sesquicentennial in June 1952. In October of that year, President Truman and his daughter whistle-stop in Bloomsburg, campaigning for Adlai Stevenson. An estimated crowd of 2,500 to 3,500 hear him speak for five minutes, describing the GOP candidate, General Eisenhower, as "a man who jumps around on the issues," and "asks you to sign a blank check." The president also advises the audience to beware of the press, which he alleges holds a bias against the Democratic party.
- The Bloomsburg Fair celebrates its centennial in 1954. Afternoon entertainment at the grandstand includes "Linon, the Tramp: One of the World's Greatest Pantomime Artists."
- A former Berwick woman, Betty Winkler, wife of New York actor George Keane, is identified as a Communist during hearings at the House Un-American Activities Committee in August 1955.
- Days before the 1956 presidential election, Vice President and Mrs. Nixon campaign in Berwick. According to *The Morning Press,* between 4,000 and 5,000 people welcome him at the train station. He is introduced by Senator Alvin Bush, who calls him "Dick Simpson." "The president," says Mr. Nixon, "should be a symbol of honesty."

WATER SUPPLY

To The Editor:

My four-year-old son was admitted to the hospital today because of severe infection caused by tooth decay.

I understand that fluoridation of Danville's water would reduce dental decay in Danville and help prevent this sort of infection.

I hope the City Council sees to it that our children have the advantage of fluoridated water supply without delay.

> Mrs. Marlene Fitzgerald
> Mr. Donald Fitzgerald
> *The Danville News*
> May 6, 1957

CHARLEY WEAVER SAYS . . .

The one thing that surprises me about the teenage problem is that it's a problem at all. To my way of thinking, the entire thing could be settled in about 15 minutes if we still had woodsheds.

These days, being a teen-ager is fashionable. Too many things are for the teen-ager alone. That racket they call rock 'n' roll is a good example.

I look on rock 'n' roll about the same as I do poison ivy. As soon as I recognize it, I keep my distance.

Mt. Idy has a rock 'n' roll singer named Willy Sump. Willy got to be a rock 'n' roll singer by calling hogs. He felt extra good one day and he let out a huge beller. In sight of half an hour, he had forty hogs and Mitch Miller on his back porch. The only trouble now is, whenever one of his records is played in Mt. Idy the town fills with hogs.

> Syndicated column
> Copyright Col. Flea, Inc.
> *Berwick Enterprise*
> December 1, 1959

DELINQUENTS

Dear Editor:

I came across another one of those articles last night knocking the teenagers and rock and roll by "Charlie Weaver." If they aren't knocking sarcasm at them in the papers, it is on television programs. It gets to be pretty disgusting and I've wanted to get this out of my system for a long time. I'm not a teenager, I'm a middle-aged mother and I have nothing against or see nothing wrong in the teenager and rock and roll.

Let me tell you something! It's the older people who are delinquents. People who think they are so good and can't see a bit of good in teenagers. Look around you and what do you see? All kinds of commandments being broken by adults. I've come to the conclusion that they are to blame for plenty of the wrong ways of some teenagers. A person can't even watch a straight honest television quiz show by these so called respectable and wonderful big people. What's the matter, didn't that shock you, you "Teen Age Criticizers?" What do you think a thing like that does to a teenager?

What about all the adult adulterers and adulteresses? The teenagers are surrounded by this contamination. What do you think that does to them? How about these glamour women who expose their upper halves with no shame on television, who have no self respect and have the gall to call it "art?" That is worse than anything any teenager can do. If that is the only way they can gain glamour then I feel spiritually sorry for them. Understand, I have nothing against bare shoulders. I think the bare shouldered gowns and dresses beautiful, but there is such a thing as being bare too far down and I think a person has to be vulgar to wear gowns that way. If anything, Charley Weaver's "hog calling" would not attract as many human dogs as those bare bosomed dames and he seems to love it when he is near them. And they ridicule teenagers and rock and roll! Some joke!

So you see what I mean. Everybody wants to know the answer to the delinquent teenager problem. My answer is this: When adults all over the world make up their minds to live a God fearing life (the Commandments were meant for adults too, not only teenagers) then they will set an example for living for yours, mine and everybody's teenagers, set them on the right road.

And the way they condemn Elvis. He has done nothing indecent ever, lived a good life. He could never be as vulgar and indecent as some of the people who talked about him. I wish "Charlie" could read this article. And who is "he" to criticize?

> A teen-age sympathizer
> *Berwick Enterprise*
> December 4, 1959

WATER FLUORIDATION

To the editor:

The Danville Junior Woman's Club would like to go on record as being in favor of the Water Fluoridation Program for Danville Community.

Our organization has many members who have children and are extremely interested in the promotion of this worthwhile and necessary health measure.

> Recording Secretary
> Sincerely,
> (Mrs.) Grace S. Cope
> *The Danville News*
> May 20, 1957

"FEELIES"

A news item in your October 22 *Enterprise* told of a new thing in films called "Feelies." This adds a new dimension to our communication

CHET'S, ROUTE 11, BLOOMSBURG, CIRCA 1960.

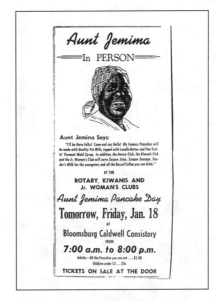

THE MORNING PRESS,
JANUARY 17, 1957.

media where one not only sees and hears but also feels. "Any emotion can be evoked by the process—hate, envy, lust, fear, laughter. . . . The messages are invisible on the screen because they are beamed too fast for the conscious eye to see. But they register on the subconscious." It might be added that this process is not confined to the movie theatre but can be done wherever there are moving pictures—on T.V., in the lobby of a bank, store or railroad station.

FIRST NATIONAL BANK,
BLOOMSBURG, CIRCA 1959.

The item was written in a light vein so that one would easily laugh it off. I am sure, however, that the more thoughtful people are concerned with its import. Up to now we could hear and see T.V. or movies and evaluate what we saw with considered judgement. Now we can be made to feel, believe and act without our knowing why and without our knowledge or consent.

The complete structure of our democratic process can be demolished by this thing. Democracy is based on the considered judgement of informed people, and capitalism is the flowering of independent, creative, competitive minds. Diversity has made us great. This could make us uniform—in religion, in politics, in culture. If this "Precon" does register on the subconscious as the article states, were one to receive conflicting suggestions mental disorder could result.

I am not alarmed about Sputnik because I believe the American people rise to problems they are aware of. But I am writing our Congressmen and Senators about "Precon" in the hope that the strict control or elimination of this device will benefit everyone.

Sincerely yours,
Mrs. Bruce Fessenden
Berwick Enterprise
October 31, 1957

FAVORING FLUORIDATION

To The Editor:

At the May meeting of the Acacia Club the History and effects of Fluoridation was discussed.

After learning more about this matter the members felt that Fluoridation would be beneficial to Danville and went on record as favoring Fluoridation of the Danville Water Supply.

Acacia Club
The Danville News
May 8, 1957

Teen Talk

During good old summertime, a picnic is The Thing.

A picnic is a perfect excuse for a boy-girl get-together as any maiden knows. A group of girls offering promises of home-prepared food and cool drinks can entice the most popular boys in their set to a day in the outdoors. If you agree to combine luscious food with some outdoor sport—swimming, boating, fishing, tennis—the lads surely will beat their feet to your retreat.

A summer picnic is the perfect occasion for man snaring, too. Or didn't you know? It is the time when you can be bait without being suspect:

(1) *Feminine*—Sunnybrook farm dress, home-cooked food,

(2) *A good sport*—enjoying the outdoors, playing his favorite game,

(3) *Romantic*—walking through the woods, listening to a bird sing, admiring the wonders of nature, cooing,

(4) *Complimentary*—admiring his prowess in building a fire, finding the right path, etc.

You don't want to fall down on any of these opportunities to win his admiration, if not his class ring. So here are some ideas for picnic food we hope will hit him in the right spot:

Dime bank budget: Chili Mac and Fruit Skewer.

To make Chili-Mac, empty a can of chili con carne with beans into a pot and heat. Cook spaghettina al dente (firm, not too soft). Pour Chili over top of spaghetti and serve with chopped onions sprinkled over the top. (So it's not romantic! But the boys will love the onions!)

Fruit Skewer: Put alternate chunks of pineapple, marshmallows and pear on a skewer and toast over a fire. This makes a fun dessert for the boys.

Fair-to-middlin allowance: Hot dogs, black-eyed peas and salad.

The hot dogs can be cooked over a grill of course, and the boys will certainly fight to see who is chef on that deal. Black-eyed peas can be cooked at home, heated up at the picnic spot.

Fat wallet menu: Fried Chicken, Macaroni salad, Grilled bananas.

Fry the chicken at home, wrap in waxed paper so that each gets at least leg and breast. Or thigh.

Grilled bananas are made by peeling and brushing with melted butter or margarine. Split bananas lengthwise, being careful not to cut them entirely in half. Place a marshmallow in each banana slit. Grill bananas over hot coals and grill until marshmallows are melted and bananas are heated. Sprinkle with chopped peanuts.

Syndicated column
The Morning Press
July 2, 1953

STOP, LOOK, LISTEN

Dear Editor:

I'm writing this letter to point out something to today's teen-agers. I'm not some old maid writing a protest: I'm a 16-year-old Shickshinny girl who has at least one ounce of sense at the top of my head, where every other teen-ager should have some. I'm not a wall flower. I'm in the middle of "the crowd" just as all my friends are.

Tonight I went to the local movies to see Elvis Presley in "Loving You." On my way home a carload of boys from Berwick and Beach Haven pulled up to turn around in a side street. Then it started! I kept walking home and these supposedly "growing boys" began yelling the most filthy, vile language that I've ever heard and I've heard some.

What I'm trying to point out is that the kids today should stop, look, listen.

It isn't just the incident that happened tonight because I realize that they were just riding around "showing off" and trying to "unsuccessfully" be grown up.

Teen-agers, STOP and think what you're doing. LOOK at yourself and the world that your own family has to live in. LISTEN to the stories of today's teen-agers.

People are blaming some of today's teenage trouble on misguidance from their parents. But if today's teen-agers are like they are, what guidance can they give their own children? What will on-coming generations be?

Sure some say, "well, there are the good and the bad." But what are the good doing about the bad? We all are being raised in a world of conflict. But someone must keep his or her head. Why not show the teen-age condemners that we too can and will keep our heads.

Wise up gang! Grow up! Use a little common sense!

Let's live to be the right kind of mothers and fathers to straighten out this crazy mixed-up world.

Stop and realize how great everything around us is and we're so small! But we're here, we're someone, we occupy space just as will the next guy.

Show the world that we too can do our part no matter how small it is.

Sincerely,
Teen-Ager
Berwick Enterprise
September 11, 1957

SUPPORT FLUORIDATION

To the Editor:

In behalf of the Business and Professional Women's Club, I am pleased to tell you that our organization wishes to support fluoridation in Danville.

Corresponding Secretary
Laura Hoffmaster
The Danville News
May 20, 1957

LIKE ME

Dear Office Window:

Now no sly remarks from you Editor, but what our town needs is a slenderizing salon for fat women like me. We take pills to curb our appetites and we go on strict diets. Then we get too strict with those around the house, due to our nerves, and get mean, mean, mean. When I'm fat I'm jolly and people like to be round me. But I don't like to be round, and that is the truth.

Tiz Too
Berwick Enterprise
December 4, 1954

FLUORIDATION NOW

To the Editor:

The members of the 1st Ward P.T.A. would like to go on record as being in favor of fluoridation now.

> 1st Ward P.T.A.
> Peg Curry, Secretary
> *The Danville News*
> May 20, 1957

RUSSIAN PARTY

Editor:

If at any time in the future the management of the Underground Tavern should care to use my name in an advertisement, I wish they would consult me first.

In that way I could give them the proper information and thus avoid the printing of incorrect material such as appeared in *The News* last week.

My name is Petro Venarchick, not Peter Venarchick. I am of Ukrainian ancestry and definitely not Russian.

Also, if they wish to so honor me with a party on Russian New Years, I wish it would be on the

```
┌──────────────────────────────────────┐
│  FUN  —  FUN  —  FUN  —  FUN          │
│         Special                       │
│F  RUSSIAN NEW YEARS DANCE          F  │
│U                                   U  │
│N  Everybody      │  Tuesday Night  N  │
│   Welcome        │    Jan. 15th       │
│  Honoring Danville's Oldest         | │
│  Russian Resident, Peter Venarchick F │
│F  Hats - Favors  │  Supper 50c      U │
│U  Noise Makers   │ Pigs in a Blanket N│
│N        Come Early                  | │
│   BUZZ BADERS ORCHESTRA               │
│   Starts Promptly at 9:00 P. M.     F │
│F   UNDERGROUND TAVERN               U │
│U      MONTOUR HOTEL                 N │
│N  FUN  —  FUN  —  FUN  —  FUN          │
└──────────────────────────────────────┘
```

THE DANVILLE NEWS, JANUARY 14, 1957.

Eve of, or on the holiday, and not after it is all over.

I wish to express my apologies to any friends who may have visited said tavern expecting to join me in celebrating.

But as I said above I was not consulted about the party nor was I invited.

> Thank You,
> Petro Venarchick
> *The Danville News*
> February 25, 1957

MOOSE FOR FLUORIDATION

On the evening of May 13th, Danville Lodge 1133, Loyal Order of Moose met in regular session.

At this meeting the subject of fluoridation of the water supply of Danville was discussed.

The Loyal Order of Moose being an organization very much interested in the care and welfare of children it goes without saying that after careful consideration of the subject before mentioned, the members of Danville Lodge voted unanimously to go on record as favoring the fluoridation of the water supply of Danville immediately.

> Albert C. Johnson
> Chairman
> Civic Affairs Committee
> Danville Lodge No. 1133
> Loyal Order of Moose
> *The Danville News*
> May 17, 1957

TRAGIC RESULTS

To the Editor:

All around us we can witness the tragic results of the disregard of highway safety laws.

The truck and bus drivers are particularly at

fault, racing to arrive at their destinations, resembling mighty snorting dragons with the smaller automobiles at their mercy!

Every news dispatch bears this out!

However, there are many laws made to protect the general citizenry, but few people seem to observe or enforce them until some tragedy occurs.

Right now in Danville, boys too young to bear firearms, are allowed to roam at will, and shoot at will.

Must we wait 'til one is killed or injured or even some innocent party, child or adult injured and then get up a petition to enforce the law?

Some traffic control is being applied to protect school children, but more is needed.

The very treacherous intersection at Walnut and Railroad Street is being left uncontrolled, just lying in wait for that "tragedy."

Water holes, junked iceboxes and refrigerators, open trash fires, serious fire hazards of various types, and again unsafe road conditions can be seen with ease around Danville!

Citizens! Let us form petitions against potential tragedies!

By doing this we can save ourselves that ultimate grief which no petition can ease.

> Hopefully,
> Mrs. C. Eugene Swiger
> *The Danville News*
> February 5, 1957

FLUORIDE AND COMMUNISTS

To The EDITOR:

Why is it so many people are ready to believe lies instead of the truth, even when all of the evidence is overwhelmingly in favor of the truth?

The world has an over-abundance of scandal-mongers and gossips, and these people never lack for a gullible audience.

When Hitler first began spreading his gospel of hate and Aryan supremacy, he found a ready audience: enough people fell for his lies to put him in a position to disrupt the peace of the world.

As a result, literally millions died in extermination camps, concentration camps and in World War II. Other millions of people were displaced from their homes: Germany was devastated, and eventually Hitler himself was a victim. All this because, in the beginning enough people believed his line.

Today, communism is a threat not only to world peace, but to the very existence of the human race.

Even in our own United States, there are many who believe in the lies of communism, despite all the evidence that communism is a destructive force dedicated to the overthrow of our government.

And in our own community, cranks, crack-pots, and hate-merchants are carrying on the same kind of work.

These cranks, crack-pots, and hate-merchants are busily spreading lies and hate-inspired literature about fluoridation, and as is always the case, they are finding some people who are willing to believe these lies, even in the face of the conclusive proof that the fluoridation program is beneficial to the children of the community and is harmful to absolutely no one.

Use your intelligence and study the evidence for yourself.

Don't deprive the children of the benefits of this proven health program.

Ask your own doctor or dentist, and be governed by the word of these professional men—men who are really qualified to know what is best for the health and well-being of our children.

In the November election, be sure to go to the polls and vote for fluoridation.

You may be sure that those who are fighting this worthy cause will be at the polls bright and early. It is up to the right-thinking citizens of Danville to put this program across.

> H. L. Gilliam
> *The Danville News*
> October 23, 1957

WHY WAIT?

To the Editor:

If the plan to fluoridate the local supply of drinking water means so much to the health of the people in Danville let's have it now. Why wait?

Mrs. Mary Edmondson,
Mr. William Edmondson,
Mr. Thomas Keefer,
Mrs. Margaret Keefer,
Mrs. Helen Bitler,
Mr. Wilbur Bitler,
Mr. Fred Boyer,
Mrs. Helen Boyer,
Mrs. Mary Klock,
Mr. George Klock,
Mrs. George Buckley,
Mr. George Buckley,
Mrs. Helen Foust,
Mr. Edward Foust,
Mrs. Sarah Evans,
Mr. John Bausch,
Mrs. John Bausch,
Mr. Luther Hawk,
Mrs. Luther Hawk,
Mr. Frank Boyer,
Mrs. Evelyn Boyer,
Mr. Westley Barber,
Mrs. Edith Barber,
Mr. Stanley Weaver,
Mrs. Doris Weaver,
Mr. Harold Hack,
Mrs. Laura Hack.
The Danville News
May 7, 1957

Fluoridation Loses By 1,315-961 Vote

THE DANVILLE NEWS, NOVEMBER 6, 1957.

NEWS ITEM

Danville Borough residents turned down a proposal to fluoridate the local water supply at a special referendum held yesterday during the municipal elections.

Unofficial tallies show that the fluoridation proposal lost by a vote of 1,315 to 961, dropping all four wards.

Fluoridation had been a subject of much discussion during the past few months.

The Danville News
November 6, 1957

CHAPTER
32

⚞ LOST AND FOUND ⚟

A MUSKET

It has been 25 years since I left your town to find a home in the wild domain of the Nebraska prairie. I then parted from friends I dearly loved and comrades that I passed the hardships of war with as a member of the 3rd Pa. Artillery. How I would like to see those comrades. I would also like to find and purchase the musket I sold at my sale at the slate quarry near Bloomsburg in October 1871. I believe Thomas Russel either bought or knows who did. I will freely pay any comrade for services and expense incurred in procuring it.

  Wm. Hohnbaum
  The Columbia County Republican
  August 31, 1893

THE NEBRASKA PRAIRIE.

As a member of the Third Pennsylvania Artillery during the Civil War, William Hohnbaum is stationed at Fort Monroe on Chesapeake Bay. He participates in a variety of assignments: handling heavy artillery for sieges, light artillery for field battles, gunboats for marine encounters, and guarding prisoners of war. In this last capacity, he helps to guard Confederate president Jefferson Davis during his imprisonment at Fort Monroe.

A SADDLE

The person last week (thro' mistake)
Who did from the subscriber take
In north-way, Northumberland town,
And left in lieu thereof his own,
A bridle and a saddle too,
A swap that will by no means suit;
The fellow left him nought to boot.
Unless he soon returns the same,
In capitals shall shine his name.
  John B-D-Y

The owner cannot do without them,
And wishes not to say about them

So honest lad (as Johnny knows ye),
If soon returned he'll not expose ye.
    ANONYMOUS
    The Sunbury and
    Northumberland Gazette
    January 1, 1794

SOME CLOTHES

If the man who about four o'clock Tuesday morning very unceremoniously left a basket containing some exceedingly wet clothes, in the alley between Wm. Chrisman's and Newton Walker's, will call at 147 corner of said alley and West First Street, give his name and identify the basket, it will be restored to him without further question.
    EARLY RISER
    The Bloomsburg Daily
    January 31, 1894

BABY BROTHER

As to my baby brother who left my house on Friday, December 28, 1894, for his home in Bloomsburg, Pa. I expected to hear from him before this time and perhaps Mr. Editor, you can tell me if he arrived at home safely. He is about 46 years of age and weighs over 250 lbs.
    Very Respectfully,
    W. L. Manning
    Brighton, N.Y.

In answer to the above, after due inquiry and diligent search, we can truthfully say that the little fellow arrived home safe and sound.
    Editor
    The Bloomsburg Daily
    January 22, 1895

A CHILD

I LEFT my child, named Margaret Hogan, aged about four years, last spring, with a certain Nicholas Williams, a Frenchman, then living near Liberty-town, for him to take care of until I returned from Philadelphia, to which place I was then going on business—and now, on my return, find that said Williams is moved away, with my child, to some place that all my vigilance has failed in finding out. Therefore, any person who can give account where the said Williams now resides, or can be found, and will take the trouble to convey such intelligence to the printer in Hagers town, will thereby confer a most lasting obligation on a poor disconsolate mother, thus bereaved of her child, and who has no reward to offer other than gratitude.

MARY HOGAN

N. B. Said Williams is a silversmith, but mostly follows peddling; and I am told, that he and his wife (who is an Irish woman) call the child their own.

(*The different printers in the United States, who possess a sympathy for the maternal feelings, will be pleased to publish the above.*)

The Oracle of Dauphin and Harrisburgh Advertiser
November 11, 1792

A CAR

Dear Editor:

I'm writing to you in regard to your sarcastic implication that my mother, Mrs. Catherine Oslaski, forgot where she parked her car on Friday evening, June 20, and reported it as stolen.

I can assure you that my mother is not the "absent minded professor" you make her out to be. As far as you and your publication are con-

cerned you were sadly misinformed (as usual) when you said the police found the car.

They had no more to do with finding it than the man in the moon.

So, in the future, I suggest you get the whole, true and correct facts before you publish anything.

Dorothy Baron
Berwick Enterprise
June 23, 1958

A BUS

Thirteen persons waiting for bus 302 departing at 6:40 p.m. from the Golden Nugget Casino—this could have been an opening scene for the Twilight Zone because it never arrived. How do I know? I was one of the persons who waited anxiously, not knowing how or if we would arrive home the same day. What happened? Why weren't we picked up?

Sandra Rapchak
Press Enterprise
July 15, 1987

A LIFE

To Edward Newhart:

You are hereby notified to be and appear before the Court of Common Pleas of Columbia County, or to exhibit evidence of the fact that you are alive, on or before the 8th day of April 1929 or a final decree of the Court declaring you legally dead will be made.

BY THE COURT
C. E. Kreisher
Atty. for Petitioner, M25 Ap.1
The Morning Press
April 1, 1929

⊿ THE FATAL DEATH ⊾

To the Editor:

   We are enclosing a poem about our late president. We are only 10 yrs. old. Would you put this in the newspaper. Thank you.

   Love,
   Christine Magill and Betsy Morrison

THE FATAL DEATH

Twas November 22, 1963,
When Mr. Kennedy and Connaly,
Were shot by bullets three.
For Mr. Connaly it was sad,
For Mr. Kennedy just too bad.
Mrs. Kennedy just could not bare
"Jack!, Jack" "No!, No!" was what she declared.
With John only 3, and Caroline, 6.
The news of their father,
Their minds couldn't fix.
He laid in the Rotunda
To stay there in state
So people could come and pay respect
After this terrible fate
They crossed the Potomac
To his favorite spot
Jackie lit an eternal flame
Which will never stop
The world will never forget this man
The 35th president of our land.
   Christine Magill and Betsy Morrison
   The Danville News
   December 14, 1963

"30 Seconds": Utterly Fed Up

I just got home from the mall where I seen this lady breast-feeding. And I have to agree with my boyfriend. It's totally gross and unnatural to see. God gave women breasts for a man's pleasure, not to be used as a portable snack bar. What's next, a public milking demonstration in the cattle arena in the fairgrounds? I mean, what are we, animals, for God's sake?

> Utterly fed-up and disgusted woman
> *Press Enterprise*
> August 20, 1996

If you had spent your high school days in health class instead of a back seat of a car, you'd know what breasts are really for.

> Loving and nursing mom
> Danville
> *Press Enterprise*
> August 27, 1996

Are we not actually animals, mammals at that, whose body is to provide nourishment so we can nurture our young? I believe it is a nice side benefit that the human mammary glands are packaged in such an attractive way.

> Anonymous Caller
> *Press Enterprise*
> August 26, 1996

I'm sure whoever you saw at the mall is very proud that she is feeding her child nature's way. My mother breast-fed me until I was two years old, and it is no coincidence that my SAT scores are over 1300, and I have the fifth highest grade point average in my class.

> Bloomsburg resident
> *Press Enterprise*
> August 28, 1996

Boy, does your boyfriend have you brainwashed. I'd hate to hear what else he says a woman's body parts are for. Unnatural? Get a life, lady.

> Happy nursing mother
> Bloomsburg
> *Press Enterprise*
> August 26, 1996

If I had my way, the welfare mothers that could breast-feed their children, I would have them do so to save our taxpayers a small fortune in baby formula. Which, stating from your grammar and your line of thinking, you will be one.

> Anonymous Caller
> *Press Enterprise*
> August 27, 1996

I totally agree with the "utterly fed-up and disgusted" woman.

> Wilkes-Barre man
> *Press Enterprise*
> August 27, 1996

My theory is you are a homosexual man, couldn't get any, got a sex change and never took the time to learn the basic functions of the female anatomy. You are a disgrace. Get your facts straight and go back to being a man. Or can't you get any that way either? As far as breast-feeding in public goes, as long as you take the time and cover up and respect passers by, what's wrong? It's their pride, not yours.

> Stephanie, Berwick
> *Press Enterprise*
> August 27, 1996

Maybe she should just get rid of her boyfriend. Just to let her know, I breast-fed my children. My daughter now breast-feeds her son. It must be that this girl does not have any children. What does she think happened before they invented formula?

> Letting it all hang out in Bloomsburg
> *Press Enterprise*
> August 27, 1996

To "Utterly disgusted" about breast-feeding: Are you disgusted when you see a dog nurse her puppies or a cat her kittens? Apparently, you don't have your facts right, nor do you have children. If you did, you would know that:
1. We are animals;
2. God did not give women breasts to please men;
3. The most natural thing a mother can do is breast-feed her babies;
4. Formula can cost up to $800 the first year; and
5. Breast milk has more vitamins and helps strengthen the immune system.

As for a public demonstration on milking cows, everyone knows that cows give milk. Where do you think the stores get it?

> Anonymous Caller
> *Press Enterprise*
> August 27, 1996

Corporate America wins again. The formula companies have even a woman believing her breasts are only for a man's pleasure.

> Father of breast-fed children
> Bloomsburg
> *Press Enterprise*
> August 29, 1996

I really don't think they've ever found a Playtex nurser in an archaeological dig.

> Nescopeck woman
> *Press Enterprise*
> August 28, 1996

In 1992, President Clinton declared war on the family. Now we have increased juvenile drug and alcohol use and some women don't know what their breasts are for.

Anonymous Caller
Press Enterprise
August 29, 1996

Has it occurred to "utterly fed-up" that the woman who was breast-feeding the baby used another part of her body in delivering the child in question that she probably also thinks is for the pleasure of men only?

Bloomsburg Man
Press Enterprise
September 1, 1996

My wife and I had a baby and she breast-feeds. And I enjoy her breasts just as much as the baby does. I've learned to share. I think "Utterly fed-up" should too.

Bloomsburg Man
Press Enterprise
September 1, 1996

This is to the utterly fed-up and disgusted woman who believes my breasts are for a man's pleasure. My girlfriend totally disagrees with her.

Anonymous Woman
Press Enterprise
August 27, 1996

Breasts are for feeding? I don't believe it. I've read every issue of *Playboy* magazine and not once did they ever infer such a thing.

Anonymous Caller
Press Enterprise
September 2, 1996

"Utterly disgusted" is living proof that boobs have boobs.

Danville Man
Press Enterprise
September 1, 1996

If God had really given women breasts solely for the pleasure of men, women would have a third breast in the middle of their back for slow dancing.

Slow Dancer
Press Enterprise
September 8, 1996

While at Hess's Tavern on Friday night, August 30, a girl who is well-known locally was bragging about making the prank phone call about the breast feeding in public. She didn't even see anyone breast-feeding, she just called it in to stir up some controversy. Mr. Sachetti, couldn't you see this coming? Enough already.

Anonymous Caller
Press Enterprise
September 9, 1996

We doubt there is a reader of this column who believes that every call is based entirely on fact. A reminder, nonetheless: Take everything you read here with a grain of salt. At the same time, consider this: Fiction has always been every bit as stirring, emotionally and intellectually, as fact. The little vignette by our creative barroom braggart obviously touched a hidden nerve in the community. Getting people to think and react has been the goal of every storyteller since someone sat down to write the first book of the Bible. Her story may have been bogus, but the resulting debate was very real. Make of it what you will.

Editor
Press Enterprise
September 9, 1996

1970

KIDS TELL IT LIKE IT WAS

For once the so-called "experts" who yearly assess the value of the year's news and the "real experts" have an area of agreement in their rating of the top news stories of 1974.

In a letter addressed to "Dear Mr. Morning Press" the members of Miss Eve Krauss' First Grade class at Bloomsburg Memorial Elementary school put the news in proper perspective in the following list of 23 stories.

1. We got a new President—his name is Mr. Ford.
2. Lora's picture was in the paper.
3. Inflation is very bad—it means higher prices.
4. Sugar prices are terrible (my Mom said so).
5. We have "energies" crisis.
6. People had to go to jail because they are in the Watergate trial.
7. Mr. and Mrs. Metro died in a fire.
8. President told awful lies to our whole country.
9. The boy in the bubble can never play outside. He can't get germs.
10. Mr. Rockefeller is so rich that he is now Vice President.
11. People threw sugar in the water instead of tea.
12. President Nixon quit working and so did Vice President Agnew.
13. Patrick had his tonsils out.
14. We talked to Governor Shapp at the railroad— he took our pen.
15. We got a letter from Mrs. President Ford.
16. The Siamese babies were separated.
17. Leslie lost her tooth.
18. Miners stopped digging coal.

AROUND THE WORLD

- Acts of terrorism, unrest in the Middle East, airline hijacking, military coups, government scandals, oil prices, and space flights dominate the headlines throughout the decade.
- The Vietnam War continues. On April 30, 1970, U.S. and South Vietnamese troops invade Cambodia. They leave on June 29.
- In 1971, a worldwide monetary crisis results in the devaluation of the U.S. dollar. In Britain, Rolls-Royce declares bankruptcy.
- At the 1972 Olympic Games, held in Munich, West Germany, eleven members of the Israeli team are murdered by Arab terrorists; five terrorists and a police officer are killed at the airport.
- The United Nations declares 1975 International Women's Year.
- On April 30, 1975, Saigon falls to the Communist army of the North Vietnamese, ending the Vietnam War.
- Steven Biko dies in a South African prison on September 12, 1977. In October, Amnesty International wins the 1977 Nobel Peace Prize.
- In 1978, the first successful birth of a human test-tube baby occurs in England.

19. He had a letter from Governor Shapp.
20. Pollution is getting "worser."
21. Governor Shapp got his job back.
22. Jack Benny died—he was 80 years old.
23. We asked President Ford for some WIN buttons—we didn't get them.

Don't you think we made a good list?

The Morning Press
January 3, 1975

MAIN STREET, BLOOMSBURG, CIRCA 1970.

Dear Editor:

Many of us here in Viet Nam have been following the stories about unrest on the nation's campuses with subdued anger. It is demoralizing to read about our underprivileged counterparts vandalizing campus buildings, manhandling institution leaders, and generally making "asses" of themselves.

It is painful to the thousands of less pampered "students" here who take their lessons from instructors dressed in black pajamas and sandals; where classrooms are sandbagged, hot sweaty jungle clearings; where the Saturday night date is a cold beer and a letter from home; and where the grades are not "A," "B," "C," but sudden death, crippling wounds or maybe victory.

But we don't expect you people back in the world to be concerned. You did your share in '44 or was it '54, and now you're too tired to do more than mutter, "What's this world coming to?"

Well, don't worry people! Because someday this war

is going to be over and half a million angry men are going to descend on the 50 states with dreams of home and families and education and jobs. And when these men hit the campuses, I sincerely hope that someone tries to stop an ex-Marine from going to class, or that some sorry, smelly, flaky, social reject tries to plant a Viet Cong cross next to the artificial leg of a Seabee or spits in the burned face of an Army medic. I guarantee that it will only happen once ! ! ! ! !

> An Unknown Marine
> *The Morning Press*
> June 25, 1970

Dear Sir:

In response to last Thursday's letter from an anonymous marine, a small group of area young people decided to start a letter-writing project to military personnel on the South East Asian front. Obviously, the marine's difficult job is not made any easier by his feeling of being forgotten by home folks, so perhaps the "home folks" must let him know he is not forgotten.

We are calling for volunteer writers of all ages to join us. Also, we would appreciate further names and addresses of service men stationed in the Indo-China area or about to be transferred to or from there. We hope to keep a continuing directory of addresses on such men.

We are also interested in setting up a petition to be circulated in the community protesting the mistreatment of POWs by North Vietnam. This petition will be sent to the President in Hanoi and would inform the North Vietnamese, if only in a small way, that other U.S. citizens besides the direct relations of POWs are concerned about the POWs' conditions and identities.

All inquiries and offers of aid or addresses should be sent to the address below. We hope to hear from you, the reader. Thank-you.

> Several Area Teens
> *The Morning Press*
> June 30, 1970

Time Capsule

AROUND THE NATION

• A 1969 survey taken in Vietnam shows that 53 percent of Army enlisted men admitted using marijuana at least once and one in six said they used it 200 or more times yearly.

• On May 4, 1970, four students are killed and eight wounded by the National Guard at a Kent State protest of the escalation of the war in Southeast Asia. Neil Young writes "Ohio," which is recorded by Crosby, Stills, Nash and Young.

• Dick and Jane and Spot are discontinued by the publisher Scott, Foresman & Company in 1970 because their books are seen as symbols of outmoded teaching methods.

• Beginning on December 1, 1970, the Post Office begins an experimental service in which mail is picked up at the end of the business day, taken directly to an airport, placed on a plane, and reaches its destination in time for delivery next morning.

• In 1973, the Supreme Court decides in the landmark case *Roe v. Wade* that women may choose to abort a pregnancy in the first trimester.

• In 1975, the first American-born saint, Elizabeth Ann Bayley Seton (1774–1821), is canonized.

• On March 28, 1979, a partial nuclear meltdown occurs at the Three Mile Island generating station near Harrisburg, Pennsylvania.

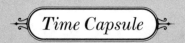

Dear Sir:

I recently received a propaganda pamphlet in the mail concerning various meanings of the "peace symbol." I feel the need to respond to the person who sent it, but as he was unwilling to reveal his identity, I can not talk with him personally.

This pamphlet would have me believe that as a Christian, I should hate and fear all Communists and hippies and I should not work for peace or nuclear disarmament. But I am a Christian and I know what Christ's message was—Love. Love from God for all men—white, black, red, American, Russian, Chinese. No one can earn this love because we are all sinners so it is a free gift—and God gives it to everyone. Jesus also said that all men are my brothers and I must love them as I love myself. So I cannot kill them. Nor can I stand by and let earthly governments destroy God's world in a nuclear holocaust. Anyone who says he is a Christian should work for peace and world harmony, not spread fear and hatred.

Love and Peace to all in Christ.

    Mrs. Paul Xander
    The Morning Press
    November 26, 1970

THE CHANGING ROLE OF NEWSPAPERS

When television and radio beam news and opinion instantly and constantly into every home, what is left for the daily newspaper? A stronger community focus and a renewed commitment to local news and sports are among the answers. The fight for survival leads to further consolidation. By the 1980s, only the *Press Enterprise* (formed from *The Morning Press* and the *Berwick Enterprise*) remains to serve Columbia County, and only *The Danville News* remains in Montour County.

CHAPTER 36

✠ ONE MILLION ✠
YEARS BEHIND

According to the scriptures, Man was placed on earth prior to Women. While no time period is mentioned, I would estimate it to be about a million years. This, of course, means that men are one million years further advanced on the evolutionary scale.

Recognizing this, men have traditionally given their protection, guidance and shelter to these less fortunates. Now a rash of laws have appeared to attempt to equalize the sexes. Should these laws be taken seriously, the only result may be to throw these poor defenseless creatures out into a cruel world to fend for themselves, with disastrous results, I fear.

There are many things women can do well such as baby-sitting, cleaning, cooking and waitressing without attempting the more difficult endeavors which are routinely performed by men.

So I urge you women to be patient in your efforts. Yes, patient for about a million years. As soon as we are convinced that you can handle our tasks, we will gladly assign them to you so that we may go on to even greater and as yet unknown horizons.

Yours truly,
Bill Spahr
The Morning Press
December 11, 1979

I was stunned by the total lack of reason, logic and mere thought that was displayed by this letter from someone who calls himself "advanced" and perhaps even superior. It would be a delight to attack the contents of Mr. Spahr's letter point by point, but that would make my letter much too long, and besides, I feel that the fallacies in his argument are obvious enough.

I would like to make clear my observation, however. Mr. Spahr unquestionably succeeded in disproving exactly what he had apparently intended to prove—the "advancedness" and, dare I say, the overall superiority of MAN. Somehow, in his infinite and advanced wisdom, Mr. Spahr has clearly shown us that his term of "less fortunate" can apply equally as well to individual MEN.

Thanks, Mr. Spahr, but NO THANKS.

Respectfully submitted,
Yvonne M.
The Morning Press
December 14, 1979

In response to Bill Spahr's letter on December 11—Just how did Man reproduce himself for

1,000,000 years? Yet, it is Scripturally true that Woman was created by God after Man had been created.

Here is how it happened.

God decided to create a human being. So God created Man. Then God took a close look at what He had made. Then God said, "Surely I can do better than this! The Man's body is so plain, so dependent on brute strength while biologically weak and unable to reproduce itself. The Man's mind has the potential to function adequately, but he's sorely lacking in the ability to express such emotions as gentleness, tenderness, sensitivity, sadness or meekness. Yes, I'll try again to create a human being. Surely I can do better next time."

So God created Woman. Again God took a close look at what he had made. Then God said, "The Woman's body is beautifully constructed, biologically strong, and able to live longer than the Man's body; it is indeed capable of taking care of itself. The Woman's body is also able to carry within it future generations of offspring in its own likeness. The Woman's mind is well developed. So is her ability to express a wide range of emotions including gentleness, joy, strength, sorrow, anger, delight and love. Yes, I surely have done better this time." And God said, "It is good."

And God was so pleased with his second attempt at creating a human being that never again did He create another sex.

Woman was the crowning glory of all of God's creation.

Diane Schmuck, Millville
The Morning Press
December 14, 1979

Dear Mr. Spahr:

Yes, we will admit that we should be patient, for a million years is a long time to wait. But I am glad to see the evolutionary process is progressing for you.

You have evolved through a number of stages.

You seem to have mastered the first basic step: the skill of manipulating tools (i.e. writing implements) to communicate.

Very good.

The difficult part now is the development of your brain's neocortical regions which are responsible for the cognitive process.

It may be difficult for you to assimilate the following facts, considering your brain's stage of development, but there is no better way than to flood it with new information and stimulus.

May we start by saying that evolution is the development of a species from its original or primitive state to its present specialized state.

According to your theory, that females appeared one million years later on the evolutionary scale, it would mean that they have a greater intellectual capacity.

Don't be afraid Mr. Spahr, for you too can learn to baby sit, cook, and clean. We will be patient with you and try to teach you these things so that someday you can take care of yourself.

Lisa Dixon
Sue Pospisil
Gayle Vassar-Ershov
Betsy Thomas
Kathy Heffner
Sharon Birt
Laurie Creasy
The Morning Press
December 14, 1979

Mr. Spahr:

In answer to Mr. Spahr's letter of 12-11-79, I have the following statements to make to Mr. Spahr:

The need for working women is sometimes necessitated by the fact that their husbands spend their whole day and my paycheck keeping places of business like Spahr's Tavern prosperous. Perhaps you justify this by thinking that you are giving protection, guidance, and shelter to the poor souls who are married to the "less unfortunates" of this world.

Knowing your wife, my sympathy goes out to her in that she must live with a person who has such a low opinion of females.

If you would take time to look at the normal daily routine of a working woman, perhaps you'd change your tune. A working woman not only puts in a full 8 hour day on an outside job, but then must go home and do the cooking, cleaning, washing, ironing, take care of the kids, all before bedtime, and then be willing and able to be a loving, obedient wife to the man of the house.

Ninety percent of the time, the MAN of the house has been sitting on his "duff" just waiting for the "less unfortunate" to cater to his needs. God did not intend for the women of His world to be the slaves of the males. They were created to be helpmates, companions, lovers, mothers and equals. Unfortunately, men of today have forced women into the working world because they can no longer accept the total responsibility of being MEN.

In closing, may I ask you, Mr. Spahr, are you on a personal basis with God, or were you there in the beginning?

One of the less unfortunates,
Bloomsburg
The Morning Press
December 12, 1979

We often wondered why even the most elementary tasks seemed to be beyond the capabilities of our male counterparts. Being one million years beyond us, it is obvious that you have participated in the phenomenon known as evolutionary momentum. That is, you and your fellow men must have reached your peak many, many years ago and are now on the downswing.

Like the dinosaurs of old, brute strength, limited intelligence and unwillingness to adapt to a changing world has hastened your downfall. Due to recent medical and biological advances, it seems that in the near future even reproduction may be possible without your (often inept) assistance.

Lynn Sabin Zelenak, Bloomsburg
Laurie Wiest, Lightstreet
The Morning Press
December 13, 1979

Dear Sir,

Bill Spahr has succeeded in doing what no one else could do. He has gotten the women out from in front of their soap operas and doing something. Bill Spahr has finally made women think. Hats off to Bill Spahr.

Elmer Nast
The Morning Press
December 17, 1979

Look. First he makes a statement that implies a denial of belief in evolution: that man was placed here by God, according to scriptures. Then when it suits him, he suddenly believes in evolution. It doesn't make sense.

What the heck was man doing, alone for a million years? Was he immortal? If he was, he wasn't evolving. And if he wasn't immortal, how did the race survive? Cloning? Maybe mitosis . . .

Jodie Thomas
The Morning Press
December 20, 1979

No further communications in response to Spahr's letter will be published.

Bob Fawcett, Editor
The Morning Press
December 20, 1979

⊠ CATAWISSA ⊠
GALILEO

Three or four years ago because of the setting sun shining in my eyes while eating supper I became aware that the sun was setting further north around Dec. 21, the shortest day when it reverses itself and starts setting further south each day until June 21, the longest day.

When it again reverses and starts setting each day further north.

But each year it (the sun) was setting further north. I talked to my neighbors and found two, Russell Nuss and Charles W. Creasy who had observed the change, too. We had our own ideas what caused this change but agreed that it had not been taking place before the launching of rockets to the moon had started.

This year, during the week of April 9, I was eating supper late and due to the sun shining in my eyes I had to pull my curtain down and use electric to eat by and when I was done with supper and I put my curtain up, the sun was just going down behind the horizon. I got a good fix on the sunset, as well as two nights later when the same thing happened. I did not think about the launching of the rocket to the moon being on April 16. But during the week of April 16, I again got supper ready and thinking I would have to pull my curtain again and started to do so when I found the sun was coming in from much further north and not shining in my face at all, but across in front of me.

By using my transit I found that before the rocket was launched the sun had set at a magnetic needle bearing of N83W from my point of observation and that after the rocket had been launched it was setting at a magnetic bearing of N56W, or a jump of 29 degrees to the north.

As no one was monkeying with the sunset but someone was monkeying with the earth during this time we must admit that it is the earth that has changed positions.

The seasons have been changing since the sunsets have been moving to the north (or the earth moving to the south) and it will be interesting to see what effect this last jump will have on our climate. I think we will have others who will check sunsets before and after the rocket launchings to see how much we have moved with the earth. Hereafter I think this last rocket has been the one using the greatest thrust of any yet and has caused the most movement.

Let's hear from someone else. I am a registered Professor of English 87 years old and have been observing these facts for some years. Maybe this is why I have been observing.

Howard Fetterolf, Catawissa
The Morning Press
June 3, 1971

EARTH DAY

To the Editor,

Earth Day, April 22, 1970, was a day which was set aside for the whole nation to learn about the Environmental Crisis which has befallen the entire world. Bloomsburg was not to be an exception, but it seemed to turn out that way.

We, the students at Bloomsburg State College prepared an exceptionally good Earth Day Program. True, the program was for the BSC students, but moreover it was for the Community of the Greater Bloomsburg Area. We the students of BSC, are only a temporary part of the Bloomsburg environment, but you, the citizens of the area, are permanent members of the environment.

We were hoping to present you the entire ramifications of the environmental problems. Unfortunately, the interested citizens of Bloomsburg must have had too many other things on your minds. . . .

Dear Daniel,

If the people of Bloomsburg did not respond to Earth Day the way you think they should have, it was not because they were not concerned, but because a lot of them were stunned and angry for a reason you don't know about or probably haven't thought of. . . .

. . . Throughout the day, I and the other members of the various committees did not see any more than about ten persons from the community of Bloomsburg. This, to me, is a sign of nothing else but apathy. Let George do it. This is the typical attitude, I am sure. Unfortunately, George alone will not solve this problem. . . .

. . . You see, that Tuesday they had received their new rate sewerage bill. In most cases, the increase was 420% or more! If you will check the going pay scale and industrial wages in Bloomsburg, you will realize that this increase is too much for the average family to bear, especially those with children. People on fixed incomes will be hard pressed. Industry and business are affected, too. . . .

Now, the following day was Earth Day. Can you understand then why Bloomsburg people were not willing or about to go out and campaign for further anti-pollution measures? . . .

. . . Just to cite one problem, statistics prove that by the year 2900 there will be 60 million billion people on the Earth. This is equivalent to 100 persons per square yard. But we don't have to look ahead to 2900. In 2600 the population of the Earth will be about 700 billion people. The total weight of these people will outweigh the total weight of the Earth and it will crumple under their very feet. . . .

. . . I don't have all the facts yet, but I'm told this is the highest charge in the nation for similar facilities. . . .

. . . But again we don't have to worry about this problem. For in only 200 years, 2100, there will be 50 billion people on Earth. It has been proven that with our rates of pollution today the atmosphere of this planet will be unable to handle these people and mankind will cease to exist on this planet. . . .

. . . Something I want you to find out after the next time you walk down Third Street to East over the bumpy road under which lies a new sewer pipe from Elwell Hall, the new 600-man dorm on campus, and later this spring when you see a trench dug on the right side (going down) of East Street into which will go the pipe to the new sewerage plant is just how much of the cost it takes to build and maintain will come from the state and how much will come from the townspeople of Bloomsburg. . . .

. . . Although these statistics are alarming, they are in the distant future. But, we have something right around the corner. Scientists predict that the rate of pollution today and the way it is increasing, all life on Earth will be gone by the year 2000. That is only 30 years away. . . .

. . . Daniel, you might get the idea from this letter that I'm only thinking about money and not putting the "real problem" out front, but I tell you,

with a great deal of honesty, that we have to think about money just to exist, not live high off the hog, but exist in 1970. . . .

. . . Therefore, I implore all you people. Whatever reasons you did not and are not doing anything for the environment, throw them all out the window and begin to take an interest in the future of your children. . . .

. . . I think it's great that young adults like yourself care enough to become involved. On the other hand, I'm telling it like it is. Try to see that, too, for your own sake.

I want you to know also that I am a concerned adult and that more adults than perhaps you realize have thoughts that agree with yours. . . .

. . . You did not participate. Today is another day. Make every day "Earth Day." Let us make the Earth a better place to live in and we will soon, I am sure, begin to enjoy good old Mother Earth once again.

Daniel J. Tearpuck, BSC Student
The Morning Press
April 25, 1970

. . . Talk to them; get to know them and let them know you. We must work together for our survival and with understanding.

Mollie H. Harter, Bloomsburg
The Morning Press
April 29, 1970

Dear Editor:

This is an answer to the B.S.C. student who wrote a letter relative to the apparent apathy of the people of Bloomsburg in the Earth Day "production" put on by the students.

The residents of Bloomsburg are interested, especially those of us who reside at the rear of Elwell Hall. We have observed Earth Day each day since Elwell Hall has been occupied. We are forced to, else we couldn't walk through our yards.

Most of us have resided in this area for years. We took great pride in the quiet, clean appearance of our tree-lined street and well kept yards. Much time, money and energy was expended in keeping it so. We felt we were part of the college campus.

We have been forced to witness the deterioration of this picture. Each day we must gather baskets of trash from our yards and gutters. Whiskey bottles, beer cans, oranges (tossed from windows) and today, a tire, litter the yard; fences are broken down and our curbs are gouged out by the parking of (undergraduate student) cars from Sunday nite to Saturday noon—signs mean nothing. Friends, relatives, doctors, etc. are forced to park blocks away when making calls.

This is representative of only one small section of Bloomsburg—there are many, many more—they were too busy to stop to watch a "production."

Don't you think, young man, that before you criticize, you had best investigate—or do you live in Elwell Hall?

> Sara Krauss
> Mr. and Mrs. Robert Goodman
> *The Morning Press*
> April 29, 1970

MOTHER NATURE

IN A FLASH

On Wednesday the 26th instant, in the afternoon about four o'clock, the lightning struck the house of Mr. Solomon Bast, one mile from the town of Mifflinsburgh, Mifflin township, and killed a boy of about 14 years of age, the son of the late captain George Poh, deceased; and on Friday following, his remains were interred in the burying place in said town.—The circumstances are remarkable. Two neighbors, Mr. Bast, and five small children, were sitting in the same room, when the lightning struck the gable end of the house—the unlucky boy was then sitting by himself, and immediately ceased to exist. The fire flew through the room to the kitchen, where a large brass kettle was hanging over the fire, which at least for the space of a minute seemed to be nothing but a lump of fire, and seemingly went up the chimney, doing happily no other misery.

The Republican Argus
July 10, 1811

JUNE 21–23, 1972

Pennsylvania suffers $2.3 billion in damage and fifty dead. Roads are washed out, bridges destroyed, 210,000 are evacuated from low-lying areas along the Susquehanna River, which crests six feet higher than the previous 1936 record. Hurricane Agnes had developed in the Gulf of Mexico, pushed up the East Coast, and was downgraded to a tropical storm before she met another storm from the west, and parked for three days over the Susquehanna Valley. As the skies open and the river rises, the people of Bloomsburg find themselves in the heart of a disaster of the first order.

FLOOD

I know that there will be many stories come out of the complete devastation here, of Agnes, many longer in significance than that which I have to relate. But I must, as a husband and father, express my gratitude and admiration to

BEFORE AND AFTER: ON JULY 4, 1910, A FIRE DEVASTATES THE
COLUMBIA COUNTY TOWN OF BENTON.

THE AGNES FLOOD IN BLOOMSBURG, 1972.

my wife, Margaret and children (David, Larry, Donna, Brian, Dean) for their wonderful effort in keeping damage to our home to a very minimum.

Beginning 2 p.m., Thursday, June 22, when water began pouring into our lower floor until 2 a.m., Friday (or some 12 hours) without any letup, my wonderful family did everything possible to keep the water from taking over.

They put down blankets on the rugs, bed spreads, towels, anything that would absorb water, stomped on these articles, then picked them up soaked with water and carried them to my wife in the laundry room.

She then ran them through the extract cycle and passed them out to the children who would put them down once again. This was repeated time and time again until everyone was nearly exhausted.

But then at 2 a.m. Friday, the flow of water subsided and the hassle was won. Never at any point did the water get over a half inch over the rugs.

I've estimated that we removed some 2,000 gallons of water, which would have put at least a foot of water in our lower floor, which contains 3 bedrooms.

Our children range from 7 years to 16 years, and at this point can only state that if in these hands our future lies, we have little to be concerned about.

Don J. Smith, Scenic Knolls
The Morning Press
July 1, 1972

BLIZZARD MEMORIES

The notorious blizzard just passed brings a flood of memories to anyone who lived through the winter and spring of 1935–36. At that time I worked out of the old Operations Headquarters of PP&L by the football field. Some names that I still remember— Henrie, Quick, Nevel, Eves, Wireman and Lee. In their very gutsy way they taught me, a naive country boy, a great deal of practical information about dealing with the public.

During that dreadful winter it was my assignment to sign up enough new customers to justify construction of a power line from Eyersgrove to Strawberry Ridge. The minimum charge was to be $4 per month and, believe it or not, about one-third of the residents could not afford that charge. Nor could they borrow money to wire their houses. When the big snow came, everything came to a halt. Snow plows, such as they were, could not cope with the deeper drifts. Gangs of 20 to 40 WPA workers were called on to shovel through the deepest places so the trucks could plow.

After two or three days the road to Jerseytown was opened for limited use so that mail and groceries could be trucked that far. About mid-morning I would put two sets of tire chains on the PP&L Chevy coupe and follow the snow-plow to Jerseytown where I made the tavern of one Benjamin Shultz my operating headquarters. There, too, I was offered much wisdom on many subjects by the worthy patrons. They were quite angry that it had taken so long for them to be offered electric service. After we discussed that for a time we got down to the business of signing contracts and right-of-way easements.

The doctor's office was near the tavern and the school just up the hill. Farmers brought their kids and their milk to Jerseytown in sleds, wagons, and even in manure spreaders. After a few days the road west was opened but, as I recall side roads were closed for days and days. To contact people living off the main road I often waded through snow up to my belt.

During the worst of the travel situation an old person died. To reach the Jerseytown Cemetery a gang of 20 WPA men shoveled for a whole day to open the driveway. That very night the spouse of the one just buried died, also, and the WPA was called once more to open the driveway. That big snow brought on the St. Patrick's Day flood and we, again, have the makings of another flood.

I have so many memories of many, many nice folks, most of the names I have forgotten. I remember Doctor Gordner and Mrs. Ben Schultz, who served delicious and bountiful "lunches" in her spacious kitchen in the back of the tavern. At least two kinds of meat and pie; and all for 35 cents.

To end on a happy note—by the fall of 1936

BLIZZARD, 1936.

the line was energized all the way from Eyersgrove to Strawberry Ridge and a new way of life was opened for those wonderful people.

William C. Wenner, Lewisburg
Press Enterprise
March 27, 1993

OPEN LETTER TO CONGRESSMAN DAN FLOOD

Dear Dan:

Due to the recent emergencies, it is very important that our flood victims who have no home or half a home, get help immediately. I can see through the various agencies that with red tape and insufficient communication, these unfortunate people are going to suffer untold miseries.

I am asking if it is possible to put into escrow at our local banks (x) number of dollars for our flood victims' homes.

I have contacted private contractors who will go street by street and assessors who will go street by street and assess these problems of property damage on the spot so that we can immediately turn cash over to these people to start their recovery of their properties. There will be no overhead, you give the Commissioners (x) number of dollars and every dollar will be spent to good use.

We have been called a farming county, but you are aware that we are hard working people in Columbia County and honest. Get the money to the Commissioners and it will be spent honestly and efficiently.

Hoping to hear from you at your earliest convenience, I remain

Sincerely,
Carl S. "Red" Canouse
Columbia County Commissioner
The Morning Press
July 7, 1972

WE SHOULD BE PROUD

I would like to say a few things about the operation that took place during the flood. First of all, I cannot see how people had the guts to condemn anyone that had to do with the operation. I think they did a great job.

There were people that condemned the Fire Company, the Army men, the way they carried on, but yet these young men were out there risking their lives to save other people and their belongings, and not even getting paid for it.

BLOOMSBURG FAIRGROUNDS, THE AGNES FLOOD, 1972.

They complain about the college. It wasn't the people that were involved in the flood that complained, but those who just sat back and watched. They complained about the young men and women who were out there working just as hard as anyone else.

As far as the Water Company, they were working day and night, doing everything they could to restore the water to customers.

All I can say is that the people of Bloomsburg should be proud that they have a Mayor, town council, chamber of commerce, town police and state police as they have.

No hard feelings,
Herschel Klinger
The Morning Press
July 7, 1972

INTO THE EARTH

Dear Editor:

The heavy ground soaking rains of a few weeks ago are blamed for a situation fraught with danger, now threatening life and limb of West Fifth St., Nescopeck, residents. They tread the ground of their backyards cautiously as long forgotten johnnie holes suddenly appear.

One lady while weeding a newly planted flower bed was frightened out of two pounds weight when a leg suddenly plunged into the earth up to the knees. The Rev. Lynn Brooks, recent pastor of the First Methodist Church, now serving in New Jersey, while tending the manse garden, leaned too heavily on the wrong end of the rake. He fell flat on his face as the handle pierced the dome of what at one time had been an important adjunct of the church premises.

Yesterday I was engaged in removing a hedge planted almost a half century ago to serve as a sort of semi-private screen for one of those pieces of typically American architecture, wholly unimaginative in conception but 100 per cent functional in design when, an ominous rumble underground gave warning that the walls of Jericho were crumbling. I am now advertising for a truck load of head-size rocks.

An interest was added to the excavation in that a pre-Fordian artifact was found, a rusty horse shoe. My wife says she remembers that very horse shoe—it hung above the door as you entered. I wonder why?

West Fifth Street Resident
Berwick Enterprise
May 23, 1959

GROCERIES

Dear Citizens,

During and after the recent flood we have witnessed many acts of self-sacrifice and togetherness in our community. The concerted effort to restore life to normalcy has been encouraging and heart-warming.

Thus it was with great dismay and sadness that on my first post-flood shopping trip to the A&P WEO Supermarket on Market Street I noticed a substantial price increase on many products. There can be no doubt that the management of A&P WEO is taking advantage of the present situation.

After returning the foodstuffs that my family had intended to buy to their proper place on the shelves, I inquired as to why the sudden increase in prices since the flood. An A&P WEO employee responded, "because they are creeps." I presume "they" is the management of A&P WEO.

I wish to assure the A&P management that my experience will be reported to the proper authorities. (located at BSC)

Perhaps the citizens of Bloomsburg can do even more—boycott A&P WEO until foodstuffs return to their pre-flood prices.

With regret,
James S. Ritter, Bloomsburg
The Morning Press
July 12, 1972

1996 FLOOD.

IT'S A BLIZZARD

To Pine Township Residents:

I am married to one of our supervisors. The recent blizzard has confirmed my thoughts that some people are sadly lacking common sense and have no thoughts for anyone but themselves.

The interstates and most every road was closed due to the storm and people were urged by government officials at the state level not to travel, yet my telephone was frequently ringing with people complaining that their road wasn't plowed.

For goodness sakes, people, it's a blizzard!

My husband left our home at 8 a.m. on Saturday morning to get started working on the roads. He returned home Sunday at 11 p.m. to sleep. Saturday night he was stranded at the township building—luckily the township road foreman lived within walking distance.

While other townships and municipalities were closing their roads late Saturday afternoon and early evening our road crews were still working. They finally stopped at 1 a.m. Sunday to rest.

I know there will likely be criticism of this let-

WINTER OF 1996.

ter by numerous township residents who believe that the road crews deliberately neglected their road.

Residents need to have realistic expectations as to the amount of time necessary for snow removal after a storm especially one of this magnitude. With many miles of roads to clear and cinder it is unrealistic to expect all roads to be cleared instantly after the last snowflake hits the ground!

There is much more to plowing snow than getting into a truck, dropping the blade and driving.

Last but not least is the safety aspect. As of 9 p.m. Saturday when the storm was at its worst, I had no idea where my husband was or if he was safe. Our township trucks are equipped with ra-

dios, but the road crews were not responding to calls by the township secretary. It is a very helpless feeling not knowing if the men were safe. I'm quite sure many of you would have been worried if it was your family member out in the storm.

Please remember, these men are doing the best job they can in extremely adverse conditions. Also remember they are human—they still need to eat and sleep. If an accident occurs due to the crew being fatigued, injuries and damage to the township equipment only slows down the process.

Please, folks, use your heads and be realistic about this issue. If you think it is an easy task try it! While I've addressed this letter to my home township, I'm sure the issue I've raised is applicable in every township across the area.

Terri Reichenbach
Press Enterprise
March 25, 1993

P.S. It's 9 p.m. Monday, my husband is out plowing your road, where's your spouse?

AFTERMATH

Dear Sirs:

I would like to tell anybody who is interested that we people in Fernville who were in the flood got a tax rebate last week.

I got $1.14. My sister-in-law got a check for 63 cents. My neighbor got 98 cents and his brother got 45 cents.

I think it cost more to hire somebody to make out the checks and pay the postage. I paid $250.65 last year.

Do they think that $1.14 cents means anything?

If they would have used that money to put up at least one street light it would have made more sense.

Lucy Kingston
The Morning Press
January 17, 1974

FLOOD, 1904.

CHAPTER 40

ᴀ FAITH ᴁ

MY OWN CONSCIENCE

Editor Sentinel:

I have been so often asked in stores and on street corners, which is the most useful: Infidelity or Christianity. This seems to be a favorite chestnut of the church. I am an Infidel myself. I want to know whether I am to worship God according to the dictates of my own conscience or whether I am to worship according to somebody else's conscience.

Thomas Paine, Thomas Jefferson, Benjamin Franklin were all Infidels and they done more for mankind than all the churches ever did. It was such men that rid the country of king and priest and had it not been for such men the church would have been killing and roasting witches yet. The church can scorn an Infidel, but I would rather be an Infidel than a paper idolater.

Now let me say, Mr. Krickbaum please print this article whether it agrees with your religious opinions or not. Help me to my just rights— free speech and free press. This right was dedicated to each individual and your subscribers should remember that your subscriptions are from varied religions. There is no use of each man having a press of his own, let the press be free, let the error have its way and reason free to combat it and if you do I will be buried inside the yard yet. It was the intentions of the Fathers of the Republic that I should.

Written Jan. 7th in the 119th year of the American Republic. Benton, Pa.

Geo. R. Hess
Democratic Sentinel
January 18, 1895

OPEN YOUR EYES

I'm calling about the Mifflinburg man who claims that we're religious zealots because we want God back in our schools. Let me tell you something, mister. You're probably one of them uneducated morons that come out of the present-day education system. Undoubtably, you don't have any brains more than an ant. If you do, you don't know where they're at. Secondly, our country was founded on Christianity principles, not Hindu, Muslims, or any of you other morons. Now let me tell you another thing, mister. This country has been going totally to hell. And the only way to salvage it is to get God back into society. You don't like that, that's too bad. But that's the way it is. Open your eyes and see the blessings that we're missing in this country.

Anonymous Caller
30 Seconds
Press Enterprise
February 16, 1996

INTERIOR OF FIRST PRESBYTERIAN CHURCH,
BLOOMSBURG, CIRCA 1905.

MY LITTLE SHARE

DANSALAN, LANAO, PHILIPPINES
FEB. 1, 1931
My dear Father,

After a trip to the warm lowlands I am back in the cool invigorating air of Lanao, determined to make life an endless succession of wonderful hours. Nothing, it seems to me, is wrong excepting to be miserable and to make others miserable spiritually. Nothing is right excepting to live wonderfully and to help others to live wonderfully. God is pulsating in the very atmosphere around us all the time, aching to give himself to us. It does not matter what happens to us, whether we are sick or well, successful or penniless, we can still have Him.

And yet—yet—one cannot well feel that way unless one has the right vitamins! One CAN, probably, but most people do not, unless they have the spiritual energy plus the physical energy to feel optimistic.

But we are going to have the right feeds in this world. The machine age is going to give them to us. Machinery is going to make the world overflow with abundance. The question of sufficient food, shelter, clothing, will be solved.

Our real question is whether we can learn to be thrillingly happy in this new world of comforts, or whether we shall find ways to make one another miserable. Machines must be supplemented by the will to be beautiful.

The new note to be struck all over the world is this: Eat the food, form the habits, think the thoughts, show the kindness, that will make all lives vibrant with joy. Listen for music in nature and in human souls. Where there are groans strive to change them to songs.

Many of the books we had to read in philosophy said that nobody could find happiness by looking for it. You found it when you sought duty, so the books said. I think now that this is nonsense, though it does contain a truth. As an individual I cannot find happiness by looking for it ALONE. Nor can I find anything else alone—food, books, clothing, automobiles. Working with the rest of humanity to produce my little share of these things I can also have my share of all these things for myself. Happiness is the same way. If we cooperate in a quest for the highest, most lasting forms of happiness, then we shall find it together. Much of our enjoyment shall be collective—parks, radios, talkies, baseball games. We learn to enjoy things which once learned, give keenest delight. Masterpieces of music, literature, painting, and especially the peculiar delight of seeing others enjoying themselves.

John Calvin thought that God made hell so that the fortunate ones who went to heaven would then be happier when they realized how much worse off the damned were than themselves. It is one of the meanest ideas ever expressed in the name of religion—and there have been plenty of others!

As for me, I mean to rule out hell, here and hereafter. I admit it is still here. It is in the starvation of China, the terrorized slavery of women, the hatreds that people nurse, the habits which suck the life out of people. But our business is to stamp out hell wherever we find it. With the aid of machines this can be done, if we breed and educate a race that will use its powers for mutual happiness. This is the most hopeful age we have ever seen, for we are nearer the goal of human happiness than ever before.

But having ruled out hell, one wonders whether one can rule out the devil. I have seen something devilish at work in so many people of late. . . .

Dear Me! Starting out with happiness as our goal and arriving here! Is this too the devil's work?

Which leads me to one more observation. One requirement for perfect happiness is the ability to laugh at one's self.

The Moros were greatly pleased at the fact that we published the first Sura of the Koran in our paper this week. It is, I think, appropriate for any religious service. What could be nobler than these words:

> "In the name of God,
> The compassionate, the merciful!
> Praise be to God, Lord of the worlds!
> The compassionate, the merciful!
> King on the day of Judgement!
> Thee only do we worship.
> And to thee do we cry for help!
> Guide us in the straight path,
> The path of those to whom thou art gracious,
> With whom thou art not displeased
> And who go not astray."

I have not quite come to the point of opening our service with that beautiful psalm, for perhaps some of our members might object. But is there a more beautiful psalm in the Old Testament?

Affectionately,
Frank Laubach
with the American Board of Missions
The Philippines
The Benton Argus
April 9, 1931

Dr. Frank C. Laubach (1884–1970) was born in Benton, Pennsylvania. In 1912, he went to the Philippines as a Congregationalist missionary, but finding that the native peoples had no written language and could not read the Koran, the primary scripture of their own Islamic faith, he was inspired to make worldwide literacy his real mission. He developed "Each One Teach One" literacy materials for 312 languages in 103 countries, reaching about 70 million people in Asia, Africa, Latin America, as well as the United States. His many letters to *The Benton Argus* have been collected and published, along with his sermons and speeches on prayer, peace, and justice. Other books by this "Apostle of Literacy" include *The Silent Billion Speak* and *The Laubach Way to Reading.* Laubach Literary International in Syracuse, New York, continues his work. In 1988, Dr. Laubach was commemorated on a U.S. postage stamp.

Lord's Prayer in our school system. A motion passed unanimously with all members present, voting yes.

Our forefathers came to America so they could worship as they wished. When a person takes an oath, he places his hand on the Bible. We also see on our coins "In God We Trust." Indeed, America is a "great nation." By taking the Bible away, we are losing our American heritage and we cannot afford to be a godless nation, can we? Of course not. We do not burn our Bibles in America and our children certainly need to know about God at an early age.

The youth of our nation who are our future leaders are now threatened by the recent action of the Supreme Court. As president of the Central Joint Board, I wish to congratulate my fellow board members on their stand. "God Bless America."

Boyd C. Laycock
The Morning Press
August 19, 1963

Dear Sir:

As an inveterate reader of "Letters to the Editor" columns, I have been both delighted and appalled with the public response to the Supreme Court decision on Bible reading in the public schools. Indicative of most of the letters on the issue was Mr. Laycock's.

Mr. Laycock implies that our youth is doomed or at least threatened by the Supreme Court action. Since the steady increase of juvenile delinquency and childhood marriages was accomplished during "Bible-reading" years, it would appear that the moral effect of such reading has been negligible. Somehow, the Bible, the most beautiful piece of literature in Western culture, loses something when ten verses are read out of context by an amateur who seldom grasps the meaning and importance of what he is reading. Somehow the Lord's Prayer, that most beautiful supplication, loses something when pronounced in dull rep-

1988 FRANK C. LAUBACH 30-CENT
U.S. POSTAGE STAMP.

CHURCH AND STATE: 1963

As president of the Central Columbia Joint School Board, I wish to make clear to the public that at our regular meeting held August 5, 1963, the entire board composed of six districts acted upon the matter of Bible reading and the

etition morning after morning until meaning is lost and only words remain. This cheapening of something so great, so pure, so inspiring probably does more harm than good.

With the freedom to believe comes the freedom to doubt. The Supreme Court is to be congratulated for making it easier for the American student to do both.

David Laubach
The Morning Press
August 24, 1963

EVANGELIST, CIRCA 1910.

Dear Sir:

It was with dismay that I read that a few of the School Boards in our county have ordered their administrators and teachers to violate the law of the land and thereby teach civil disobedience to the children and young people under their authority. As an ordained Minister of the Gospel I have given my life to the teaching and proclamation of the Word of God as found in the Bible. As an elected public official serving on a school board I have taken an oath to support, obey and defend the Constitution of the United States of America. The Supreme Court of the United States has the final authority in interpreting the Constitution of this nation and the Supreme Court has declared that it is unconstitutional to require the reading of the Bible or the recitation of prayer in the Public Schools as a part of a required religious exercise.

Regardless of how one may personally feel about the decision of the Court, this is now the law of the land. In our free and democratic society the Constitution of the United States may be amended by due process if the majority of the citizens of the nation feel that a change should be made. No citizen or group of citizens has the right or authority flagrantly to violate the Constitution as it is interpreted by the Supreme Court.

The cause of religion is not served when the Bible is made a political football. The Bible itself requires of us obedience to the governing authorities and the magistrates. (Romans 13:1–2 and Titus 3:1) No one is more concerned than I that the Bible be respected and that children and adults revere the Word of God. When one uses the Bible to break the law, it becomes an object of derision and contempt. If one does not agree with Constitution, then let him proceed in the proper way to try and have it amended but let us as school directors not break the oaths we have taken before God and the people by encouraging our children to have disrespect for the law of the land.

Rev. Robert C. Angus
School Director
Bloomsburg School District
The Morning Press
September 3, 1963

A FLOWER IN THE PATH OF LIFE

In an editorial printed in *The Sunbury and Northumberland Gazette* of April 27, 1799, Thomas Cooper lambasted President John Adams for proclaiming a general fast, claiming that such an action was "not within the pale of the President's constitutional authority" and united "two subjects which in my opinion ought never to be joined together, POLITICS and RELIGION."

A response was written by Elizabeth Priestley, whose father-in-law was Joseph Priestley, the English chemist who discovered oxygen in 1774. The Priestleys had emigrated to the United States in 1794 to escape persecution for their Unitarian beliefs. They settled in Northumberland, Pennsylvania, where the Priestley home is now a historic site.

I propose on all occasions to keep this paper open to both sides of every question of importance; and I cannot give a better proof of my intentions than by inserting the following answer to my own observations. I am sure my readers will agree, that if my remarks were ill founded, I could not have received a more good-tempered or elegant refutation of them.

The EDITOR
The Sunbury and Northumberland Gazette

Mr. Editor,

PERMIT me to send you a few comments respecting the late Fast.

That the observance of a Fast was merely recommended by the President, cannot I think admit of doubt, since the constitution vests him with no power to appoint them, and no penalty is consequent on non-observance.

I see no ground for the alarm you manifest of an alliance of Church and State from this assumption (as you would call it) on the part of the President. In calculating the probable consequences of public acts, the spirit of the times is an important consideration. In the present day, when religion has lost and continues to lose ground, and when infidelity with dauntless front makes rapid strides among us, we need be under no apprehension of the State seeking so old fashioned a coadjutor as the Church. The spirit of the times is a pledge of security on this score.

That the President should recommend industry and attention to commerce, to agriculture, to education, or to objects of public utility in general, would be considered fit and laudable. On what principle, then, can it be thought unbecoming in him to recommend religious exercises, which he may deem equally important in promoting the welfare of society? If no compulsory means are used to enforce their observance, and every person is free to follow the dictates of his own mind, where is the reasonable ground of complaint? And when the interests of religion are visibly declining, I think it highly desirable that influential characters should manifest their respect for it.

Jesus Christ, you observe, says his kingdom is not of this world. It is true that its rewards and punishments are not; but it will not be denied that the object of it, which is to render men more virtuous and useful, concerns this life; and religious acts may be fairly considered as a means to this ends. Whatever promotes friendly intercourse between man and man and calls the kind affections into play, is as favorable to virtue as to pleasure; and a holiday of this kind is, to the mass of the people, a flower in the path of life: a sentiment in which I dare say you will agree with me.

You entertain fears that this example may induce future Presidents, with less respect for religion, to make it subservient to purposes of state intrigue; I have no apprehensions of this kind. The mere garb of piety will not go far in this country. The people have too much good sense, and too little predilection for religion, to be deceived by it.

If, Mr. Editor, you think the above remarks are worth inserting in your paper, they are much at your service.

E. P.
Northumberland, Pennsylvania
The Sunbury and Northumberland Gazette
May 4, 1799

HOW CAN IT BE?

Messrs. Editor:

You will permit me, through your columns, to make a few remarks about a sermon delivered in Grace Church, New York, by Rev. Dr. Hare, on Sunday the 2nd day of April, 1871. Gentlemen, the foundation of the Jewish faith is "Love thy neighbor as thyself"; the same words Christ said should be the foundation of the Christian faith. The minister of Grace Church must have forgotten this on the 2nd day of April; we find in this sermon this most abominable sentence: "The Jews would think it wrong to steal from a brother Jew, but right from a Gentile." How can it be, in the nineteenth century, in this blessed land of freedom, that such a man is permitted in a church filled with intelligent persons to poison the hearts of his congregation by such a disgraceful statement? It is not only an injustice to the Jews, but a disgrace to Christians, and a slander to Christ, who was born of a Jewish mother.

What an injustice to Christ himself, that God, the Almighty, could not find, in this whole world, a maiden, except one coming from a nation of thieves and robbers, to bear His beloved Son! God's commandment was "Thou shalt not steal." It does not say from a Jew or Gentile. Our laws are plain, for they say, "The stranger who comes in thy land shall have the same right with you and one law is to govern all." It almost seems that some Christian ministers can find no more solid arguments in behalf of the religion which they preach, than in lowering sister religions in the estimation of their hearers. Christian preachers should consider that a degradation of the Jewish religion is a degradation of the mother of the Christian faith.

A Jew
The Montour American
May 11, 1871

ALL OVER THE WORLD

The writer having an invitation to visit the Quaker settlement about ten miles from Bloomsburg April tenth to speak, found the people waiting the arrival of the man of African descent. Their treatment religiously, socially and politically, without the notice of cast, is highly commendable, which made me think a man is a man all over the world if he behaves himself.

Yours truly,
W. H. Palmer
Pastor of Bloom. Church
The Bloomsburg Journal
April 20, 1881

ON THIS PLANET

On May 22 of this year, President Reagan issued a statement about persecution of Bahais in Iran and urged the Iranian government to halt the planned execution of the Bahais. Khomeini, the head of the Iranian revolutionary government, in reply expressed that the Bahai faith is not a religion.

This opens an interesting subject—he is not the only one that does not believe in other religions. On this planet, there are about 15 million Jews who do not believe that Jesus Christ is the Son of God; there are about 500 million Buddhists and over 330 million Hindus that do not believe in Moses and his faith; and even among 500 million Moslems of the world, 90 percent do not believe in Ali, the son-in-law of Mohammed, as the first guardian after Mohammed, as Iranian "Shiite," a brand of Moslems, believe.

Among all of these religions, the Bahai faith is the only one that believes that Jesus, Moses, Mohammed, Buddha, all had been sent as messengers of God to guide the human race.

Moeen Kiani
Press Enterprise
October 20, 1983

INTERIOR OF ST. PAUL'S EPISCOPAL CHURCH, BLOOMSBURG, 1907.

INTERIOR OF ST. MATTHEW'S LUTHERAN CHURCH, BLOOMSBURG, CIRCA 1910.

BETTER UNDERSTANDING

Dear Editor,

I'm writing in behalf of the editorial written by the Paulist Fathers.

I, as a Catholic, enjoy these articles and I believe that my many Protestant friends enjoy them also as they will get a better understanding of my religion. Many things which are misunderstood are explained clearly.

Please continue these Paulist Editorials. Will be looking forward to reading them.

Lorraine Lovecchio, Sec'y
Parish Council of Catholic Women
St. Joseph's Church
Berwick Enterprise
August 28, 1957

MORE

Thank you for giving us more religion world news lately.

Everyday we get pages and pages of politics, sports, economics, crime, social life, etc.; pages and pages of this every day.

Well, religion can play a great part in world peace which is important to all of us. So please tell us just a little about such things.

We young folks are more interested than you may think. Our lives are at stake. Do hear us pleading.

J. M. for A NICE BUNCH OF KIDS
Press Enterprise
February 15, 1983

THE STILL, SMALL VOICE OF GOD

We all ponder over conditions about us. We have glue-sniffing in our community, militancy in our state organizations, confusion in our national policies, and havoc abroad. Why?

The pieces of life seem to fit together like a giant puzzle, but there is one piece missing and that piece is personal integrity. If we have integrity in every little thing, aren't we promised integrity in each big thing?

This is an individual responsibility and it comes back to each one of us.

Now is the season to strive for integrity—the beautiful season of the Passover and the Resurrection—for isn't integrity just listening to the still, small voice of God?

Jacqueline S. Creasy
The Morning Press
March 28, 1968

☒ HUMAN NATURE ☒

About Judge Thomas: Now here is a man divorced from his first wife, probably lonesome, taking his right-hand helper that he worked with home, having a few beers, talking sex with her—now there is nothing wrong with this. But he should have tried a couple of shots of moonshine, it always works better. But he denies he talked sex or said anything out of the way. I don't believe him. This is not human nature. The one letter said they talked about business 99 percent of the time. I wonder what they talked about in the other one percent of time. Maybe monkey business. I've lived almost 84 years on this earth and I seen a lot of this kind of business going on. I got to know human nature pretty well.

CHARLIE KARNS AT AGE NINETY.

But I always thought that sex is something between two people, man and woman, who love each other. Not to be thrown around like a dirty dish rag. I think Anita Hill was telling the truth. She took a lie detector test and passed but Judge Thomas didn't. I don't think he would of passed it. What Anita Hill was put through by senators especially Arlen Spector who all had a skeleton in their closet as Ted Kennedy was shameful.

The three women who came to his defense and said they worked around Judge Thomas and he never made a pass at them or said anything out of the road to them. Well the first lady from Chicago talked too much, if he would of got mixed up with her she would have talked him to death. Then there would have been no Judge Thomas. The second lady, a little black lady, put me in a mind of a little dog we had always barking and yuping at people. The third lady had a face like a bull dog. I have a Rottweiler dog that was better looking than her. I have to give Judge Thomas credit, he knows how to pick good looking women. Look at the beautiful white lady he married.

Charlie Karns, Millville
Press Enterprise
November 2, 1991

⊿ No Harm ⊾
Is Meant

To the 72-year-old who called 30 Seconds saying he worked, went to school and played with blacks and all others, and feels qualified to judge the level of racism in Bloomsburg, a few facts:

- _Blacks were not allowed to join the fire company._
- _Blacks were not allowed to buy burial space at Elan until the latest managers took over._
- _Blacks were not allowed to buy Fair shares like their fellow employees at the carpet mill._
- _After graduating from the high school and BSC my sister was told Bloomsburg was not ready for a black teacher._
- _After attending Sunday School a letter was sent to a black family stating you have your own church, go to it. . . ._

Our observations of the Negroes character shows us plainly that they are not capable of self-government and history teaches the same. Our northern towns are pestered enough with black vagrants now. And the equal distribution of nearly four millions of Negroes through the whole of the States, would be a nuisance almost unendurable, and to give them equal rights among us, and amalgamate them with the whites at the ballot box, and in our legislative halls, or place one in the Presidential Chair, would be destroying the pride and self-respect of the Nation.

The Negro is naturally adapted to slavery. Give them liberty and they are indolent and lazy. There are several hundred of them here that have the benefit of the president's Proclamation and some of the most intelligent of them acknowledge that their condition was better in slavery, than the way it is. I have heard them say it.

A Soldier
Columbia Democrat
May 23, 1863

I've no doubt racism exists, but I want these people who expressed themselves to know that not all white people are bigoted and that there are many in our community who feel as I do; namely, that the color of our skins has nothing to do with our worth as individuals. Before moving to this area I lived in a predominantly black neighborhood and found many of the people there to be wonderful, good citizens.

If there is anything that we as Bloomsburg citizens can do to make you feel more welcome, let us know. I for one feel our community is a better place because people of all backgrounds are in it.

We can choose to segregate ourselves by referring only to labels such as black, white, Oriental, etc. Or we can put them aside and realize we are all brothers and sisters and sons and daughters of our Father in Heaven. The choice is ours.

Cindy Sanford
Press Enterprise
May 12, 1989

. . . The church secretary did apologize in later years and said the church board and minister told her to write the letter.

After announcing their engagement, the family of a black couple received several vicious letters with words like "mongrel children" and "kill the groom." It seems they were thought to be a mixed couple. . . .

I am commenting about the Virginian who commented about the fat people in Pennsylvania. I totally agree. There are just too many fat people. They are just disgusting. I think they should all go to a fat farm.

Anonymous Caller
Press Enterprise
September 1, 1992

I attend Bloomsburg High School and my complaint is that some teachers at school are going around saying not to come to A CHORUS LINE because who wants to watch a bunch of players act like gays. There is only one character in the play that is gay and not in real life. I wish teachers and faculty would stop going around telling students not to attend our play.

Anonymous Caller
Press Enterprise
March 24, 1992

Christian ministers should not forget that the Christian religion is based and founded upon the Jewish religion and that without the Jewish prophets, Jewish morality, and Jewish commandments, the Christian religion would lack all reason of existence and all claims to divine origin would vanish into nothingness. Christian ministers belittling the Jewish religion display their own ignorance and lack of appreciation for truth and justice.

> A Jew
> *The Montour American*
> May 11, 1871

Over the past few months on a lot of talk shows there have been a lot of strange people with different problems who claim they are coming out of the closet. Homosexuals. Lesbians. Transvestites. And child abusers. I mean, what is the world coming to? If anyone knows where this closet is could they please call me so I could go blow it up because God only knows what is going to come out of it next.

> Espy Man
> *Press Enterprise*
> September 5, 1992

The Jewish Bolshevik Revolution in Russia resulted in the murder of 66 million Christians from 1918–1957. Karl Marx was a German Jew born to Jewish parents in 1818. Lenin, in some literature, is described as a Kalmuck Jew. In 1920, the so called Russian government was 90 percent Jewish. Let me know if you want some reading material with the truth.

> Bloomsburg man
> *Press Enterprise*
> September 5, 1996

Why don't you people of the press ask those who served in Viet Nam what they think of those "slant eyes"? I spent a year there and everyday I had the local people tell the G.I.'s to go home, they didn't want us over there. I feel the same way about their coming here.

If the people of the United States are suckers enough to donate food, housing, cars and jobs to those Slant Eyes then those same people deserve to get burnt. The only thing I would like to donate to any one of the Slant Eyes is a bullet between the eyes. Sign me,

> A Vietnam Vet
> *Saturday/Sunday*
> July 28–29, 1979

Bloomsburg is a German name and all German names must be dropped and real American names substituted.

Though Bloomsburg has a population of thousands, consider its anti-American name with a "burg" at the end.

Do not be outdone by real patriots who have done away with all things German. Down with the germ of Germanism!

Patriots of all Orders
The Morning Press
January 6, 1925

My Dear Sir:—

The slogan of "Freedom" has brought the oppressed toilsmen of Europe here; and we ask only a cot for a home, and a chance to earn an honest living by the sweat of our brow. We seek not to subsist in luxury or by speculation upon the hard earnings of others. Many are unlearned, except in the promptings of an honest mind, and the experience of the oppressed, and all are so unused to the manners, customs and arts of the land as to be incapable of plots, stratagems and conspiracies. We know of no oath more solemn or binding than that of fidelity when we adopt republican America as our country. Our countrymen, our parents, brethren and children are here, and we have nothing to look for but their happiness and ours, in the prosperity of the republic, and the perpetuity of its institutions. If we are treated as citizens, our children will grow up with grateful recollections. Only a spirit of intolerance and bigotry can ever make them remember that they have any feature of character distinct from the mass of the million.

I have been told by Know-Nothings that they have no "hard feeling" toward Irishmen, and are only opposed to the "Dutch"—my German neighbor is told that only the Irish are to be proscribed—Catholics are told that only foreigners are to be put down, and foreign Protestants that the opposition is only to Catholics. And then at the end, all of us are informed that no harm is meant to us.

From a Catholic
The Star of the North
September 21, 1854

. . . So until you go to a restaurant and the waitress says we don't serve niggers; until you buy a drink and they break the glass; until you have to go to the dentist, the beauty parlor after hours or the back door to buy food at an eating place, or apply for a job and the boss asks the other workers if they care if a black works there . . . until then, I don't feel you're qualified to say what the conditions for blacks in Bloomsburg are or have been.

Isabel Tarr
Press Enterprise
March 24, 1992

ISABEL TARR.

⊿ YOUR NEXT-DOOR ⊾
NEIGHBOR

There have been many articles recently in the *Press Enterprise* in regards to perpetrators of childhood sexual abuse and the judicial decisions in each individual case.

On Oct. 19, when I picked up the *Press Enterprise* and once again this topic was in print, I felt compelled to write.

The article that I am referring to is the one describing this recent plea agreement. Under this agreement this woman would spend at least 30 days in jail. It is my understanding that it is likely that she will spend only 30 days in jail and then serve the rest of her sentence on probation. When I see sentences like this being handed down from our judicial system, I become enraged—because I am a survivor of sexual abuse.

It seems to me that the forgotten ones in this recent case are the children who were victimized. Everyone conveniently forgets that, while the perpetrators receive 30 days to five years in jail (with very good chances for only probation), the victim/survivor gets the life sentence. Everyone, except the victim can easily forget, in a little while, what has happened. But the victim/survivor can never forget. No, my perpetrator was never charged nor sentenced for what he did to me, and I must struggle daily just to survive.

I must pay for the counseling that has become a rather permanent part of my life. Believe me, I have other things that I would much rather spend my hard-earned dollars, but counseling is a necessity, not a luxury. I am the one who must worry each time I go out of my house if I will have to face my abuser. I am the one who must live with the pained looks on my families when I talk about my abuse. I am the one who is left to deal with the psychological aftermath in whatever way I can, while my perpetrator goes on his merry way.

I also believe that there are many who will never be able to call themselves survivors because they found the battle of surviving to be too much and are now dead. Think about all those who commit suicide, or overdose on drugs and/or alcohol—could it be that they were victims who were trying to kill the pain of sexual abuse? I understand why they wanted to die because I, too, wanted to die. It seemed like the only way that the pain, caused by my abuse, would ever go away. But I'm one of the fortunate victims. I've gotten very good help from many places.

As a survivor, I can't sign my name to this letter because too many people would recognize my name and undoubtedly be shocked and want to know who the perpetrator of my abuse was. All I can tell you is that he lives right in our community and has been confronted by my family. We keep his name to ourselves because he would make my life even more difficult than it already is. Just remember, he could be your next-door neighbor, your local policeman, your clergyman, etc.; so please, please, people, protect your defenseless children. Next time you read an article about a perpetrator of child sexual abuse, say a prayer for the victim. The victims need to know that someone remembers them.

 Name Withheld
 Press Enterprise
 November 6, 1993

CHAPTER 44

✎ "30 MORE ✍ SECONDS"

Did anybody watch David Letterman, Friday, July 8, and see that guy drank milk up his nose and it came out his eye? How did he do that?

Anonymous Caller
Press Enterprise
July 12, 1994

In response to the semi-literate religious fanatic claiming that Mideast religions are Satan worship. I'm a practicing Satanist and as far as I know, we're in no way affiliated with Hindus, Muslims, or the Psychic Friends Network. Just want to clear up that misconception.

Anonymous Caller
Press Enterprise
August 12, 1995

I'm not an area native, but I feel this needs to be said. Pat Buchanan is the man to vote for. His ideas are ahead of their time. He wants us to unify under his foresight and rally to rule the world. Because we're better than the rest and anybody else. We are Americans. I also understand he supports the purchase of Alaska and hopes it will be a state someday.

Vermonter Passing Through
Press Enterprise
March 6, 1996

I would like to address the Berwick R.R. 4 woman who complained about cow manure on holidays, weekends and washdays. If you have lived in the country for 20 years, you must understand that cows do produce manure. And this is life in the country. If it bothers you that much, I suggest you buy some Pampers and go over to the dairy farm and put them on the cows. Good luck. My husband and I have cows as well and you're welcome to try it at our place, too.

Bloomsburg Woman
Press Enterprise
August 4, 1995

To the nice family who came and adopted mama and her three kittens. We think about them and wonder if you could put a notice in 30 Seconds and tell us how they are doing. We hope they are all well.

> Briar Creek Couple
> *Press Enterprise*
> October 20, 1997

When we first marry and learn to can, we use the open kettle method, just a few pints at a time. As our family grows, we use the canner method, eight quarts at a time. When we become senior citizens, we go back to canning three or four pints at a time and are so happy to hear each lid snap shut, we could joyously go out and say "my lid snapped" but afraid our neighbors might agree.

> Anonymous Caller
> *Press Enterprise*
> September 3, 1996

I'm calling about the sneezing in the paper. I, too, am that way and when I read your paper I sneeze and sneeze. I have some of my neighbors says so. It must be in your ink or something that you are using. I don't know what it is, but it really has us worked up here when you read the paper. Besides that the ink rubs off on your clothing as you read the paper. Thank you.

> Millville woman
> *Press Enterprise*
> January 12, 1993

Speaking about your paper. It gets very boring at times. Try to put articles of interest in, life

CITIZENS BAND, 1911.

history, science, maybe a couple of short stories and maybe people would think differently about your paper. Have a good day.

Beach Haven man
Press Enterprise
January 11, 1993

Having survived more than 72 years, I've seen quite a bit. I can recall many meals of stewed tomatoes and boiled potatoes during the Great Depression. I have vivid memories of more than three years during World War II, from here to Japan and, thank God, back home. I've watched folks suffer the ravages of floods and droughts and fires. But the woman whose daughter had to make do with a plain Band-Aid at Geisinger [Medical Center] because there weren't any with cartoon characters, your story has touched my heart. By damn, you and your family have known hardship.

Anonymous Caller
Press Enterprise
June 29, 1996

This is to the Bloomsburg woman about getting her services hooked up. You should have someone you trust come over to your place, give them all your information and write a note that explains everything. Maybe that can help you get your services turned on if you are not available to be home at that time.

Nescopeck Woman
Press Enterprise
March 2, 1996

THE ABCS

Education in the deepest sense is continuous and lifelong and in essence, unfinishable. What we think we know is often less helpful than the desire to learn. If parents and teachers stifle a child's curiosity by teaching rote, trying to pour information into the child's head, they have failed in the most important job in the world, forming our children into thoughtful, knowledgeable and responsible adults.

> Benton Woman
> 30 Seconds
> *Press Enterprise*
> July 12, 1994

RULES AND REGULATIONS

To those whom it may concern the following rules and regulations are proposed for their due observance.

Imprimus: The scholars shall during the summer season, meet at the schoolhouse, precisely at 8 o'clock; and in the winter at nine, (that is) when the days are longer than the nights, they shall meet at eight; and when the nights are longer than the days, at nine.

The scholars shall enter the schoolhouse soberly, salute the teacher (if present) with the usual salutations, and take their seats without disturbance or delay; observing likewise, in the evening, to take their leave of him in the common expressions of valediction.

The scholars must have their hands and face washed clean, their hair well combed, and nails decently pared. If the scholars meet any persons as they are coming to, or going from school, if spoken to, they shall accost them civilly, give them no impertinent or abusive language, nor treat them in any other rude or uncivil manner. When in school, they shall diligently attend to their respective studies, make no grimaces or uncouth gesticulations, nor behave in any other manner, which may tend to divert others, or cause themselves to neglect their proper business.

Any scholar having the itch or other infectious disorders, and being sensible of the same, shall not attend school, or associate with the scholars: but the teacher shall dismiss him or her, with a few lines to the parents, or guardians, intimating his reasons for so doing, and the parents or guardians of said scholar, shall detain him or her at home until perfectly

cured, or the teacher's apprehensions on that score removed. If any scholar shall prove so contumacious or refractory as not to be corrigible by the teacher, or if any whose years will not prudently suffer them to be chastised, shall refuse to obey the precepts of the teacher, such person or persons in either case, persisting in their obstinacy and disobedience shall be expelled.

Finally, it is earnestly recommended to, and anxiously requested of all, who belong to this academy, to behave themselves with modesty, sobriety and temperance; to live in peace, harmony and concord; doing good and showing kindness to one another, as it becometh brothers and sisters—children of one great parent.

PHILANDER
The Oracle of Dauphin and Harrisburgh Advertiser
June 8, 1795

Many citizens declare that "the money paid for our schools this winter might as well be thrown away." Some say, "it were better to close our schools, send the teachers home, pay them their full term of salary, and save the expense of fuel." From current reports on every hand, our schools are demoralized, broken up, with no reasonable hope for reorganizing them to good working order.

John C. Wenner
The Columbian
November 30, 1905

Education may be carried to such an extent as to be injurious to the individual and to the body politic. The proposition is now being agitated to have our common schools kept open eight months in each year. I take the position that this is an unwarranted expense upon the taxpayer.

Old Fogy
The Columbian
January 27, 1893

DRESS CODE

Why can't we wear them? It won't hurt anybody.

At Southern Columbia High School, our dress code says that we can't wear "Co-ed Naked" t-shirts, flip-flops, backless sandals or hats in school. I don't think that it is right that we can't wear what we want to school.

It's what everybody is wearing. Recently we were told that we wouldn't be allowed to wear "Co-ed Naked" t-shirts in school. I don't see why we can't wear them. It's not like it is hurting anybody by wearing them.

If flip-flops or backless sandals look good with your outfit you wear them. In our school handbook it says that flip-flops or backless sandals are not permitted. If people feel comfortable wearing them, then they should be allowed to wear them.

If hats are what people want to wear they should be allowed to wear them in school. This is another thing we can't wear. It says in our handbook that hats are not acceptable in school. Hats are another thing. If they look good with the outfit you should be allowed to wear them.

If you feel comfortable by wearing these things then you should be allowed to. I don't think any of these things are going to hurt anybody. This is what kids want to wear in school.

Jodi Levan, Elysburg
Press Enterprise
December 27, 1993

But says one, "When I went to school I done my sums on a slate and there was no use for the blackboard." "And I," says another, "learned geography in the book, which was much better than to spend time looking at a big map on the wall." While another says he can't see any use in the teacher spending his time in talking so much about some little balls, and counting them over and over, to the little boys and girls, who are too young yet to *"larn cipherin'."*

Alpha
The Star of the North
February 6, 1861

Look at our teachers! What interest have they as a class shown in our schools? None, scarcely excepting to demand their stipulated salary. They go into the school either because they can do nothing else in the winter, or because that secures the best and easiest pay.

They don't know how to teach, and don't care how to learn how.

Berwick
Democratic Investigator
November 3, 1853

A GOOD MOVIE

I am a 16-year-old girl. The other day in social studies my teacher showed us a movie about AIDS. It was a good movie! I paid close attention to it. I thought it was very interesting to watch. I would love to study about AIDS. Every time I watch a program about AIDS I learn something new that I didn't know. I think kids these days should learn more about AIDS! Because to me, I think AIDS is very scary because

some person could be carrying this and they might not know. They could end up giving it to someone else. And I think when you reach an age you should be tested for it! I don't think it is fair when someone catches it because then they have to suffer. Because I know I wouldn't want to suffer with it.

It hurts me to think about the people that are suffering from it. The way some people get it I don't think it is fair. What I think they should do is have a free testing day for it! Because what if someone gets raped? That person that raped them could have AIDS. Then that person has to suffer.

Hopefully someone who cares is reading this. I think they should have special shows on about AIDS for people who don't know much about it.

Melody Zubler, Millville
Press Enterprise
December 13, 1989

Can it be possible that for the next hundred years this marvelous improvement in education will accelerate and outdo the last hundred years? If so, what can we imagine Bloomsburg to be like at the end of the 20th Century? This is a thought that impresses us with wonderful possibilities!

J. C. W.
The Columbian
December 11, 1901

I'm just curious. Why do all the people on the West Coast get to find out about the O.J. trial at 10 a.m. and we have to wait until 1 p.m.? I just wondered.

Nescopeck man
"30 Seconds"
Press Enterprise
October 13, 1995

PARTING THOUGHTS

THE LAST GOOD

As the last good I can do for you in the world, I join, to the trifles I leave to you, these few directions, which I beg of you to read for my sake, who always loved you.

Above all things fear God, as the supreme author of all good; love Him with all your heart, and be religious, but detest every tincture of hypocrisy.

Regard well your neighbour, that is all mankind, of whatever nation, profession, or faith, while they are honest; and be ever so yourself. It is the best policy in the end, depend upon it.

Guard against indolence, it is the root of every evil; to which bad company gives the finishing stroke. Love economy without avarice, and be ever thyself thy best friend.

Fly from intemperance and debauchery, they will rot thy body while they will be a canker to thy mind. To keep both sound, allow thyself never to be behind hand with thy correspondents, with thy creditors, with thy daily occupation, and thy soul shall enjoy peace. By using moderate diet, exercise, recreation, thy body shall possess health and vigour.

Dear John, should fortune frown, which depend on it, she sometimes will, do then look round on thousands more wretched than thyself, and who, perhaps, did less deserve to be so, and be content. Contentment is better than gold.

Wish not for death, because it is a sin; but scorn to fear it; be prepared for it each hour, since come it must; while the good mind smiles at its sting, and defies, through Christ, its point.

Beware of passion and cruelty; the bravest men are always the most humane. Rejoice in good nature, not only to man, but to the meanest insect, yea, to the whole creation; scorn to hurt any living being but for thy food or thy defense.

To be cruel is the portion of the coward; while to be brave and humane goes hand in hand and pleases God. Obey as your duty those who are set over you, since without knowing how to be obedient none ever knew how to command.

Now, dear boy, love Mrs. Stedman and her little children from your heart, if ever you had a love for your dead father, who made this request. She has most tenderly proved a help; whilst thou art a brother to her helpless little ones, prove also a parent and guardian by your kindness and conduct.

Let your good sense keep peace and harmony in my dear family; then may the blessing of Almighty God overspread you and them, and we, together with your beloved mother, my dear Johanna, have a chance once more to meet. When in the presence of our Heavenly Father and Merciful Benefactor, our joy and happiness shall be eternal and complete, which is the ardent wish, the sincere prayer, and only hope of your once loving father, who, my dear child, when you read this, shall be no more, and rests, with an affectionate heart to eternity, yours,

J. G. Stedman.

P.S. Let not your grief for my decease overcome you; let your tears flow with moderation and trust that I am happy.

The Oracle of Dauphin and Harrisburgh Advertiser
April 25, 1796

A SMALL TOWN WOULD BE DIFFERENT

I am twelve years old and I have something important to say. I have lived in this area for more than one year and will soon be moving. I move a lot.

I was happy about moving to a small town because I thought it would be easy to make friends and I thought people would be friendlier. I would like to tell what its really like here. I never had the guts to do it like this but will now because I know my friends feel this way too but won't say it because no one will believe it. Also my friends have to stay here. I hope this helps them.

The kids in this area are good. Some of them get into trouble but I think it's because of the way some people are. I told my mother and she said it was in my head so I told my friends and we watched people for hours and hardly no one smiled.

I'm talking mostly about adults because they run the town. They make the rules and have stores and work everywhere and we have to deal with these people. We have to go to school and it's the same except for a couple teachers and the kids. I know they have problems too but I think we have to deal with ours and theres too.

I have to say that my friends get in trouble and me too. But most of my friends can't talk to there parents who are adults and don't have much time to listen. I know some of them try but they mostly say its the kids fault. I think my parents listen a lot more than most except for one thing. They don't like my friends cause they get in trouble.

I think I have these friends because they were lonely when I was, when I first moved here. And I think they were lonely because they can't talk to their parents. Then we get in trouble because we do things for fun to fix the people who act like they care but don't really or don't have time.

Sometimes I think that adults can't talk to each other like me and my friends can. And here's something important too.

Adults can complain to kids about taxes and bills and our grades and the way we wear our hair and the friends we pick but if we can't criticize there friends or complain about the way they are. They think we don't have feelings and don't care about anyone but ourselves. Sometimes I think its the other way around.

My friends that get in trouble have some pretty sad problems. And that's why we get together, to talk about them and to laugh. We can complain and we don't get lectured and there parents don't throw a fit and tell them there wrong.

Maybe kids would be nicer if adults could smile and accept them as part of the human race instead of pretending there not around or giving them dirty looks. I thought that a small town would have more time or be different. I know some adults that do listen and do understand and I hope they keep there heads together and can help my friends. And I hope the streets don't get torn up again.

Name Withheld
The Morning Press
November 28, 1978

⨞ EPILOGUE ⨞

Dear Sir:

I am writing this to thank the Bloomsburg Police Dept. for bringing my lawn chair back to me. I did not report it stolen, being that it was not a very expensive chair, but it made me feel good that they took the time to find the owner of the chair. Where they found it, I do not know, but I feel very thankful to them.

        Mrs. John Moyle, Bloomsburg
        The Morning Press
        July 28, 1971

⚘ AFTERWORD ⚘

LETTERS TO THE EDITOR
AS THEATRE OF PLACE

BY TODD LONDON

In Thornton Wilder's *Our Town,* you might remember, the Stage Manager welcomes us into Grover's Corners with exquisite specificity. He points out all the churches—each denomination—the town hall, the post office and jail, a row of stores, schools, houses, down to the burdock in Mrs. Gibbs's garden and the butternut tree "right here." By the end of Act I, the playwright/tour guide connects this pinpoint locale with a universe beyond imagining. We hear tell of a letter addressed "Jane Crofut; The Crofut Farm; Grover's Corners; Sutton County; New Hampshire; United States of America; Continent of North America; Western Hemisphere; the Earth; the Solar System; the Universe; the Mind of God." So all such correspondence has the potential to travel: from a single soul on a tiny plot of land to the mind of God. . . .

Letters to the Editor is the Bloomsburg Theatre Ensemble's *Our Town,* and we follow this book, and the stage version that preceded it, the way we do Jane Crofut's letter: First we glimpse an individual life, that of a war vet, a teenage mother, a concerned citizen, or a neighborhood crank reaching for a pad, typewriter, or pay phone. The message crosses the literal streets of one east-central Pennsylvania town, and as it goes, we begin to notice the contours of the town itself. The picture that emerges of Bloomsburg today, like the slides that accompanied the stage version of *Letters,* carries traces of older pictures, as frontier Bloomsburg bleeds into industrial Bloomsburg, as the Civil War dissolves into Desert Storm. Because this townscape makes such a typically American scene (the sign welcoming westward travelers to

Pennsylvania once boasted, "America Starts Here"), it calls our attention to America as a whole, first at a moment in history—March 16, 1894, for instance, or May 1957—then as it is now. Finally we get a glance at America in its essence—"America," the idea of America.

All theatre is local. It happens here and now in a space shared by performers and audience. For this reason, dramatic events are always, on some significant level, *about* the people together in the theatre, whether they're ancient Greeks watching their mythologies enacted, Elizabethans at the Globe seeing their royal history unfold, or the folks who read the *Press Enterprise*. The Bloomsburg Theatre Ensemble knows and lives this fact, and so, over twenty years, it has grown into something both ordinary and radical, something more uniquely American than the European-modeled institutional theatres found in most U.S. cities: a professional, activist community theatre of place.

"Theatre of place" describes a phenomenon of America's nonprofit art theatre that has emerged especially over the past two decades. Its roots are traceable, at least, to the Works Progress Administration's Federal Theatre Project, the first government-sponsored attempt to democratize the art form and create employment for theatre artists nationally. This activist, community-based artistic movement consists of a diverse body of theatres and artists that have found themselves propelled to the most unlikely spots: rural byroads, urban housing projects, quiet towns, and communities in crisis. It includes solo performers who re-create communities onstage; itinerant companies that, through extended residences, work with locals to theatricalize oral history and foster community; and frankly political troupes working in prisons, schools, and homeless shelters and committed to saving lives through art.

Theatre of place also covers the quieter radicalism of BTE, an impossible theatre that came to Middle America and stayed. Since its official opening in 1978, this unique company has defined its ideal in concrete and unusual terms. BTE is a fully professional theatre existing in a rural community—a town that, with just over twelve thousand inhabitants, should never be able to sustain a repertory company—where it aims to be as central to that community as schools, libraries, hospitals, and churches. Ensemble members join that community at every level (including governance), as would doctors, farmers, restaurant managers, or factory hands. BTE runs collectively not unlike a sixties experimental theatre troupe, but it fits into its community like a medieval craft guild. The ambition, which this company inherited from its eighty-plus-year-old founder, Alvina Krause, a Northwestern University master acting teacher who'd retired to this area, is a quantum leap over the regional theatre movement, which has, in roughly thirty-five years, established institutional theatres in most major cities. Krause envisioned a theatre in every corner of the country, in each and every community.

This book offers tangible proof of BTE's radical purpose, its deep belief in cultural democracy. Unlike the vast canon of world drama, *Letters* springs not from a singular genius, but from the inadvertent genius of a very specific people: the folks living in and around Bloomsburg, Pennsylvania, past and present. It also flies in the face of accepted wisdom about what lasts as art. If Ezra Pound was right when he proclaimed that "literature is news that *stays* news," then how foolhardy it seems to assume that actual news (and the daily responses it activates) could rise to the level of literature. But it does. And it does because this town stands in for Everytown, because the depth of this exploration of one small circle on the map over time unearths great and simple human riches.

Letters to the Editor exemplifies the kind of deep listening that can only happen when artists turn their intense, loving focus on something they know intimately. BTE has found its place—and with *Letters* it has found a multivocal expression of its relation to that place. The nascent theatre-of-place movement makes a mission of what's always been true: Theatre works best when it reflects or challenges a specific community's ideas about itself. I wish, therefore, that I'd been able to see this piece in the theatre as Bloomsburgers could see it, as an infinitely detailed and knowing reflection of a homeland. Maybe that's the spiritual dimension Wilder was pointing to when he stretched a farm address to the "mind of God." The notion of a homeland evokes the power of spiritual community and the connective mysteries of life. In his journal, Emerson, similarly, meditated on this continuum between place and spirit: *"The place which I have not sought, but in which my duty places me, is a sort of royal palace. If I am faithful to it, I move in it with a pleasing awe at the immensity of the chain of which I hold the last link in my hand and am led by it. . . ."*

Todd London is the artistic director of New Dramatists in New York, a center for the support and development of playwrights. He is a former managing editor of American Theatre *magazine and the author of* The Artistic Home *(Theatre Communications Group); his essays on theatre and culture have appeared nationally and abroad. He is a winner of the 1996–97 George Jean Nathan Award for Dramatic Criticism.*

BIBLIOGRAPHY

REFERENCES

Barton, Edwin M. *Columbia County Two Hundred Years Ago.* Orangeville, Pa.: Columbia County Historical Society, 1976.

Battle, J. H., ed. *History of Columbia and Montour Counties, Pennsylvania.* Chicago: A. Warner and Company, 1887.

Beers, J. H., and Company. *Historical and Biographical Annals of Columbia and Montour Counties, Pennsylvania.* Chicago: J. H. Beers, 1915.

Benton, William. *The Annals of America,* vols. 1–19. Chicago: Encyclopaedia Britannica, Inc., 1968–1974.

Bomboy, Robert Phillip, ed. *Danville: The Bicentennial History.* Danville, Pa.: The Danville Bicentennial Committee, 1992.

The Book of Key Facts. New York: The Queensbury Group, 1978.

Brasch, Walter M. *Columbia County Place Names,* rev. ed. Elmwood, Ill.: Mayfly Productions, 1997.

Brigham, Clarence S. *History and Bibliography of American Newspapers: 1690–1820,* vol. II. Worcester, Mass.: American Antiquarian Society, 1947.

Bruccoli, Matthew J., and Layman, Richard, eds. *American Decades: 1970–1979.* Detroit: Gale Research, Inc., 1995.

Davis, Kenneth C. *Don't Know Much About History.* New York: Avon Books, 1995.

Freeze, John G. *A History of Columbia County, Pennsylvania.* Bloomsburg, Pa.: Elwell and Bittenbender, 1883.

Gale, Robert L. *The Gay Nineties in America.* Westport, Conn.: Greenwood Press, 1992.

Godcharles, Frederic A. *Chronicles of Central Pennsylvania,* vol. II. New York: Lewis Historical Publishing Co., Inc., 1944.

Greenspan, Karen. *The Timetable of Women's History.* New York: Simon & Schuster, 1994.

Gregory, Winifred, ed. *American Newspapers 1821–1936: A Union List of Files Available in the United States and Canada.* New York: Bibliographical Society of America, Kraus Reprint Corporation, 1967.

Grun, Bernard. *The Timetables of History* (based on Werner Stein's *Kulturfahrplan*). New York: Touchstone/Simon & Schuster, 1991.

Layman, Richard, ed. *American Decades,* vols. 1–9. Detroit: Gale Research, Inc., 1994.

Lewis, Joan M. *Berwick: As It Was Then, As It Is Now.* Berwick, Pa.: Berwick Area School District, Keystone Publishing Company, 1985.

Lupiano, Vincent dePaul, and Sayers, Ken W. *It Was a Very Good Year: A Cultural History of the United States from 1776 to the Present.* Holbrook, Mass.: Bob Adams, Inc., 1994.

Morris, Richard B. *The Framing of the Federal Constitution.* Washington, D.C.: Division of Publications, National Park Service, U. S. Department of the Interior, 1979.

Newton, Craig A., ed. "Local War Letters from the Philippines: 1899–1900." *The Columbian,* journal of the Columbia County Historical Society, vol. 3, no. 4, April 1974.

Roberts, Jeanne B., and Rev. John R. Albright, eds. *A History of Catawissa, Pennsylvania.* Catawissa, Pa.: Catawissa Bicentennial Commission, 1974.

Trager, James. *The People's Chronicle*. New York: Henry Holt & Co., 1992.

Turner, George A. *Civil War Letters from Soldiers and Citizens of Columbia County, Pennsylvania*. New York: American Heritage Custom Publishing, 1996.

United States Newspaper Program National Union List, vol. 1, A–Cou. Dublin, Ohio: Online Computer Library, June 1985.

Williams, Neville. *Chronology of the Modern World*. New York: David McKay Co., Inc., 1966.

NEWSPAPER SOURCES

The lion's share of our letters come from Bloomsburg newspapers, with others from newspapers published in the neighboring Columbia or Montour County towns of Benton, Berwick, Catawissa, and Danville. We have looked to sources farther afield when the letters touched on Bloomsburg, such as the letters to *The Shenandoah Herald* (Shenandoah, Pennsylvania) in the chapter focusing on the Bloomsburg trial of the Mollie Maguires in 1877.

For the late eighteenth and early nineteenth centuries, before there was a Montour or a Columbia County (both were part of Northumberland County) and before there was an incorporated Town of Bloomsburg, we looked to the nearest towns of size with newspapers that settlers in this valley might have been reading or writing to, including Sunbury, Northumberland, Wilkes-Barre, and Harrisburg. Our search for early mentions of Bloomsburg or references to this region brought us to several late-eighteenth-century Philadelphia newspapers, including *The Aurora and General Advertiser.* Here is a complete list of source newspapers used in compiling *Letters to the Editor:*

    The Aurora and General Advertiser, Philadelphia, Pennsylvania
    Benton Argus, Benton, Pennsylvania
    Berwick Conservator, Berwick, Pennsylvania
    Berwick Enterprise, Berwick, Pennsylvania
    Berwick Gazette, Berwick, Pennsylvania
    Berwick News, Berwick, Pennsylvania
    Berwick Sentinel, Berwick, Pennsylvania
    The Bloomsburg Daily, Bloomsburg, Pennsylvania
    Bloomsburg Journal, Bloomsburg, Pennsylvania
    Catawissa News Item, Catawissa, Pennsylvania
    Chambersburg Repository, Chambersburg, Pennsylvania
    Columbia County Republican, Bloomsburg, Pennsylvania
    Columbia Democrat, Bloomsburg, Pennsylvania

The Columbian, Bloomsburg, Pennsylvania

Columbia Democrat, Bloomsburg, Pennsylvania

The Danville Evening News, Danville, Pennsylvania

Danville Intelligencer, Danville, Pennsylvania

The Danville Morning News, Danville, Pennsylvania

The Danville News, Danville, Pennsylvania

Dauphin Guardian, Harrisburg, Pennsylvania

Democratic Investigator, Berwick, Pennsylvania

Democratic Sentinel, Bloomsburg, Pennsylvania

The Gem, Danville, Pennsylvania

The Independent Weekly, Bloomsburg, Pennsylvania,
and Orangeville, Pennsylvania

Lewisburg Chronicle, Lewisburg, Pennsylvania

Millville Weekly Tablet, Millville, Pennsylvania

Montour American, Danville, Pennsylvania

The Morning Press, Bloomsburg, Pennsylvania

Old Warrior, Harrisburg, Pennsylvania

The Oracle of Dauphin and Harrisburgh Advertiser,
Harrisburg, Pennsylvania

Pennsylvania Republican, Harrisburg, Pennsylvania

People's Advocate, Lewisburg, Pennsylvania

Pottsville Evening Herald, Pottsville, Pennsylvania

Pottsville Republican, Pottsville, Pennsylvania

Press Enterprise, Bloomsburg, Pennsylvania

Republican Argus, Northumberland, Pennsylvania

Saturday/Sunday, Bloomsburg, Pennsylvania

The Shenandoah Herald, Shenandoah, Pennsylvania

Star of the North, Bloomsburg, Pennsylvania

The Sunbury and Northumberland Gazette, Sunbury,
Pennsylvania

Sunbury Times, Sunbury, Pennsylvania

Whig State Journal, Harrisburg, Pennsylvania

PICTURE CREDITS

Pages 19, 22 (top), 39, 49, 62, 63, 88, 98, 99, 107, 108, 110 (top left), 112, 113 (top), 115 (bottom), 116, 117, 121, 122 (top), 128, 136, 151, 161, 163, 166 (bottom), 174 (left), 175 (middle), 186, 194, 195, 201 (top), 202, 229, 232 (bottom): Collection of Mary and Reuel Hartman, Bloomsburg, Pennsylvania. Susquehanna Valley Post Card Club, Inc.

Pages 21, 27, 64, 94, 109, 122 (bottom), 134, 168, 170 (top), 173, 174 (right), 177, 187 (top), 192, 216, 234, 253 (top): Collection of Columbia County Historical Society.

Pages 22 (bottom), 36, 59, 60 (bottom), 66, 79, 96, 137, 179 (bottom), 188, 191, 209, 224, 225, 250, 253 (middle and bottom), 257: Gordon R. Wenzel.

Pages 25, 28, 30: *The Oracle of Dauphin and Harrisburgh Advertiser,* Harrisburgh, Pennsylvania.

Pages 32, 33, 56 (bottom), 60 (top), 77, 170 (bottom), 175 (top), 179 (top), 184, 226, 241, 245, 259: Marlin R. Wagner.

Pages 34 (left column), 146, 150, 153, 201 (bottom): *The Morning Press,* Bloomsburg, Pennsylvania.

Page 34 (right column): King Features Syndicate.

Pages 35, 37, 56 (top), 57 (top left), 105, 106, 115 (top), 119, 127, 129, 130, 143, 145, 155, 157, 164, 166 (top), 167, 172 (bottom), 182, 187 (bottom), 190, 198, 208, 228 (top and middle), 236, 237, 252: Collection of Gerard Stropnicky.

Pages 42, 45 (bottom): *Lewisburg Chronicle,* Lewisburgh, Pennsylvania.

Page 45 (top): *Chambersburg Repository,* Chambersburg, Pennsylvania.

Pages 50, 53, 101, 102, 103, 126: Mary and Reuel Hartman, Bloomsburg, Pennsylvania. Susquehanna Valley Post Card Club, Inc. Photograph by Marlin R. Wagner.

Pages 51, 57 (bottom left and right), 61, 125, 154, 158, 175 (bottom), 240: Collection of Harry Ward.

Pages 69, 70, 72, 73: *Star of the North,* Bloomsburg, Pennsylvania.

Page 71: George A. Turner.

Page 74: *Columbia Democrat,* Bloomsburg, Pennsylvania.

Pages 80, 81: *Pottsville Evening Herald,* Pottsville, Pennsylvania.

Page 87: Columbia County Historical Society. Photograph by Greg Lehr and Marlin R. Wagner.

Page 110 (bottom right): *The Bloomsburg Daily,* Bloomsburg, Pennsylvania.

Pages 113 (bottom), 231, 232 (top): Veronica Snyder-McHenry.

Pages 118, 172 (top), 178, 189, 249: Collection of Roy Shoop, Watsontown, Pennsylvania. Susquehanna Valley Post Card Club, Inc.

Pages 205, 207: *The Danville News,* Danville, Pennsylvania.

Pages 228 (bottom), 230: Glen Edwards Studio.